History of the Soviet Union from 1917 to 1991 and its dissolution

Compiled by

Terra Pitta

Scribbles

Year of Publication 2018

ISBN : 9789352979301

Book Published by

Scribbles

(An Imprint of Alpha Editions)

email - alphaedis@gmail.com

Produced by: PediaPress GmbH
Limburg an der Lahn
Germany
http://pediapress.com/

Contents

Introduction to Soviet Union

Soviet Union

<indicator name="pp-default"> 🔒 </indicator>

Union of Soviet Socialist Republics
Союз Советских Социалистических Республик   *Soyuz Sovetskikh Sotsialisticheskikh Respublik*
1922–1991[1]
  Flag   State emblem
Motto   "Workers of the world, unite!"   Пролетарии всех стран, соединяйтесь!   (*Proletarii vsekh stran, soyedinyaytes'!*   **Literally**: "Proletarians of all countries, unite!")

Anthem
The Internationale
(1922–1944)
State Anthem of the Soviet Union
(1944–1977)

State Anthem of the Soviet Union
(modified version)
(1977–1991)

The Soviet Union during the Cold War

Capital	Moscow
Languages	**Official:** Russian[2,3]
Demonym	Soviet, Russian
Government	**1922–90** Federal Marxist–Leninist one-party socialist state[4,5,6,7] **1990–91:** Federal semi-presidential republic
General Secretary	
•	1922–1952	Joseph Stalin (first)
•	1991	Vladimir Ivashko (last)
Head of state	
•	1922–1938	Mikhail Kalinin (first)

	1988–1991	Mikhail Gorbachev (last)
Head of government		
•	1922–1924	Vladimir Lenin (first)
•	1991	Ivan Silayev (last)
Legislature		Supreme Soviet
•	Upper house	Soviet of Nationalities
•	Lower house	Soviet of the Union
Historical era		20th century
•	Treaty of Creation	30 December 1922
•	Admitted to the United Nations	25 October 1945
•	Constitution adopted	9 October 1977
•	Union dissolved	26 December 1991[1]
Area		
•	1991	22,402,200 km^2 (8,649,500 sq mi)
Population		
•	1991 est.	293,047,571
Density		13/km^2 (34/sq mi)
Currency		Soviet ruble (руб) (SUR)
Internet TLD		.su[8]
Calling code		+7

Preceded by	Succeeded by
	Russian Federation
	Ukraine
Russian SFSR	Belarus
Transcaucasian SFSR	Armenia
Ukrainian SSR	Azerbaijan
Byelorussian SSR	Estonia
Bukharan People's Soviet Republic	Georgia
Khorezm People's Soviet Republic	Kazakhstan
Estonia	Kyrgyzstan
Latvia	Latvia
Lithuania	Lithuania
Kingdom of Romania	Moldova
Tuvan People's Republic	Tajikistan
	Turkmenistan
	Uzbekistan

Notes

1. ^ Declaration № 142-H of the Soviet of the Republics of the Supreme Soviet of the Soviet Union, formally establishing the dissolution of the Soviet Union as a state and subject of international law. (in Russian)
2. ^ Original lyrics used from 1944 to 1956. No lyrics from 1956 to 1977. Revised lyrics from 1977 to 1991.
3. ^ All-union official since 1990, constituent republics had the right to declare their own official languages.
4. ^ Assigned on 19 September 1990, existing onwards.

The **Soviet Union**, (Russian: Сове́тский Сою́з, tr. *Sovétsky Soyúz*, IPA: [sɐ'vʲɛt͡skʲɪj sɐ'jus] (◄» listen)) officially the **Union of Soviet Socialist Republics** (Russian: Сою́з Сове́тских Социалисти́ческих Респу́блик (СССР), tr. *Soyúz Sovétskikh Sotsialistícheskikh Respúblik*, IPA: [sɐ'jus sɐ'vʲɛt͡skʲɪx sətsɨəlʲɪs'tʲit͡ɕɪskʲɪx rʲɪ'spublʲɪk] (◄» listen)) (**USSR**), was a socialist federation in Eurasia that existed from 1922 to 1991. Nominally a union of multiple national Soviet republics,[9] its government and economy were highly centralized. The country was a one-party state, governed by the Communist Party with Moscow as its capital in its largest republic, the Russian Soviet Federative Socialist Republic (Russian SFSR). The Russian nation had constitutionally equal status among the many nations of the union, but exerted *de facto* dominance in various respects. Other major urban centres were Leningrad, Kiev, Minsk, Alma-Ata and Novosibirsk. The Soviet Union was one of the five recognized nuclear weapons states and possessed the largest stockpile of weapons of mass destruction. It was a founding permanent member of the United Nations Security Council as well as a member of the Organization for Security and Co-operation in Europe (OSCE) and the leading member of the Council for Mutual Economic Assistance (CMEA) and the Warsaw Pact.

The Soviet Union had its roots in the October Revolution of 1917, when the Bolsheviks led by Vladimir Lenin overthrew the Russian Provisional Government which had replaced Tsar Nicholas II during World War I. In 1922, the Soviet Union was formed by the Treaty on the Creation of the USSR which legalized the unification of the Russian, Transcaucasian, Ukrainian and Byelorussian republics that had occurred from 1918. Following Lenin's death in 1924 and a brief power struggle, Joseph Stalin came to power in the mid-1920s. Stalin committed the state's ideology to Marxism–Leninism (which he created) and constructed a command economy which led to a period of rapid industrialization and collectivization. During this period of totalitarian rule, political paranoia fermented and the late-1930s Great Purge removed Stalin's opponents within and outside of the party via arbitrary arrests and persecutions of many people, resulting in over 600,000 deaths. Suppression of political critics, forced labor were carried out by Stalin's government. In 1933, a major famine that became known as the Holodomor in Soviet Ukraine struck multiple Soviet grain-growing regions, causing the deaths of some 3 to 7 million people.[10]

In August 1939, days before the start of World War II, the USSR signed the Molotov–Ribbentrop Pact agreeing to non-aggression with Nazi Germany, after which the two countries invaded Poland in September 1939. In June 1941, the pact collapsed as Germany turned to attack the Soviet Union, opening the largest and bloodiest theatre of war in history. Soviet war casualties accounted for the highest proportion of the conflict in the effort of acquiring the upper hand over Axis forces at intense battles such as Stalingrad and Kursk. The territories overtaken by the Red Army became satellite states of the Soviet Union and the postwar division of Europe into capitalist and communist halves would lead to increased tensions with the West, led by the United States of America.

The Cold War emerged by 1947 as the Eastern Bloc, united under the Warsaw Pact in 1955, confronted the Western Bloc, united under NATO in 1949. On 5 March 1953, Stalin died and was eventually succeeded by Nikita Khrushchev, who in 1956 denounced Stalin and began the de-Stalinization of Soviet society through the Khrushchev Thaw. The Soviet Union took an early lead in the Space Race, with the first artificial satellite and the first human spaceflight. Dissatisfied with Khrushchev's policies, the Communist Party's conservative wing led a coup d'état against Khrushchev in 1964, quietly ousting him without any bloodshed. In the early 1970s, there was a brief détente of relations with the United States, but tensions resumed with the Soviet–Afghan War in 1979. In the mid-1980s, the last Soviet leader, Mikhail Gorbachev, sought to reform and liberalize the economy through his policies of *glasnost* (openness) and *perestroika* (restructuring). Under Gorbachev, the role of the Communist Party in governing the state was removed from the constitution, causing a surge of severe political instability to set in. The Cold War ended during his tenure in 1989 as Soviet satellite states in Eastern Europe and overthrew their respective communist governments.

With the rise of strong nationalist and separatist movements inside the union republics, Gorbachev tried to avert a dissolution of the Soviet Union in the post-Cold War era. A March 1991 referendum, boycotted by some republics, resulted in a majority of participating citizens voting in favor of preserving the union as a renewed federation. Gorbachev's power was greatly diminished after Russian President Boris Yeltsin played a high-profile role in facing down an abortive August 1991 coup d'état attempted by Communist Party hardliners. On 25 December 1991, Gorbachev resigned and the remaining twelve constituent republics emerged as independent post-Soviet states. The Russian Federation—formerly the Russian SFSR—assumed the Soviet Union's rights and obligations and is recognized as the successor state of the Soviet

Union.[11,12,13] In summing up the international ramifications of these events, Vladislav Zubok stated: "The collapse of the Soviet empire was an event of epochal geopolitical, military, ideological and economic significance".

Name

Part of **a series** on the

History of Russia

Maykop	37th–30th century BCE
Yamna	34th–27th century BCE
Afanasevo	34th–26th century BCE
Corded Ware	30th–24th century BCE
Catacomb	29th–23rd century BCE
Poltavka	28th–22nd century BCE
Sintashta	22nd–19th century BCE
Andronovo	21st–10th century BCE
Srubna	19th–13th century BCE
Cimmerians	12th–7th century BCE
Scythians	8th–4th century BCE
Sarmatians	5th century BCE–4th century CE
Early Slavs/Rus'	pre-9th century
Old Great Bulgaria	632–668
Khazar Khaganate	650-969
Rus' Khaganate	9th century
Volga Bulgaria	9th–13th century
Kievan Rus'	882–1240
Vladimir-Suzdal	1157–1331
Novgorod Republic	1136–1478
Mongol Yoke	1240s–1480
Grand Duchy of Moscow	1283–1547
Tsardom of Russia	1547–1721
Russian Empire	1721–1917
Russian Republic	1917

Russian SFSR	1917–1991
Soviet Union	1922–1991
Russian Federation	1991–present

Timeline ▦ Russia portal

- v
- t
- e[14]

The word "Soviet" is derived from a Russian word meaning council, assembly, advice, harmony, concord[15] and all ultimately deriving from the proto-Slavic verbal stem of *vět-iti* ("to inform"), related to Slavic *věst* ("news"), English "wise", the root in "ad-vis-or" (which came to English through French), or the Dutch *weten* ("to know"; cf. *wetenschap* meaning "science"). The word *sovietnik* means "councillor".

A number of organizations in Russian history were called "council" (Russian: совéт). For example, in the Russian Empire the State Council, which functioned from 1810 to 1917, was referred to as a Council of Ministers after the revolt of 1905.

During the Georgian Affair, Vladimir Lenin envisioned an expression of Great Russian ethnic chauvinism by Joseph Stalin and his supporters, calling for these nation-states to join Russia as semi-independent parts of a greater union, which he initially named as the Union of Soviet Republics of Europe and Asia (Russian: Сою́з Совéтских Респу́блик Евро́пы и А́зии, tr. *Soyúz Sovétskikh Respúblik Evrópy i Ázii*).[16] Stalin initially resisted the proposal, but ultimately accepted it, although with Lenin's agreement changed the name of the newly proposed state to the Union of Soviet Socialist Republics, albeit all the republics began as "Socialist Soviet" and did not change to the other order until 1936. In addition, in the national languages of several republics the word "Council/Conciliar" in the respective language was only quite late changed to an adaptation of the Russian "Soviet" and never in others, e.g. Ukraine.

The names of the Soviet Union are as follows in several languages of its 15 constituent republics:

- **Russian**: Союз Советских Социалистических Республик; *Soyuz Sovetskikh Sotsialisticheskikh Respublik*
- **Ukrainian**: Союз Радянських Соціалістичних Республік; *Soyuz Radyans'kykh Socialistychnykh Respublik*
- **Belarusian**: Саюз Савецкіх Сацыялістычных Рэспублік; *Sajuz Savieckich Sacyjalistyčnych Respublik*
- **Uzbek**: Совет Социалистик Республикалари Иттифоқи; *Sovet Sotsialistik Respublikalari Ittifoqi*

- **Kazakh**: Кеңестік Социалистік Республикалар Одағы; *Keñestik Socïalïstik Respwblïkalar Odağı*
- **Georgian**: საბჭოთა სოციალისტური რესპუბლიკების კავშირი (sabch'ota sotsialist'uri resp'ublik'ebis k'avshiri)
- **Azerbaijani**: Совет Сосиалист Республикалары Иттифагы; *Sovet Sosialist Respublikaları İttifaqı*
- **Lithuanian**: Tarybų Socialistinių Respublikų Sąjunga
- **Moldovan**: Униуня Републичилор Советиче Сочиалисте; *Uniunea Republicilor Sovietice Socialiste*
- **Latvian**: Padomju Sociālistisko Republiku Savienība
- **Kyrgyz**: Советтик Социалисттик Республикалар Союзу; *Sovettik Socialisttik Respublikalar Soyuzu*
- **Tajik**: Иттиходи Чумхурихои Шӯравии Сосиалистӣ; *Ittihodi Chumhurihoi Shūravii Sosialistī*
- **Armenian**: Խորհրդային Սոցիալիստական Հանրապետությունների Միություն; *Xorhrdayin Socialistakan Hanrapetowtyownneri Miowtyown*
- **Turkmen**: Совет Социалистик Республикалары Союзы; *Sovet Sosialistik Respublikalary Soýuzy*
- **Estonian**: Nõukogude Sotsialistlike Vabariikide Liit

In some cases, due to the length of its name the state was referred to as the Soviet Union or the USSR, especially when used in the Western media. It was also informally called Russia (and its citizens Russians), though that was technically incorrect since Russia was only one of the republics.

Geography, climate and environment

With an area of 22,402,200 square kilometres (8,649,500 sq mi), the Soviet Union was the world's largest country, a status that is retained by the Russian Federation.[17] Covering a sixth of Earth's land surface, its size was comparable to that of North America. The European portion accounted for a quarter of the country's area, and was the cultural and economic center. The eastern part in Asia extended to the Pacific Ocean to the east and Afghanistan to the south, and, except some areas in Central Asia, was much less populous. It spanned over 10,000 kilometres (6,200 mi) east to west across 11 time zones, and over 7,200 kilometres (4,500 mi) north to south. It had five climate zones: tundra, taiga, steppes, desert and mountains.

The Soviet Union had the world's longest border, like Russia, measuring over 60,000 kilometres (37,000 mi), or 1 $^1/_2$ circumferences of Earth. Two-thirds of it was a coastline. Across the Bering Strait was the United States. The Soviet Union bordered Afghanistan, China, Czechoslovakia, Finland, Hungary, Iran,

Mongolia, North Korea, Norway, Poland, Romania, and Turkey from 1945 to 1991.

The Soviet Union's highest mountain was Communism Peak (now Ismoil Somoni Peak) in Tajikistan, at 7,495 metres (24,590 ft). The Soviet Union also included most of the world's largest lakes; the Caspian Sea (shared with Iran), and Lake Baikal, the world's largest and deepest freshwater lake that is also an internal body of water in Russia.

History

Part of a series on the
History of the Union of Soviet Socialist Republics (Soviet Union)
1917–1927 Revolutionary Beginnings
• Revolution • Civil War • New Economic Policy • 1922 Treaty • National delimitation
1927–1953 Stalinist rule
• Socialism in One Country • Great Purge

Soviet famine of 1932–33

- (Holodomor
- Kazakhstan famine of 1932-1933)

World War II

- (Molotov–Ribbentrop Pact
- Great Patriotic War
- Operation Barbarossa
- Occupation of the Baltic states
- Soviet occupation of Bessarabia and Northern Bukovina
- Battle of Berlin
- Soviet invasion of Manchuria)

- Soviet deportations
- Soviet famine of 1946–47
- Cold War
- Korean War

1953–1964

Post-Stalin era

- Berlin blockade
- 1954 transfer of Crimea
- Khrushchev Thaw
- On the Cult of Personality and Its Consequences
- We will bury you
- 9 March riots
- Wage reforms
- Cuban Revolution
- Sino-Soviet split
- Space program
- Cuban Missile Crisis

1964–1982

Brezhnev era

- Brezhnev Doctrine
- Era of Stagnation
- 50th anniversary of the Armenian Genocide protests

- Prague Spring

Vietnam War

- (Laotian Civil War
- Operation Menu
- Cambodian Civil War
- Fall of Saigon)

- Six-Day War
- Détente
- Yom Kippur War
- Dirty War

Wars in Africa

- (Angolan War of Independence
- Angolan Civil War
- Mozambican War of Independence
- Mozambican Civil War
- South African Border War
- Rhodesian Bush War)

- Cambodian-Vietnamese War
- Soviet–Afghan War
- 1980 Summer Olympics

Olympic boycotts

- (1980 Olympic boycott
- 1984 Olympic boycott)

- Polish strike
- Death and funeral of Brezhnev

1982–1991

Leadership changes and collapse

- Invasion of Grenada
- Glasnost
- Perestroika
- Soviet withdrawal from Afghanistan

Singing Revolution

- (Estonian Sovereignty Declaration

- Baltic Way
- Act of the Re-Establishment of the State of Lithuania
- On the Restoration of Independence of the Republic of Latvia)

Revolutions of 1989

- (Pan-European picnic
- Die Wende
- Peaceful Revolution
- Fall of the Berlin Wall
- Velvet Revolution
- End of communist rule in Hungary
- Romanian Revolution
- German reunification)

Dissolution

- (Jeltoqsan
- Nagorno-Karabakh War
- 9 April tragedy
- Black January
- Osh riots
- War of Laws
- Dushanbe riots
- January Events
- The Barricades
- Referendum
- Union of Sovereign States
- August Coup
- Ukrainian independence (referendum)
- Belavezha Accords
- Alma-Ata Protocol)

History of

- Russia
- Moscow
- Kiev
- Minsk
- Former Soviet Republics

Soviet leadership
• 1. Lenin • 2. Stalin • 3. Malenkov • 4. Khrushchev • 5. Brezhnev • 6. Andropov • 7. Chernenko • 8. Gorbachev
• Culture • Economy • Education • Geography • Politics
▬ Soviet Union portal
• v • t • e[18]

The last Russian Tsar, Nicholas II, ruled the Russian Empire until his abdication in March 1917 in the aftermath of the February Revolution, due in part to the strain of fighting in World War I, which lacked public support. A short-lived Russian Provisional Government took power, to be overthrown in the October Revolution (N.S. 7 November 1917) by revolutionaries led by the Bolshevik leader Vladimir Lenin.

The Soviet Union was officially established in December 1922 with the union of the Russian, Ukrainian, Byelorussian, and Transcaucasian Soviet republics, each ruled by local Bolshevik parties. Despite the foundation of the Soviet state as a federative entity of many constituent republics, each with its own political and administrative entities, the term "Soviet Russia" – strictly applicable only to the Russian Federative Socialist Republic – was often applied to the entire country by non-Soviet writers and politicians.

Figure 1: *Vladimir Lenin, Leon Trotsky and Lev Kamenev celebrating the second anniversary of the October Revolution*

Revolution and foundation

Modern revolutionary activity in the Russian Empire began with the Decembrist revolt of 1825. Although serfdom was abolished in 1861, it was done on terms unfavorable to the peasants and served to encourage revolutionaries. A parliament—the State Duma—was established in 1906 after the Russian Revolution of 1905, but Tsar Nicholas II resisted attempts to move from absolute to constitutional monarchy. Social unrest continued and was aggravated during World War I by military defeat and food shortages in major cities.

A spontaneous popular uprising in Petrograd, in response to the wartime decay of Russia's economy and morale, culminated in the February Revolution and the toppling of the imperial government in March 1917. The tsarist autocracy was replaced by the Russian Provisional Government, which intended to conduct elections to the Russian Constituent Assembly and to continue fighting on the side of the Entente in World War I.

At the same time, workers' councils, known in Russian as "Soviets", sprang up across the country. The Bolsheviks, led by Vladimir Lenin, pushed for socialist revolution in the Soviets and on the streets. On 7 November 1917, the Red Guards stormed the Winter Palace in Petrograd, ending the rule of the Provisional Government and leaving all political power to the Soviets. This

Figure 2: *The Russian SFSR as a part of the USSR in 1922*

event would later be officially known in Soviet bibliographies as the Great October Socialist Revolution. In December, the Bolsheviks signed an armistice with the Central Powers, though by February 1918, fighting had resumed. In March, the Soviets ended involvement in the war for good and signed the Treaty of Brest-Litovsk.

A long and bloody Civil War ensued between the Reds and the Whites, starting in 1917 and ending in 1923 with the Reds' victory. It included foreign intervention, the execution of the former tsar and his family, and the famine of 1921, which killed about five million people. In March 1921, during a related conflict with Poland, the Peace of Riga was signed, splitting disputed territories in Belarus and Ukraine between the Republic of Poland and Soviet Russia. Soviet Russia had to resolve similar conflicts with the newly established Republic of Finland, the Republic of Estonia, the Republic of Latvia, and the Republic of Lithuania.

Unification of republics

On 28 December 1922, a conference of plenipotentiary delegations from the Russian SFSR, the Transcaucasian SFSR, the Ukrainian SSR and the Byelorussian SSR approved the Treaty on the Creation of the USSR[19] and the Declaration of the Creation of the USSR, forming the Union of Soviet Socialist Republics.[20] These two documents were confirmed by the 1st Congress of Soviets of the USSR and signed by the heads of the delegations,[21] Mikhail

Figure 3: *The Russian SFSR as a part of the*
USSR after 1936 Russian territorial changes

Kalinin, Mikhail Tskhakaya, Mikhail Frunze, Grigory Petrovsky, and Alexander Chervyakov,[22] on 30 December 1922. The formal proclamation was made from the stage of the Bolshoi Theatre.

On 1 February 1924, the USSR was recognized by the United Kingdom. The same year, a Soviet Constitution was approved, legitimizing the December 1922 union.

An intensive restructuring of the economy, industry and politics of the country began in the early days of Soviet power in 1917. A large part of this was done according to the Bolshevik Initial Decrees, government documents signed by Vladimir Lenin. One of the most prominent breakthroughs was the GOELRO plan, which envisioned a major restructuring of the Soviet economy based on total electrification of the country. The plan was developed in 1920 and covered a 10 to 15-year period. It included construction of a network of 30 regional power stations, including ten large hydroelectric power plants, and numerous electric-powered large industrial enterprises. The plan became the prototype for subsequent Five-Year Plans and was fulfilled by 1931.[23]

Stalin era

Joseph Stalin and Nikolai Yezhov in a photo together, but after being executed he was edited out of the image

From its creation, the government in the Soviet Union was based on the one-party rule of the Communist Party (Bolsheviks).[24] After the economic policy of "War communism" during the Russian Civil War, as a prelude to fully developing socialism in the country, the Soviet government permitted some private enterprise to coexist alongside nationalized industry in the 1920s and total food requisition in the countryside was replaced by a food tax.

The stated purpose of the one-party state was to ensure that capitalist exploitation would not return to the Soviet Union and that the principles of democratic centralism would be most effective in representing the people's will in a practical manner. Debate over the future of the economy provided the background for a power struggle in the years after Lenin's death in 1924. Initially, Lenin was to be replaced by a "troika" consisting of Grigory Zinoviev of the Ukrainian SSR, Lev Kamenev of the Russian SFSR, and Joseph Stalin of the Transcaucasian SFSR.

On 3 April 1922, Stalin was named the General Secretary of the Communist Party of the Soviet Union. Lenin had appointed Stalin the head of the Workers' and Peasants' Inspectorate, which gave Stalin considerable power. By gradually consolidating his influence and isolating and outmaneuvering his rivals within the party, Stalin became the undisputed leader of the Soviet Union and, by the end of the 1920s, established totalitarian rule. In October 1927, Grigory Zinoviev and Leon Trotsky were expelled from the Central Committee and forced into exile.

In 1928, Stalin introduced the first five-year plan for building a socialist economy. In place of the internationalism expressed by Lenin throughout the Revolution, it aimed to build Socialism in One Country. In industry, the state assumed control over all existing enterprises and undertook an intensive program of industrialization. In agriculture, rather than adhering to the "lead by example" policy advocated by Lenin, forced collectivization of farms was implemented all over the country.

Famines ensued, causing millions of deaths; surviving kulaks were persecuted and many sent to Gulags to do forced labour. Social upheaval continued in the mid-1930s. Stalin's Great Purge resulted in the execution or detainment of many "Old Bolsheviks" who had participated in the October Revolution with Lenin. According to declassified Soviet archives, the NKVD arrested more than one and a half million people in 1937 and 1938, of whom 681,692 were shot. Over those two years there were an average of over one thousand executions a day. According to historian Geoffrey Hosking, "...excess deaths during the 1930s as a whole were in the range of 10–11 million", although historian Timothy D. Snyder claims that archival evidence suggests a maximum excess mortality of nine million during the entire Stalin era.[25] Historian and archival researcher Stephen G. Wheatcroft asserts that around a million "purposive killings" can be attributed to Stalinist regime, along with the premature deaths of roughly two million more amongst the repressed populations (i.e., in camps, prisons, exile, etc.) through criminal negligence.[26] Despite the turmoil of the mid-to-late 1930s, the Soviet Union developed a powerful industrial economy in the years before World War II.

Under the doctrine of state atheism in the Soviet Union, there was a "government-sponsored program of forced conversion to atheism" conducted by Communists.[27,28] The communist regime targeted religions based on State interests, and while most organized religions were never outlawed, religious property was confiscated, believers were harassed, and religion was ridiculed while atheism was propagated in schools.[29] In 1925 the government founded the League of Militant Atheists to intensify the propaganda campaign.[30] Accordingly, although personal expressions of religious faith were not explicitly banned, a strong sense of social stigma was imposed on them by the official structures and mass media and it was generally considered unacceptable for members of certain professions (teachers, state bureaucrats, soldiers) to be openly religious. As for the Russian Orthodox Church, Soviet authorities sought to control it and, in times of national crisis, to exploit it for the regime's own purposes; but their ultimate goal was to eliminate it. During the first five years of Soviet power, the Bolsheviks executed 28 Russian Orthodox bishops and over 1,200 Russian Orthodox priests. Many others were imprisoned or exiled. Believers were harassed and persecuted. Most seminaries were closed, and the publication of most religious material was prohibited. By 1941 only 500 churches remained open out of about 54,000 in existence prior to World War I.

Figure 4: *"Strengthen working discipline in collective farms",*
a Soviet propaganda poster issued in Uzbekistan, 1933

1930s

Closer cooperation between the Soviet Union and the West developed in the early 1930s. From 1932 to 1934, the Soviet Union participated in the World Disarmament Conference. In 1933, diplomatic relations between the United States and the USSR were established when in November the newly elected President of the United States, Franklin D. Roosevelt, chose to formally recognize Stalin's Communist government and negotiated a new trade agreement between the two nations.[31] In September 1934, the Soviet Union joined the League of Nations. After the Spanish Civil War broke out in 1936, the USSR actively supported the Republican forces against the Nationalists, who were supported by Fascist Italy and Nazi Germany.

In December 1936, Stalin unveiled a new Soviet Constitution. Supporters around the world hailed it as the most democratic Constitution imaginable. Historian J. Arch Getty concludes:

> *Many who lauded Stalin's Soviet Union as the most democratic country*
> *on earth lived to regret their words. After all, the Soviet Constitution of*
> *1936 was adopted on the eve of the Great Terror of the late 1930s; the*
> *"thoroughly democratic" elections to the first Supreme Soviet permitted*
> *only uncontested candidates and took place at the height of the savage vi-*
> *olence in 1937. The civil rights, personal freedoms, and democratic forms*

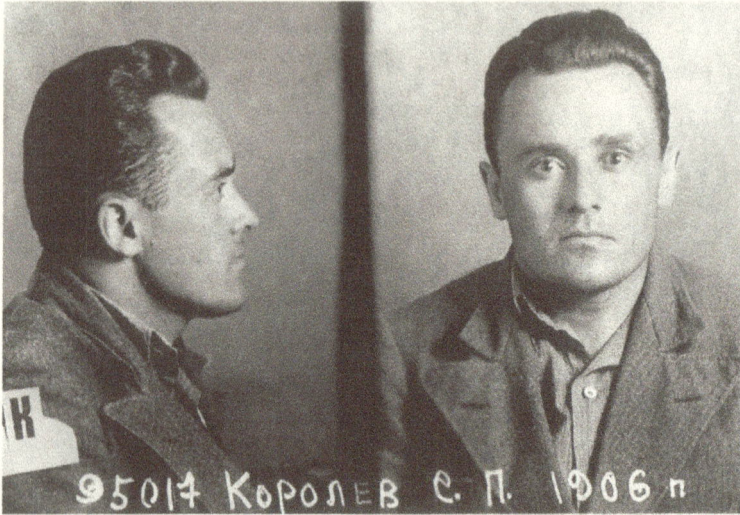

Figure 5: *Sergei Korolev, the father of the Soviet space program, shortly after his arrest during Stalin's Great Terror*

promised in the Stalin constitution were trampled almost immediately and remained dead letters until long after Stalin's death.[32]

In 1939, the Soviet Union made a dramatic shift toward Nazi Germany. Almost a year after Britain and France had concluded the Munich Agreement with Germany, the Soviet Union made agreements with Germany as well, both militarily and economically during extensive talks. The two countries concluded the Molotov–Ribbentrop Pact and the German–Soviet Commercial Agreement in August 1939. The nonaggression pact made possible Soviet occupation of Lithuania, Latvia, Estonia, Bessarabia, northern Bukovina, and eastern Poland. In late November, unable to coerce the Republic of Finland by diplomatic means into moving its border 25 kilometres (16 mi) back from Leningrad, Joseph Stalin ordered the invasion of Finland.

In the east, the Soviet military won several decisive victories during border clashes with the Empire of Japan in 1938 and 1939. However, in April 1941, USSR signed the Soviet–Japanese Neutrality Pact with the Japan, recognizing the territorial integrity of Manchukuo, a Japanese puppet state.

Figure 6: *The Battle of Stalingrad is considered by many*
historians as a decisive turning point of World War II

World War II

Although it has been debated whether the Soviet Union intended to invade Germany once it was strong enough,[33] Germany itself broke the treaty and invaded the Soviet Union on 22 June 1941, starting what was known in the USSR as the "Great Patriotic War". The Red Army stopped the seemingly invincible German Army at the Battle of Moscow, aided by an unusually harsh winter. The Battle of Stalingrad, which lasted from late 1942 to early 1943, dealt a severe blow to the Germans from which they never fully recovered and became a turning point in the war. After Stalingrad, Soviet forces drove through Eastern Europe to Berlin before Germany surrendered in 1945. The German Army suffered 80% of its military deaths in the Eastern Front.

The same year, the USSR, in fulfillment of its agreement with the Allies at the Yalta Conference, denounced the Soviet–Japanese Neutrality Pact in April 1945[34] and invaded Manchukuo and other Japan-controlled territories on 9 August 1945.[35] This conflict ended with a decisive Soviet victory, contributing to the unconditional surrender of Japan and the end of World War II.

The Soviet Union suffered greatly in the war, losing around 27 million people. Approximately 2.8 million Soviet POWs died of starvation, mistreatment, or executions in just eight months of 1941–42.[36] During the war, the Soviet Union together with the United States, the United Kingdom and China were considered the Big Four Allied powers in World War II , and later became the Four Policemen, which formed the basis of the United Nations Security Council. It emerged as a superpower in the post-war period. Once denied diplomatic recognition by the Western world, the Soviet Union had official relations with practically every nation by the late 1940s. A member of the United Nations at its foundation in 1945, the Soviet Union became one of the five permanent members of the United Nations Security Council, which gave it the right to veto any of its resolutions.

Figure 7: *Left to right: Soviet Premier Joseph Stalin, U.S. President Franklin D. Roosevelt and British Prime Minister Winston Churchill confer in Tehran in 1943*

The Soviet Union maintained its status as one of the world's two superpowers for four decades through its hegemony in Eastern Europe, military strength, economic strength, aid to developing countries, and scientific research, especially in space technology and weaponry.

Cold War

During the immediate postwar period, the Soviet Union rebuilt and expanded its economy, while maintaining its strictly centralized control. It took effective control over most of Eastern Europe (except Yugoslavia and Albania), turning them into satellite states. The Soviet Union bound its satellite states in a military alliance (the Warsaw Pact) in 1955; and an economic organization (The Council for Mutual Economic Assistance or Comecon), a counterpart to the European Economic Community, from 1949 to 1991. The Soviet Union concentrated on its own recovery. It seized and transferred most of Germany's industrial plants and it exacted war reparations from East Germany, Hungary, Romania, and Bulgaria, using Soviet-dominated joint enterprises. It used trading arrangements deliberately designed to favor the Soviet Union. Moscow controlled the Communist parties that ruled the satellite states, and they followed orders from the Kremlin. Historian Mark Kramer concludes:[37]

Figure 8: *Globe showing the greatest territorial extent of the Soviet Union
and states that were dominated politically, economically and/or militarily
by it (which was in 1960), namely the period of time just after the Cuban
Revolution of 1959 and just before the official Sino-Soviet split of 1961*

*The net outflow of resources from eastern Europe to the Soviet Union was
approximately $15 billion to $20 billion in the first decade after World
War II, an amount roughly equal to the total aid provided by the United
States to western Europe under the Marshall Plan.*

Later, the Comecon supplied aid to the eventually victorious Communist Party
of China, and saw its influence grow elsewhere in the world. Fearing its ambitions, the Soviet Union's wartime allies, the United Kingdom and the United
States, became its enemies. In the ensuing Cold War, the two sides clashed
indirectly using mostly proxies.

Khrushchev era

Stalin died on 5 March 1953. Without a mutually agreeable successor, the
highest Communist Party officials initially opted to rule the Soviet Union jointly
through a troika headed by Georgy Malenkov. This did not last, however, and
Nikita Khrushchev eventually won the power struggle by the mid-1950s. He
shortly afterward denounced Stalin's use of repression in 1956 and proceeded

Figure 9: *Soviet leader Nikita Khrushchev (left)*
with John F. Kennedy in Vienna, 3 June 1961

to ease Stalin's repressive controls over party and society. This was known as de-Stalinization.

Moscow considered Eastern Europe to be a critically vital buffer zone for the forward defense of its western borders, in case of another major invasion such as the German invasion of 1940. For this reason, the USSR sought to cement its control of the region by transforming the Eastern European countries into satellite states, dependent upon, and subservient to, its leadership. Soviet military force was used to suppress anti-Stalinist uprisings in Hungary and Poland in 1956.

In the late 1950s, a confrontation with China regarding the USSR's rapprochement with the West, and what Mao Zedong perceived as Khrushchev's revisionism, led to the Sino–Soviet split. This resulted in a break throughout the global Marxist–Leninist movement, with the governments in Albania, Cambodia and Somalia choosing to ally with China in place of the USSR.

During this period of the late 1950s and early 1960s, the Soviet Union continued to realize scientific and technological exploits in the Space Race, rivaling the United States: launching the first artificial satellite, Sputnik 1 in 1957; a living dog named Laika in 1957; the first human being, Yuri Gagarin in 1961; the first woman in space, Valentina Tereshkova in 1963; Alexey Leonov, the first person to walk in space in 1965; the first soft landing on the moon by space-craft Luna 9 in 1966; and the first moon rovers, Lunokhod 1 and Lunokhod 2.

Khrushchev initiated "The Thaw", a complex shift in political, cultural and economic life in the Soviet Union. This included some openness and contact with other nations and new social and economic policies with more emphasis on commodity goods, allowing living standards to rise dramatically while maintaining high levels of economic growth. Censorship was relaxed as well. Khrushchev's reforms in agriculture and administration, however, were generally unproductive. In 1962, he precipitated a crisis with the United States over the Soviet deployment of nuclear missiles in Cuba. An agreement was made between the Soviet Union and the United States to remove enemy nuclear missiles from both Cuba and Turkey, concluding the crisis. This event caused Khrushchev much embarrassment and loss of prestige, resulting in his removal from power in 1964.

Era of Stagnation

The Era of Stagnation was a period of negative economic, political, and social effects in the Soviet Union, which began during the rule of Leonid Brezhnev and continued under Yuri Andropov and Konstantin Chernenko.

Following the ousting of Khrushchev, another period of collective leadership ensued, consisting of Leonid Brezhnev as General Secretary, Alexei Kosygin as Premier and Nikolai Podgorny as Chairman of the Presidium, lasting until Brezhnev established himself in the early 1970s as the preeminent Soviet leader.

In 1968, the Soviet Union and Warsaw Pact allies invaded Czechoslovakia to halt the Prague Spring reforms. In the aftermath, Brezhnev justified the invasion along with the earlier invasions of Eastern European states by introducing the Brezhnev Doctrine, which claimed the right of the Soviet Union to violate the sovereignty of any country that attempted to replace Marxism–Leninism with capitalism.

Brezhnev presided over a period of *détente* with the West that resulted in treaties on armament control (SALT I, SALT II, Anti-Ballistic Missile Treaty) while at the same time building up Soviet military might.

In October 1977, the third Soviet Constitution was unanimously adopted. The prevailing mood of the Soviet leadership at the time of Brezhnev's death in 1982 was one of aversion to change. The long period of Brezhnev's rule had come to be dubbed one of "standstill", with an aging and ossified top political leadership.

Figure 10: *Soviet General Secretary Leonid Brezhnev and U.S. President Jimmy Carter sign the SALT II arms limitation treaty in Vienna on 18 June 1979*

Gorbachev era

Two developments dominated the decade that followed: the increasingly apparent crumbling of the Soviet Union's economic and political structures, and the patchwork attempts at reforms to reverse that process. Kenneth S. Deffeyes argued in *Beyond Oil* that the Reagan administration encouraged Saudi Arabia to lower the price of oil to the point where the Soviets could not make a profit selling their oil, so the USSR's hard currency reserves became depleted.[38]

Brezhnev's next two successors, transitional figures with deep roots in his tradition, did not last long. Yuri Andropov was 68 years old and Konstantin Chernenko 72 when they assumed power; both died in less than two years. In an attempt to avoid a third short-lived leader, in 1985, the Soviets turned to the next generation and selected Mikhail Gorbachev.

Gorbachev made significant changes in the economy and party leadership, called *perestroika*. His policy of *glasnost* freed public access to information after decades of heavy government censorship.

Gorbachev also moved to end the Cold War. In 1988, the Soviet Union abandoned its nine-year war in Afghanistan and began to withdraw its forces. In the late 1980s, he refused military support to the governments of the Soviet Union's satellite statesWikipedia:Please clarify, which paved the way for Revolutions of 1989. With the tearing down of the Berlin Wall and with East

Figure 11: *Mikhail Gorbachev in one-to-one dis-cussions with U.S. President Ronald Reagan*

Figure 12: *Reagan greets a young boy while touring Red Square with Gorbachev during the Moscow Summit, 31 May 1988*

Germany and West Germany pursuing unification, the Iron Curtain between the West and Soviet-controlled regions came down.

In the late 1980s, the constituent republics of the Soviet Union started legal moves towards potentially declaring sovereignty over their territories, citing Article 72 of the USSR constitution, which stated that any constituent republic was free to secede.[39] On 7 April 1990, a law was passed allowing a republic to secede if more than two-thirds of its residents voted for it in a referendum.[40] Many held their first free elections in the Soviet era for their own national legislatures in 1990. Many of these legislatures proceeded to produce legislation contradicting the Union laws in what was known as the "War of Laws".

In 1989, the Russian SFSR, which was then the largest constituent republic (with about half of the population) convened a newly elected Congress of People's Deputies. Boris Yeltsin was elected its chairman. On 12 June 1990, the Congress declared Russia's sovereignty over its territory and proceeded to pass laws that attempted to supersede some of the USSR's laws. After a landslide victory of Sąjūdis in Lithuania, that country declared its independence restored on 11 March 1990.

A referendum for the preservation of the USSR was held on 17 March 1991 in nine republics (the remainder having boycotted the vote), with the majority of the population in those nine republics voting for preservation of the Union. The referendum gave Gorbachev a minor boost. In the summer of 1991, the New Union Treaty, which would have turned the Soviet Union into a much looser Union, was agreed upon by eight republics.

The signing of the treaty, however, was interrupted by the August Coup—an attempted coup d'état by hardline members of the government and the KGB who sought to reverse Gorbachev's reforms and reassert the central government's control over the republics. After the coup collapsed, Yeltsin was seen as a hero for his decisive actions, while Gorbachev's power was effectively ended. The balance of power tipped significantly towards the republics. In August 1991, Latvia and Estonia immediately declared the restoration of their full independence (following Lithuania's 1990 example). Gorbachev resigned as general secretary in late August, and soon afterward the Party's activities were indefinitely suspended—effectively ending its rule. By the fall, Gorbachev could no longer influence events outside Moscow, and he was being challenged even there by Yeltsin, who had been elected President of Russia in July 1991.

Figure 13: *Boris Yeltsin stands on a tank in Moscow to defy the August Coup, 1991*

Dissolution

The remaining 12 republics continued discussing new, increasingly looser, models of the Union. However, by December all except Russia and Kazakhstan had formally declared independence. During this time, Yeltsin took over what remained of the Soviet government, including the Moscow Kremlin. The final blow was struck on 1 December when Ukraine, the second most powerful republic, voted overwhelmingly for independence. Ukraine's secession ended any realistic chance of the Soviet Union staying together even on a limited scale.

On 8 December 1991, the presidents of Russia, Ukraine and Belarus (formerly Byelorussia), signed the Belavezha Accords, which declared the Soviet Union dissolved and established the Commonwealth of Independent States (CIS) in its place. While doubts remained over the authority of the accords to do this, on 21 December 1991, the representatives of all Soviet republics except Georgia signed the Alma-Ata Protocol, which confirmed the accords. On 25 December 1991, Gorbachev resigned as the President of the USSR, declaring the office extinct. He turned the powers that had been vested in the presidency over to Yeltsin. That night, the Soviet flag was lowered for the last time, and the Russian tricolor was raised in its place.

The following day, the Supreme Soviet, the highest governmental body of the Soviet Union, voted both itself and the Soviet Union out of existence. This

Figure 14: *Changes in national boundaries after the end of the Cold War*

is generally recognized as marking the official, final dissolution of the Soviet Union as a functioning state. The Soviet Army originally remained under overall CIS command, but was soon absorbed into the different military forces of the newly independent states. The few remaining Soviet institutions that had not been taken over by Russia ceased to function by the end of 1991.

Following the dissolution of the Soviet Union on 26 December 1991, Russia was internationally recognized[41] as its legal successor on the international stage. To that end, Russia voluntarily accepted all Soviet foreign debt and claimed overseas Soviet properties as its own. Under the 1992 Lisbon Protocol, Russia also agreed to receive all nuclear weapons remaining in the territory of other former Soviet republics. Since then, the Russian Federation has assumed the Soviet Union's rights and obligations. Ukraine has refused to recognize exclusive Russian claims to succession of the USSR and claimed such status for Ukraine as well, which was codified in Articles 7 and 8 of its 1991 law On Legal Succession of Ukraine. Since its independence in 1991, Ukraine has continued to pursue claims against Russia in foreign courts, seeking to recover its share of the foreign property that was owned by the USSR.

The dissolution of the Soviet Union was followed by a severe economic contraction and catastrophic fall in living standards in post-Soviet states[42] including a rapid increase in poverty, crime,[43] corruption, unemployment, homelessness, rates of disease, demographic losses, income inequality and the rise

Figure 15: *Internally displaced Azerbaijanis from Nagorno-Karabakh, 1993*

of an oligarchical class, along with decreases in calorie intake, life expectancy, adult literacy, and income. Between 1988/1989 and 1993/1995, the Gini ratio increased by an average of 9 points for all former socialist countries. The economic shocks that accompanied wholesale privatization were associated with sharp increases in mortality. Data shows Russia, Kazakhstan, Latvia, Lithuania and Estonia saw a tripling of unemployment and a 42% increase in male death rates between 1991 and 1994.[44,45] In the following decades, only five or six of the post-communist states are on a path to joining the wealthy capitalist West while most are falling behind, some to such an extent that it will take over fifty years to catch up to where they were before the fall of the Soviet Bloc.

In summing up the international ramifications of these events, Vladislav Zubok stated: "The collapse of the Soviet empire was an event of epochal geopolitical, military, ideological, and economic significance

Post-Soviet states

The analysis of the succession of states with respect to the 15 post-Soviet states is complex. The Russian Federation is seen as the legal *continuator* state and is for most purposes the heir to the Soviet Union. It retained ownership of all former Soviet embassy properties, as well as the old Soviet UN membership and permanent membership on the Security Council.

There are additionally four states that claim independence from the other internationally recognized post-Soviet states, but possess limited international recognition: Abkhazia, Nagorno-Karabakh, South Ossetia, and Transnistria.

Figure 16: *Country emblems of the Soviet Republics before and after the dissolution of the Soviet Union*Note that the Transcaucasian Soviet Federative Socialist Republic (fifth in the second row) no longer exists as a political entity of any kind and the emblem is unofficial*

The Chechen separatist movement of the Chechen Republic of Ichkeria lacks any international recognition.

Foreign affairs

Organizations

Stalin always made the final policy decisions, 1925–1953. Otherwise Soviet foreign policy was set by the Commission on the Foreign Policy of the Central Committee of the Communist Party of the Soviet Union, or by the Party's highest body the Politburo. Operations were handled by the separate Ministry of Foreign Affairs. It was known as the People's Commissariat for Foreign Affairs (or Narkomindel), until 1946. The most influential spokesmen were Georgy Chicherin (1872–1936), Maxim Litvinov (1876–1951), Vyacheslav Molotov (1890–1986), Andrey Vyshinsky (1883–1954) and Andrei Gromyko (1909–1989). Intellectuals were based in the Moscow State Institute of International Relations.[46]

Figure 17: *1960s Cuba-Soviet friendship poster with Fidel Castro and Nikita Khrushchev*

Figure 18: *Gerald Ford, Leonid Brezhnev and Henry Kissinger speaking informally at the Vladivostok Summit in 1974*

Figure 19: *Mikhail Gorbachev and George H. W. Bush signing bilateral documents during Gorbachev's official visit to the United States in 1990*

Figure 20: *1987 Soviet stamp*

- Comintern (1919–1943), or Communist International, was an international communist organization based in the Kremlin that advocated world communism. The Comintern intended to "struggle by all available means, including armed force, for the overthrow of the international bourgeoisie and the creation of an international Soviet republic as a transition stage to the complete abolition of the state". It was abolished as a conciliatory measure toward Britain and the United States.[47]
- Comecon, the Council for Mutual Economic Assistance (Russian: Совет Экономической Взаимопомощи, *Sovet Ekonomicheskoy Vzaimopomoshchi*, СЭВ, SEV) was an economic organization from 1949 to 1991 under Soviet control that comprised the countries of the Eastern Bloc along with a number of communist states elsewhere in the world. Moscow was concerned about the Marshall Plan and Comecon was meant to prevent countries in the Soviets' sphere of influence from moving towards that of the Americans and South-East Asia. Comecon was the Eastern Bloc's reply to the formation in Western Europe of the Organization for European Economic Co-Operation (OEEC).[48,49]
- The Warsaw Pact was a collective defence alliance formed in 1955 among the Soviet Union and seven Soviet satellite states of Central and Eastern Europe during the Cold War. The Warsaw Pact was the military complement to the Comecon, the regional economic organization for the socialist states of Central and Eastern Europe. The Warsaw Pact was created in reaction to the integration of West Germany into NATO.[50]
- The Cominform (1947–1956), informally the Communist Information Bureau and officially the Information Bureau of the Communist and Workers' Parties, was the first official agency of the international communist movement since the dissolution of the Comintern in 1943. Its role was to coordinate actions between communist parties under Soviet direction. Stalin used it to order Western European communist parties to abandon their exclusively parliamentarian line and instead concentrate on politically impeding the operations of the Marshall Plan.[51] It also coordinated international aid to communist insurgents during the Greek Civil War in 1947–1949.[52] It expelled Yugoslavia in 1948 after Josip Broz Tito insisted on an independent program. Its newspaper, *For a Lasting Peace, for a People's Democracy!*, promoted Stalin's positions. The Cominform's concentration on Europe meant a deemphasis on world revolution in Soviet foreign policy. By enunciating a uniform ideology, it allowed the constituent parties to focus on personalities rather than issues.[53]

Early Soviet foreign policies (1919–1939)

The Communist leadership the Soviet Union intensely debated foreign policy issues and change directions several times. Even after Stalin assumed dictatorial control in the late 1920s, there were debates and he frequently changed positions.[54]

The first stage (1917–1921), assumed that Communist revolutions would break out very soon in every major industrial country, and it was the Soviet responsibility to assist them. The Comintern was the weapon of choice. A few revolutions did break out, but they were quickly suppressed (the longest lasting one was in Hungary)—the Hungarian Soviet Republic—lasted only from 21 March 1919 to 1 August 1919. The Russian Bolsheviks were in no position to give any help.

By 1921, the second stage came with the realization by Lenin, Trotsky, and Stalin that capitalism had stabilized itself in Europe and there would not be any widespread revolutions anytime soon. It became the duty of the Russian Bolsheviks to protect what they had in Russia, and avoid military confrontations that might destroy their bridgehead. Russia was now in it a pariah state, along with Germany. The two came to terms in 1922 with the Treaty of Rapallo that settled long-standing grievances. At the same time the two countries secretly set up training programs for illegal German army and air force operations at hidden camps in the Soviet Union.[55]

At the same time, Moscow stopped threatening other states, and instead worked to open peaceful relationships in terms of trade, and diplomatic recognition. United Kingdom, dismissed the warnings of Winston Churchill and a few others about a continuing communist threat, and opened trade relations and de facto diplomatic recognition in 1922. There was hope for a settlement of the prewar tsarist debts, but that issue was repeatedly postponed. Formal recognition came when the new Labour Party came to power in 1924.[56] All the other major countries opened trade relationships. Henry Ford opened large-scale business relationships with the Soviets in the late 1920s, hoping it would lead to a long-term peace. Finally, in 1933, the United States officially recognized the Soviet Union, a decision backed by public opinion and especially by American business interests that expected a new profitable market would open up.[57]

A third stage came in the late 1920s and early 1930s, when Stalin ordered Communist parties across the world to strongly oppose non-communist political parties, labor unions or other organizations on the left. Stalin reversed himself in 1934 with the Popular Front program the called on all Communist parties to join together with all anti-Fascist political, labor, and organizational forces that were opposed to fascism, especially of the Nazi variety.[58,59]

Politics

There were three power hierarchies in the Soviet Union: the legislature represented by the Supreme Soviet of the Soviet Union, the government represented by the Council of Ministers, and the Communist Party of the Soviet Union (CPSU), the only legal party and the ultimate policymaker in the country.[61]

Communist Party

At the top of the Communist Party was the Central Committee, elected at Party Congresses and Conferences. The Central Committee in turn voted for a Politburo (called the Presidium between 1952–1966), Secretariat and the General Secretary (First Secretary from 1953 to 1966), the de facto highest office in the Soviet Union. Depending on the degree of power consolidation, it was either the Politburo as a collective body or the General Secretary, who always was one of the Politburo members, that effectively led the party and the country (except for the period of the highly personalized authority of Stalin, exercised directly through his position in the Council of Ministers rather than the Politburo after 1941). They were not controlled by the general party membership, as the key principle of the party organization was democratic centralism, demanding strict subordination to higher bodies, and elections went uncontested, endorsing the candidates proposed from above.

Figure 21: *The Grand Kremlin Palace, seat of the Supreme Soviet of the Soviet Union, 1982*

The Communist Party maintained its dominance over the state largely through its control over the system of appointments. All senior government officials and most deputies of the Supreme Soviet were members of the CPSU. Of the party heads themselves, Stalin in 1941–1953 and Khrushchev in 1958–1964 were Premiers. Upon the forced retirement of Khrushchev, the party leader was prohibited from this kind of double membership, but the later General Secretaries for at least some part of their tenure occupied the largely ceremonial position of Chairman of the Presidium of the Supreme Soviet, the nominal head of state. The institutions at lower levels were overseen and at times supplanted by primary party organizations.

However, in practice the degree of control the party was able to exercise over the state bureaucracy, particularly after the death of Stalin, was far from total, with the bureaucracy pursuing different interests that were at times in conflict with the party. Nor was the party itself monolithic from top to bottom, although factions were officially banned.

Government

The Supreme Soviet (successor of the Congress of Soviets and Central Executive Committee) was nominally the highest state body for most of the Soviet history, at first acting as a rubber stamp institution, approving and implementing all decisions made by the party. However, the powers and functions of the Supreme Soviet were extended in the late 1950s, 1960s and 1970s, including the creation of new state commissions and committees. It gained additional powers relating to the approval of the Five-Year Plans and the Soviet government budget. The Supreme Soviet elected a Presidium to wield its power between plenary sessions, ordinarily held twice a year, and appointed the Supreme Court, the Procurator General and the Council of Ministers (known before 1946 as the Council of People's Commissars), headed by the Chairman (Premier) and managing an enormous bureaucracy responsible for the administration of the economy and society. State and party structures of the constituent republics largely emulated the structure of the central institutions, although the Russian SFSR, unlike the other constituent republics, for most of its history had no republican branch of the CPSU, being ruled directly by the union-wide party until 1990. Local authorities were organized likewise into party committees, local Soviets and executive committees. While the state system was nominally federal, the party was unitary.

The state security police (the KGB and its predecessor agencies) played an important role in Soviet politics. It was instrumental in the Stalinist terror, but after the death of Stalin, the state security police was brought under strict party control. Under Yuri Andropov, KGB chairman in 1967–1982 and General Secretary from 1982 to 1984, the KGB engaged in the suppression of political dissent and maintained an extensive network of informers, reasserting itself as a political actor to some extent independent of the party-state structure, culminating in the anti-corruption campaign targeting high party officials in the late 1970s and early 1980s.

Separation of power and reform

The Union constitutions, which were promulgated in 1918, 1924, 1936 and 1977, did not limit state power. No formal separation of powers existed between the Party, Supreme Soviet and Council of Ministers that represented executive and legislative branches of the government. The system was governed less by statute than by informal conventions, and no settled mechanism of leadership succession existed. Bitter and at times deadly power struggles took place in the Politburo after the deaths of Lenin and Joseph Stalin, as well as after Khrushchev's dismissal, itself due to a decision by both the Politburo and the Central Committee. All leaders of the Communist Party before Gorbachev died in office, except Georgy Malenkov and Khrushchev, both dismissed from the party leadership amid internal struggle within the party.

Between 1988 and 1990, facing considerable opposition, Mikhail Gorbachev enacted reforms shifting power away from the highest bodies of the party and

Figure 22: *Nationalist anti-government riots in Dushanbe, Tajikistan, 1990*

making the Supreme Soviet less dependent on them. The Congress of People's Deputies was established, the majority of whose members were directly elected in competitive elections held in March 1989. The Congress now elected the Supreme Soviet, which became a full-time parliament, much stronger than before. For the first time since the 1920s, it refused to rubber stamp proposals from the party and Council of Ministers. In 1990, Gorbachev introduced and assumed the position of the President of the Soviet Union, concentrated power in his executive office, independent of the party, and subordinated the government, now renamed the Cabinet of Ministers of the USSR, to himself.

Tensions grew between the union-wide authorities under Gorbachev, reformists led in Russia by Boris Yeltsin and controlling the newly elected Supreme Soviet of the Russian SFSR, and communist hardliners. On 19–21 August 1991, a group of hardliners staged an abortive coup attempt. Following the failed coup, the State Council of the Soviet Union became the highest organ of state power "in the period of transition". Gorbachev resigned as General Secretary, only remaining President for the final months of the existence of the USSR.

Judicial system

The judiciary was not independent of the other branches of government. The Supreme Court supervised the lower courts (People's Court) and applied the law as established by the Constitution or as interpreted by the Supreme Soviet. The Constitutional Oversight Committee reviewed the constitutionality of laws and acts. The Soviet Union used the inquisitorial system of Roman law, where the judge, procurator, and defense attorney collaborate to establish the truth.

Administrative divisions

Constitutionally, the USSR was a federation of constituent Union Republics, which were either unitary states, such as Ukraine or Byelorussia (SSRs), or federal states, such as Russia or Transcaucasia (SFSRs), all four being the founding republics who signed the Treaty on the Creation of the USSR in December 1922. In 1924, during the national delimitation in Central Asia, Uzbekistan and Turkmenistan were formed from parts of the Russia's Turkestan ASSR and two Soviet dependencies, the Khorezm and Bukharan SSRs. In 1929, Tajikistan was split off from the Uzbekistan SSR. With the constitution of 1936, the Transcaucasian SFSR was dissolved, resulting in its constituent republics of Armenia, Georgia and Azerbaijan being elevated to Union Republics, while Kazakhstan and Kirghizia were split off from Russian SFSR, resulting in the same status. In August 1940, Moldavia was formed from parts of the Ukraine and Bessarabia and Northern Bukovina. Estonia, Latvia and Lithuania (SSRs) were also admitted into the union which was not recognized by most of the international community and was considered an illegal occupation. Karelia was split off from Russia as a Union Republic in March 1940 and was reabsorbed in 1956. Between July 1956 and September 1991, there were 15 union republics (see map below).

While nominally a union of equals, in practice the Soviet Union was dominated by Russians. The domination was so absolute that for most of the Soviet Union's existence, it was commonly (but incorrectly) referred to as "Russia". While the RSFSR was technically only one republic within the larger union, it was by far the largest (both in terms of population and geography), most powerful, and most highly developed. Historian Matthew White wrote that it was an open secret that the Soviet Union's federal structure was "window dressing" for Russian dominance. For that reason, the people of the Soviet Union were usually called "Russians", not "Soviets", since "everyone knew who really ran the show".

	Flag	Republic	Capital	Map of the Soviet Union
		The Republics of the Soviet Union (1956–1991)		
1		Russia	Moscow	
2		Ukraine	Kiev	
3		Byelorussia	Minsk	
4		Uzbekistan	Tashkent	
5		Kazakhstan	Alma-Ata	
6		Georgia	Tbilisi	
7		Azerbaijan	Baku	
8		Lithuania[a]	Vilnius	
9		Moldavia	Kishinev	
10		Latvia[a]	Riga	
11		Kirghizia	Frunze	
12		Tajikistan	Dushanbe	
13		Armenia	Yerevan	
14		Turkmenia	Ashkhabad	
15		Estonia[a]	Tallinn	

[a] The annexation of the Baltic republics in 1940 was illegal occupation by the current Baltic governments and by a number of Western countries, including the United States, United Kingdom, Canada, Australia and the European Union.[62,63] Their position is supported by the European Union,[64] the European Court of Human Rights,[65] the United Nations Human Rights Council and the United States. The Soviet Union and the current government of the Russian Federation considered the annexation legal, but officially recognized their independence on September 6, 1991, three months prior to its final dissolution.

Economy

The Soviet Union became the first country to adopt a planned economy, whereby production and distribution of goods were centralized and directed by the government. The first Bolshevik experience with a command economy

Figure 23: *The DneproGES, one of many hydroelectric power stations in the Soviet Union*

Figure 24:
The Soviet Union in comparison to other countries by GDP (nominal) per capita in 1965 based on a West-German school book (1971)

Figure 25: *Picking cotton in Armenia in the 1930s*

was the policy of War communism, which involved the nationalization of industry, centralized distribution of output, coercive requisition of agricultural
production, and attempts to eliminate money circulation, private enterprises
and free trade. After the severe economic collapse, Lenin replaced war communism by the New Economic Policy (NEP) in 1921, legalising free trade and
private ownership of small businesses. The economy quickly recovered.

After a long debate among the members of Politburo about the course of
economic development, by 1928–1929, upon gaining control of the country,
Joseph Stalin abandoned NEP and pushed for full central planning, starting
forced collectivization of agriculture and enacting draconian labor legislation.
Resources were mobilized for rapid industrialization, which greatly expanded
Soviet capacity in heavy industry and capital goods during the 1930s. A main
motivation for industrialization was preparation for war, mostly due to distrust
of the outside capitalistic world. As a result, the USSR was transformed from
a largely agrarian economy into a great industrial power, leading the way for
its emergence as a superpower after World War II. The war hugely devastated
Soviet economy and infrastructure and they required extensive reconstruction.

By the early 1940s, the Soviet economy had become relatively self-sufficient;
for most of the period until the creation of Comecon, only a very small share of
domestic products was traded internationally. After the creation of the Eastern
Bloc, external trade rose rapidly. Still, the influence of the world economy

on the USSR was limited by fixed domestic prices and a state monopoly on foreign trade. Grain and sophisticated consumer manufactures became major import articles from around the 1960s. During the arms race of the Cold War, the Soviet economy was burdened by military expenditures, heavily lobbied for by a powerful bureaucracy dependent on the arms industry. At the same time, the Soviet Union became the largest arms exporter to the Third World. Significant amounts of Soviet resources during the Cold War were allocated in aid to the other socialist states.

From the 1930s until its dissolution in late 1991, the way the Soviet economy operated remained essentially unchanged. The economy was formally directed by central planning, carried out by Gosplan and organized in five-year plans. However, in practice the plans were highly aggregated and provisional, subject to *ad hoc* intervention by superiors. All key economic decisions were taken by the political leadership. Allocated resources and plan targets were normally denominated in rubles rather than in physical goods. Credit was discouraged, but widespread. Final allocation of output was achieved through relatively de-centralized, unplanned contracting. Although in theory prices were legally set from above, in practice they were often negotiated, and informal horizontal links (between producer factories etc.) were widespread.

A number of basic services were state-funded, such as education and health care. In the manufacturing sector, heavy industry and defense were prioritized over consumer goods. Consumer goods, particularly outside large cities, were often scarce, of poor quality and limited choice. Under command economy, consumers had almost no influence on production, so the changing demands of a population with growing incomes could not be satisfied by supplies at rigidly fixed prices.[66] A massive unplanned second economy grew up at low levels alongside the planned one, providing some of the goods and services that the planners could not. Legalization of some elements of the decentralized economy was attempted with the reform of 1965.

Although statistics of the Soviet economy are notoriously unreliable and its economic growth difficult to estimate precisely, by most accounts, the economy continued to expand until the mid-1980s. During the 1950s and 1960s, it had comparatively high growth and was catching up to the West. However, after 1970, the growth, while still positive, steadily declined much more quickly and consistently than in other countries, despite a rapid increase in the capital stock (the rate of capital increase was only surpassed by Japan).

Overall, between 1960 and 1989, the growth rate of per capita income in the Soviet Union was slightly above the world average (based on 102 countries).Wikipedia:Citation needed According to Stanley Fischer and William

Figure 26: *Workers of the Salihorsk potash plant, Belarus, 1968*

Easterly, growth could have been faster. By their calculation, per capita income of Soviet Union in 1989 should have been twice higher than it was, considering the amount of investment, education and population. The authors attribute this poor performance to low productivity of capital in the Soviet Union. Steven Rosenfielde states that the standard of living declined due to Stalin's despotism, and while there was a brief improvement after his death, it lapsed into stagnation.

In 1987, Mikhail Gorbachev tried to reform and revitalize the economy with his program of *perestroika*. His policies relaxed state control over enterprises, but did not replace it by market incentives, resulting in a sharp decline in output. The economy, already suffering from reduced petroleum export revenues, started to collapse. Prices were still fixed, and property was still largely state-owned until after the dissolution of the Soviet Union. For most of the period after World War II until its collapse, Soviet GDP (PPP) was the second largest in the world, and 3rd in the world during the mid-1980s to 1989, although per-capita it was behind that of First World countries. Compared to countries with similar per-capita GDP in 1928, the Soviet Union experienced significant growth.

In 1990, the Soviet Union had a Human Development Index of 0.920, placing it in the "high" category of human development. It was the third-highest in the

Figure 27: *Soviet stamp depicting the 30th anniversary of the International Atomic Energy Agency, published in 1987, a year following the Chernobyl nuclear disaster*

Eastern Bloc, behind Czechoslovakia and East Germany, and the 25th in the world of 130 countries.

Energy

The need for fuel declined in the Soviet Union from the 1970s to the 1980s, both per ruble of gross social product and per ruble of industrial product. At the start, this decline grew very rapidly but gradually slowed down between 1970 and 1975. From 1975 and 1980, it grew even slower,Wikipedia:Please clarify only 2.6 percent. David Wilson, a historian, believed that the gas industry would account for 40 percent of Soviet fuel production by the end of the century. His theory did not come to fruition because of the USSR's collapse. The USSR, in theory, would have continued to have an economic growth rate of 2–2.5 percent during the 1990s because of Soviet energy fields.Wikipedia:Please clarify However, the energy sector faced many difficulties, among them the country's high military expenditure and hostile relations with the First World (pre-Gorbachev era).

In 1991, the Soviet Union had a pipeline network of 82,000 kilometres (51,000 mi) for crude oil and another 206,500 kilometres (128,300 mi) for natural gas. Petroleum and petroleum-based products, natural gas, metals,

Figure 28: *Soviet stamp showing the orbit of Sputnik 1*

wood, agricultural products, and a variety of manufactured goods, primarily machinery, arms and military equipment, were exported. In the 1970s and 1980s, the Soviet Union heavily relied on fossil fuel exports to earn hard currency. At its peak in 1988, it was the largest producer and second largest exporter of crude oil, surpassed only by Saudi Arabia.

Science and technology

The Soviet Union placed great emphasis on science and technology within its economy, however, the most remarkable Soviet successes in technology, such as producing the world's first space satellite, typically were the responsibility of the military. Lenin believed that the USSR would never overtake the developed world if it remained as technologically backward as it was upon its founding. Soviet authorities proved their commitment to Lenin's belief by developing massive networks, research and development organizations. In the early 1960s, the Soviets awarded 40% of chemistry PhDs to women, compared to only 5% who received such a degree in the United States.[67] By 1989, Soviet scientists were among the world's best-trained specialists in several areas, such as energy physics, selected areas of medicine, mathematics, welding and military technologies. Due to rigid state planning and bureaucracy, the Soviets remained far behind technologically in chemistry, biology, and computers when compared to the First World.

Figure 29: *Aeroflot's flag during the Soviet era*

Under the Reagan administration, Project Socrates determined that the Soviet Union addressed the acquisition of science and technology in a manner that was radically different from what the US was using. In the case of the US, economic prioritization was being used for indigenous research and develop-ment as the means to acquire science and technology in both the private and public sectors. In contrast, the Soviet Union was offensively and defensively maneuvering in the acquisition and utilization of the worldwide technology, to increase the competitive advantage that they acquired from the technology, while preventing the US from acquiring a competitive advantage. However, in addition, the Soviet Union's technology-based planning was executed in a cen-tralized, government-centric manner that greatly hindered its flexibility. It was this significant lack of flexibility that was exploited by the US to undermine the strength of the Soviet Union and thus foster its reform.

Transport

Transport was a key component of the nation's economy. The economic cen-tralization of the late 1920s and 1930s led to the development of infrastructure on a massive scale, most notably the establishment of Aeroflot, an aviation en-terprise. The country had a wide variety of modes of transport by land, water and air. However, due to bad maintenance, much of the road, water and Soviet civil aviation transport were outdated and technologically backward compared to the First World.

Soviet rail transport was the largest and most intensively used in the world; it was also better developed than most of its Western counterparts. By the late 1970s and early 1980s, Soviet economists were calling for the construction of more roads to alleviate some of the burden from the railways and to improve

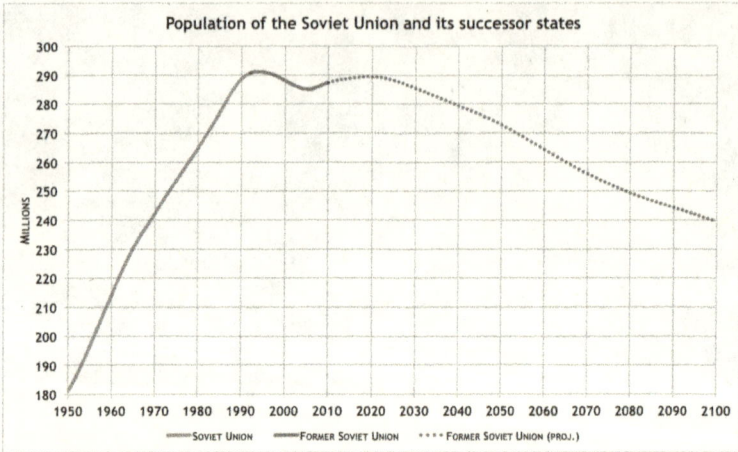

Figure 30: *Population of the Soviet Union (red) and the post-Soviet states (blue) from 1961 to 2009 as well as projection (dotted blue) from 2010 to 2100*

the Soviet government budget.[68] The street network and automotive indus-try[69] remained underdeveloped,[70] and dirt roads were common outside major cities.[71] Soviet maintenance projects proved unable to take care of even the few roads the country had. By the early-to-mid-1980s, the Soviet authori-ties tried to solve the road problem by ordering the construction of new ones. Meanwhile, the automobile industry was growing at a faster rate than road construction.[72] The underdeveloped road network led to a growing demand for public transport.[73]

Despite improvements, several aspects of the transport sector were still-Wikipedia:Manual of Style/Dates and numbers#Chronological items riddled with problems due to outdated infrastructure, lack of investment, corruption and bad decision-making. Soviet authorities were unable to meet the growing demand for transport infrastructure and services.

The Soviet merchant navy was one of the largest in the world.

Demographics

Excess deaths over the course of World War I and the Russian Civil War (in-cluding the postwar famine) amounted to a combined total of 18 million, some 10 million in the 1930s, and more than 26 million in 1941–5. The postwar Soviet population was 45 to 50 million smaller than it would have been if pre-war demographic growth had continued. According to Catherine Merridale,

"... reasonable estimate would place the total number of excess deaths for the whole period somewhere around 60 million."

The birth rate of the USSR decreased from 44.0 per thousand in 1926 to 18.0 in 1974, largely due to increasing urbanization and the rising average age of marriages. The mortality rate demonstrated a gradual decrease as well – from 23.7 per thousand in 1926 to 8.7 in 1974. In general, the birth rates of the southern republics in Transcaucasia and Central Asia were considerably higher than those in the northern parts of the Soviet Union, and in some cases even increased in the post–World War II period, a phenomenon partly attributed to slower rates of urbanization and traditionally earlier marriages in the southern republics. Soviet Europe moved towards sub-replacement fertility, while Soviet Central Asia continued to exhibit population growth well above replacement-level fertility.

The late 1960s and the 1970s witnessed a reversal of the declining trajectory of the rate of mortality in the USSR, and was especially notable among men of working age, but was also prevalent in Russia and other predominantly Slavic areas of the country. An analysis of the official data from the late 1980s showed that after worsening in the late-1970s and the early 1980s, adult mortality began to improve again. The infant mortality rate increased from 24.7 in 1970 to 27.9 in 1974. Some researchers regarded the rise as largely real, a consequence of worsening health conditions and services. The rises in both adult and infant mortality were not explained or defended by Soviet officials, and the Soviet government simply stopped publishing all mortality statistics for ten years. Soviet demographers and health specialists remained silent about the mortality increases until the late-1980s, when the publication of mortality data resumed and researchers could delve into the real causes.[74]

Education

Anatoly Lunacharsky became the first People's Commissar for Education of Soviet Russia. At the beginning, the Soviet authorities placed great emphasis on the elimination of illiteracy. People who were literate were automatically hired as teachers. Wikipedia:Citation needed For a short period, quality was sacrificed for quantity. By 1940, Joseph Stalin could announce that illiteracy had been eliminated. Throughout the 1930s social mobility rose sharply, which has been attributed to Soviet reforms in education.[75] In the aftermath of the Great Patriotic War, the country's educational system expanded dramatically. This expansion had a tremendous effect. In the 1960s, nearly all Soviet children had access to education, the only exception being those living in remote areas. Nikita Khrushchev tried to make education more accessible, making it clear to children that education was closely linked to the needs of

Figure 31: *Soviet pupils in Milovice, Czechoslovakia (now Czech Republic), 1985*

society. Education also became important in giving rise to the New Man. Citizens directly entering the work force had the constitutional right to a job and to free vocational training.

The country's system of education was highly centralized and universally accessible to all citizens, with affirmative action for applicants from nations associated with cultural backwardness. However, as part of the general antisemitic policy, an unofficial Jewish quota was applied in the leading institutions of higher education by subjecting Jewish applicants to harsher entrance examinations. The Brezhnev era also introduced a rule that required all university applicants to present a reference from the local Komsomol party secretary. According to statistics from 1986, the number of higher education students per the population of 10,000 was 181 for the USSR, compared to 517 for the U.S.

Ethnic groups

The Soviet Union was a very ethnically diverse country, with more than 100 distinct ethnic groups. The total population was estimated at 293 million in 1991. According to a 1990 estimate, the majority were Russians (50.78%), followed by Ukrainians (15.45%) and Uzbeks (5.84%).

All citizens of the USSR had their own ethnic affiliation. The ethnicity of a person was chosen at the age of sixteen[76] by the child's parents. If the parents

Figure 32: *People in Samarkand, Uzbek SSR, 1981*

Figure 33: *Svaneti man in Mestia, Georgian SSR, 1929*

did not agree, the child was automatically assigned the ethnicity of the father. Partly due to Soviet policies, some of the smaller minority ethnic groups were considered part of larger ones, such as the Mingrelians of Georgia, who were classified with the linguistically related Georgians. Some ethnic groups voluntarily assimilated, while others were brought in by force. Russians, Belarusians, and Ukrainians shared close cultural ties, while other groups did not. With multiple nationalities living in the same territory, ethnic antagonisms developed over the years.[77]Wikipedia:Neutral point of viewTalk:Soviet Union#

Figure 34: *Ethnographic map of the Soviet Union, 1941*

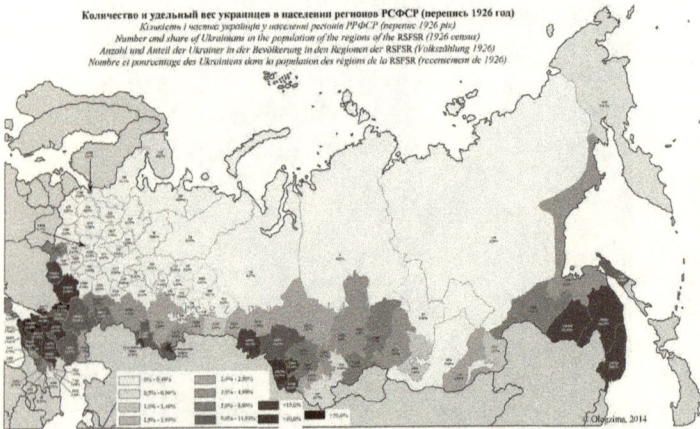

Figure 35: *Number and share of Ukrainians in the population of the regions of the RSFSR (1926 census)*

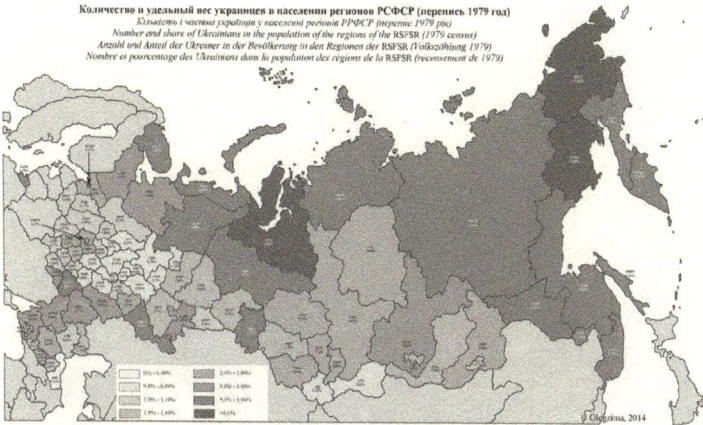

Figure 36: *Number and share of Ukrainians in the population of the regions of the RSFSR (1979 census)*

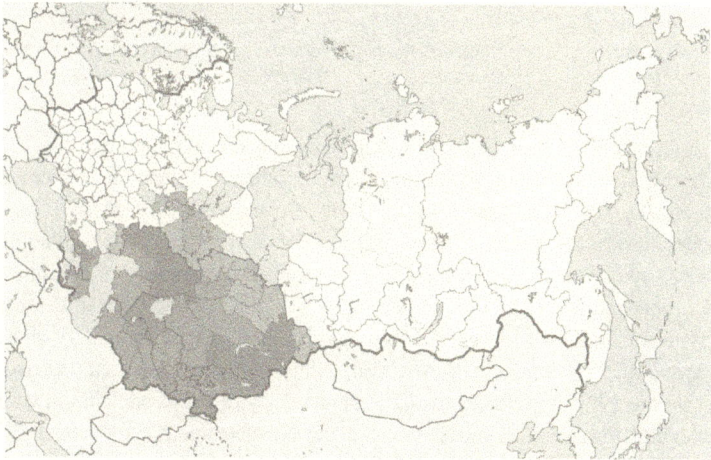

Figure 37: *Map showing the distribution of Muslims within the Soviet Union in 1979*

Health

In 1917, before the revolution, health conditions were significantly behind those of developed countries. As Lenin later noted, "Either the lice will defeat socialism, or socialism will defeat the lice". The Soviet principle of health care was conceived by the People's Commissariat for Health in 1918. Health care was to be controlled by the state and would be provided to its citizens free of

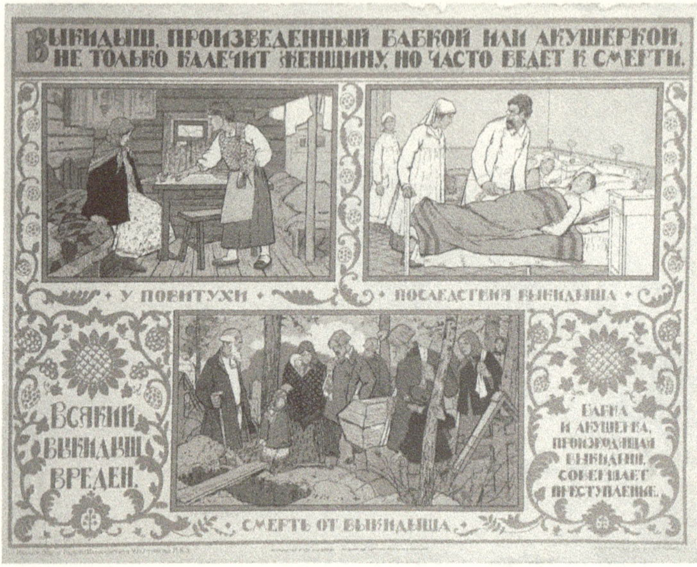

Figure 38: *An early Soviet-era poster discouraging unsafe abortion practices*

charge, this at the time being a revolutionary concept. Article 42 of the 1977 Soviet Constitution gave all citizens the right to health protection and free access to any health institutions in the USSR. Before Leonid Brezhnev became General Secretary, the healthcare system of the Soviet Union was held in high esteem by many foreign specialists. This changed however, from Brezhnev's accession and Mikhail Gorbachev's tenure as leader, the Soviet health care system was heavily criticized for many basic faults, such as the quality of service and the unevenness in its provision. Minister of Health Yevgeniy Chazov, during the 19th Congress of the Communist Party of the Soviet Union, while highlighting such Soviet successes as having the most doctors and hospitals in the world, recognized the system's areas for improvement and felt that billions of Soviet rubles were squandered.

After the socialist revolution, the life expectancy for all age groups went up. This statistic in itself was seen by some that the socialist system was superior to the capitalist system. These improvements continued into the 1960s, when the life expectancy in the Soviet Union surpassed that of the United States. It remained stable during most years, although in the 1970s, it went down slightly, possibly because of alcohol abuse. At the same time, infant mortality began to rise. After 1974, the government stopped publishing statistics on this. This trend can be partly explained by the number of pregnancies rising drastically in the Asian part of the country where infant mortality was highest, while declining markedly in the more developed European part of the Soviet Union. The USSR had several centers of excellence, such as the Fyodorov Eye Microsurgery Complex, founded in 1988 by Russian eye surgeon Svyatoslav Fyodorov.

Language

The Soviet government headed by Vladimir Lenin gave small language groups their own writing systems. The development of these writing systems was very successful, even though some flaws were detected. During the later days of the USSR, countries with the same multilingual situation implemented similar policies. A serious problem when creating these writing systems was that the languages differed dialectally greatly from each other. When a language had been given a writing system and appeared in a notable publication, that language would attain "official language" status. There were many minority languages which never received their own writing system; therefore their speakers were forced to have a second language. There are examples where the Soviet government retreated from this policy, most notable under Stalin's regime, where education was discontinued in languages which were not widespread enough. These languages were then assimilated into another language, mostly Russian. During the Great Patriotic War, some minority languages were banned, and their speakers accused of collaborating with the enemy.

As the most widely spoken of the Soviet Union's many languages, Russian *de facto* functioned as an official language, as the "language of interethnic communication" (Russian: язык межнационального общения), but only assumed the *de jure* status as the official national language in 1990.

Religion

Christianity and Islam had the greatest number of adherents among the Soviet state's religious citizens. Eastern Christianity predominated among Christians, with Russia's traditional Russian Orthodox Church being the Soviet Union's largest Christian denomination. About 90 percent of the Soviet Union's Muslims were Sunnis, with Shias being concentrated in Azerbaijan. Smaller groups included Roman Catholics, Jews, Buddhists, and a variety of Protestant denominations (especially Baptists and Lutherans).

Religious influence had been strong in the Russian Empire. The Russian Orthodox Church enjoyed a privileged status as the church of the monarchy and took part in carrying out official state functions. The immediate period following the establishment of the Soviet state included a struggle against the

Figure 39: *The Cathedral of Christ the Saviour*
in Moscow during its demolition in 1931

Orthodox Church, which the revolutionaries considered an ally of the former
ruling classes.

In Soviet law, the "freedom to hold religious services" was constitutionally
guaranteed, although the ruling Communist Party regarded religion as incompatible with the Marxist spirit of scientific materialism. In practice, the Soviet
system subscribed to a narrow interpretation of this right, and in fact utilized
a range of official measures to discourage religion and curb the activities of
religious groups.

The 1918 Council of People's Commissars decree establishing the Russian Soviet Federative Socialist Republic (RSFSR) as a secular state also decreed that
"the teaching of religion in all [places] where subjects of general instruction
are taught, is forbidden. Citizens may teach and may be taught religion privately." Among further restrictions, those adopted in 1929, a half-decade into
Stalin's rule, included express prohibitions on a range of church activities, including meetings for organized Bible study. Both Christian and non-Christian
establishments were shut down by the thousands in the 1920s and 1930s. By
1940, as many as 90 percent of the churches, synagogues, and mosques that
had been operating in 1917 were closed.

Figure 40: *Soviet stamp showing Saint Sophia's Cathedral, Kiev and statue of Bohdan Khmelnytsky, 1989*

Convinced that religious anti-Sovietism had become a thing of the past with most Soviet Christians, and with the looming threat of war, the Stalin regime began shifting to a more moderate religion policy in the late 1930s. Soviet religious establishments overwhelmingly rallied to support the war effort during the Soviet war with Nazi Germany. Amid other accommodations to religious faith after Nazi Germany attacked the Soviet Union, churches were reopened, Radio Moscow began broadcasting a religious hour, and a historic meeting between Stalin and Orthodox Church leader Patriarch Sergius of Moscow was held in 1943. Stalin had the support of the majority of the religious people in the Soviet Union even through the late 1980s. The general tendency of this period was an increase in religious activity among believers of all faiths.

The Soviet establishment under General Secretary Nikita Khrushchev's leadership clashed with the churches in 1958–1964, a period when atheism was emphasized in the educational curriculum, and numerous state publications promoted atheistic views. During this period, the number of churches fell from 20,000 to 10,000 from 1959 to 1965, and the number of synagogues dropped from 500 to 97. The number of working mosques also declined, falling from 1,500 to 500 within a decade.

Religious institutions remained monitored by the Soviet government, but churches, synagogues, temples, and mosques were all given more leeway in

Figure 41: *Soviet singer-songwriter, poet and actor Vladimir Vysotsky in 1979*

the Brezhnev era. Official relations between the Orthodox Church and the Soviet government again warmed to the point that the Brezhnev government twice honored Orthodox Patriarch Alexy I with the Order of the Red Banner of Labour. A poll conducted by Soviet authorities in 1982 recorded 20 percent of the Soviet population as "active religious believers."

Culture

The culture of the Soviet Union passed through several stages during the USSR's 69-year existence. During the first eleven years following the Revolution (1918–1929), there was relative freedom and artists experimented with several different styles to find a distinctive Soviet style of art. Lenin wanted art to be accessible to the Russian people. On the other hand, hundreds of intellectuals, writers, and artists were exiled or executed, and their work banned, for example Nikolay Gumilyov (shot for alleged conspiring against the Bolshevik regime) and Yevgeny Zamyatin (banned).[78]

The government encouraged a variety of trends. In art and literature, numerous schools, some traditional and others radically experimental, proliferated.

Communist writers Maxim Gorky and Vladimir Mayakovsky were active during this time. Film, as a means of influencing a largely illiterate society, received encouragement from the state; much of director Sergei Eisenstein's best work dates from this period.

Later, during Stalin's rule, Soviet culture was characterized by the rise and domination of the government-imposed style of socialist realism, with all other trends being severely repressed, with rare exceptions, for example Mikhail Bulgakov's works. Many writers were imprisoned and killed.

Following the Khrushchev Thaw of the late 1950s and early 1960s, censorship was diminished. During this time, a distinctive period of Soviet culture developed characterized by conformist public life and intense focus on personal life. Greater experimentation in art forms were again permissible, with the result that more sophisticated and subtly critical work began to be produced. The regime loosened its emphasis on socialist realism; thus, for instance, many protagonists of the novels of author Yury Trifonov concerned themselves with problems of daily life rather than with building socialism. An underground dissident literature, known as *samizdat*, developed during this late period. In architecture the Khrushchev era mostly focused on functional design as opposed to the highly decorated style of Stalin's epoch.

In the second half of the 1980s, Gorbachev's policies of *perestroika* and *glasnost* significantly expanded freedom of expression throughout the Soviet Union in the media & press.

Sport

Founded on 20 July 1924 in Moscow, *Sovetsky Sport* was the first sports newspaper of the Soviet Union.

The Olympic Committee of the USSR formed on April 21, 1951, and the IOC recognised the new body in its 45th session (7 May 1951). In the same year, when the Soviet representative Konstantin Andrianov became an IOC member, the USSR officially joined the Olympic Movement. The 1952 Summer Olympics in Helsinki thus became first Olympic Games for Soviet athletes.

The Soviet Union national ice hockey team won nearly every world championship and Olympic tournament between 1954 and 1991 and never failed to medal in any International Ice Hockey Federation (IIHF) tournament they competed in.

The adventWikipedia:Manual of Style/Dates and numbers#Chronological items of the state-sponsored "full-time amateur athlete" of the Eastern Bloc countries further eroded the ideology of the pure amateur, as it put the self-financed amateurs of the Western countries at a disadvantage. The Soviet

Figure 42: *Valeri Kharlamov represented the Soviet Union at 11 Ice Hockey World Championships, winning 8 gold medals, 2 silvers and 1 bronze*

Union entered teams of athletes who were all nominally students, soldiers, or working in a profession - in reality the Soviet state paid many of these competitors to train on a full-time basis. Nevertheless, the IOC held to the traditional rules regarding amateurism.

A 1989 report by a committee of the Australian Senate claimed that "there is hardly a medal winner at the Moscow Games, certainly not a gold medal winner...who is not on one sort of drug or another: usually several kinds. The Moscow Games might well have been called the Chemists' Games".

A member of the IOC Medical Commission, Manfred Donike, privately ran additional tests with a new technique for identifying abnormal levels of testosterone by measuring its ratio to epitestosterone in urine. Twenty percent of the specimens he tested, including those from sixteen gold medalists, would have resulted in disciplinary proceedings had the tests been official. The results of Donike's unofficial tests later convinced the IOC to add his new technique to their testing protocols. The first documented case of "blood doping" occurred at the 1980 Summer Olympics when a runnerWikipedia:Manual of Style/Words to watch#Unsupported attributions was transfused with two pints of blood before winning medals in the 5000 m and 10,000 m.

Documentation obtained in 2016 revealed the Soviet Union's plans for a statewide doping system in track and field in preparation for the 1984 Summer Olympics in Los Angeles. Dated prior to the USSR's decision to boycott the 1984 Games, the document detailed the existing steroids operations of the program, along with suggestions for further enhancements. Dr. Sergei Portugalov of the Institute for Physical Culture, prepared the communication, directed to the Soviet Union's head of track and field. Portugalov later became one of the main figures involved in the implementation of Russian doping prior to the 2016 Summer Olympics.

Bibliography

- Ambler, John; Shaw, Denis J.B.; Symons, Leslie (1985). *Soviet and East European Transport Problems*[79]. Taylor & Francis. ISBN 978-0-7099-0557-8.
- Comrie, Bernard (1981). *The Languages of the Soviet Union*[80]. Cambridge University Press (CUP) Archive. ISBN 978-0-521-29877-3.
- Davies, Robert; Wheatcroft, Stephen (2004). *The Industrialisation of Soviet Russia Volume 5: The Years of Hunger: Soviet Agriculture 1931–1933*[81]. Palgrave Macmillan. ISBN 978-0-230-23855-8.
- Fischer, Louis (1964). *The Life of Lenin*. London: Weidenfeld and Nicolson.
- Janz, Denis (1998). *World Christianity and Marxism*[82]. New York: Oxford University Press. ISBN 978-0-19-511944-2.
- Lane, David Stuart (1992). *Soviet Society under Perestroika*[83]. Routledge. ISBN 978-0-415-07600-5.
- Leggett, George (1981). *The Cheka: Lenin's Political Police*. Oxford: Oxford University Press. ISBN 978-0-19-822552-2.
- Lewin, Moshe (1969). *Lenin's Last Struggle*. Translated by Sheridan Smith, A. M. London: Faber and Faber.
- Rayfield, Donald (2004). *Stalin and His Hangmen: An Authoritative Portrait of a Tyrant and Those Who Served Him*. Viking Press. ISBN 978-0-375-75771-6.
- Service, Robert (2000). *Lenin: A Biography*. London: Macmillan. ISBN 978-0-333-72625-9.
- Simon, Gerard (1974). *Church, State, and Opposition in the U.S.S.R.*[84] Berkeley and Los Angeles: University of California Press. ISBN 978-0-520-02612-4.
- Volkogonov, Dmitri (1994). *Lenin: Life and Legacy*. Translated by Shukman, Harold. London: HarperCollins. ISBN 978-0-00-255123-6.

- White, James D. (2001). *Lenin: The Practice and Theory of Revolution*. European History in Perspective. Basingstoke, England: Palgrave. ISBN 978-0-333-72157-5.
- Wilson, David (1983). *The Demand for Energy in the Soviet Union*[85]. Taylor & Francis. ISBN 978-0-7099-2704-4.
- World Bank and OECD (1991). *A Study of the Soviet economy*[86]. **3**. International Monetary Fund. ISBN 9789264134683.
- Palat, Madhavan K. (2001). *Social Identities in Revolutionary Russia*[87]. UK: Palgrave. ISBN 978-0-333-92947-6. Retrieved 26 May 2012.
- Warshofsky Lapidus, Gail (1978). *Women in Soviet Society: Equality, Development, and Social Change*. Berkeley, CA: University of California Press. ISBN 978-0-520-03938-4.
- Wheatcroft, Stephen (1996). "The Scale and Nature of German and Soviet Repression and Mass Killings, 1930–45"[88] (PDF). *Europe-Asia Studies*. **48** (8): 1319–1353. doi: 10.1080/09668139608412415[89]. JSTOR 152781[90].

Further reading

<templatestyles src="Template:Refbegin/styles.css" />

Surveys

- *A Country Study: Soviet Union (Former)*[91]. Library of Congress Country Studies, 1991.
- Brown, Archie, et al., eds.: *The Cambridge Encyclopedia of Russia and the Soviet Union* (Cambridge University Press, 1982).
- Gilbert, Martin. *Routledge Atlas of Russian History* (4th ed. 2007) excerpt and text search[92]
- Gorodetsky, Gabriel, ed. *Soviet Foreign Policy, 1917–1991: A Retrospective* (2014)
- Grant, Ted. *Russia, from Revolution to Counter-Revolution*, London, Well Red Publications, 1997
- Hosking, Geoffrey. *The First Socialist Society: A History of the Soviet Union from Within* (2nd ed. Harvard UP 1992) 570pp
- Howe, G. Melvyn: *The Soviet Union: A Geographical Survey* 2nd. edn. (Estover, UK: MacDonald and Evans, 1983).
- Kort, Michael. *The Soviet Colossus: History and Aftermath* (7th ed. 2010) 502pp
- McCauley, Martin. *The Rise and Fall of the Soviet Union* (2007), 522 pages.
- Moss, Walter G. *A History of Russia*. Vol. 2: Since 1855. 2d ed. Anthem Press, 2005.

- Nove, Alec. *An Economic History of the USSR, 1917–1991.* (3rd ed. 1993)
- Pipes, Richard. *Communism: A History* (2003)
- Service, Robert. *A History of Twentieth-Century Russia.* (2nd ed. 1999)

Lenin and Leninism

- Clark, Ronald W. *Lenin* (1988). 570 pp.
- Debo, Richard K. *Survival and Consolidation: The Foreign Policy of Soviet Russia, 1918–1921* (1992).
- Marples, David R. *Lenin's Revolution: Russia, 1917–1921* (2000) 156pp. short survey
- Pipes, Richard. *A Concise History of the Russian Revolution* (1996) excerpt and text search[93], by a leading conservative
- Pipes, Richard. *Russia under the Bolshevik Regime.* (1994). 608 pp.
- Service, Robert. *Lenin: A Biography* (2002), 561pp; standard scholarly biography; a short version of his 3 vol detailed biography
- Volkogonov, Dmitri. *Lenin: Life and Legacy* (1994). 600 pp.

Stalin and Stalinism

- Daniels, R. V., ed. *The Stalin Revolution* (1965)
- Davies, Sarah, and James Harris, eds. *Stalin: A New History,* (2006), 310pp, 14 specialized essays by scholars excerpt and text search[94]
- De Jonge, Alex. *Stalin and the Shaping of the Soviet Union* (1986)
- Fitzpatrick, Sheila, ed. *Stalinism: New Directions,* (1999), 396pp excerpts from many scholars on the impact of Stalinism on the people (little on Stalin himself) online edition[95]
- Fitzpatrick, Sheila. "Impact of the Opening of Soviet Archives on Western Scholarship on Soviet Social History." *Russian Review* 74#3 (2015): 377–400; historiography
- Hoffmann, David L. ed. *Stalinism: The Essential Readings,* (2002) essays by 12 scholars
- Laqueur, Walter. *Stalin: The Glasnost Revelations* (1990)
- Kershaw, Ian, and Moshe Lewin. *Stalinism and Nazism: Dictatorships in Comparison* (2004) excerpt and text search[96]
- Kotkin, Stephen (2014). *Stalin: Paradoxes of Power, 1878–1928.* London: Allen Lane. ISBN 978-0-713-99944-0. 976pp
  - Kotkin, Stephen (2017). *Stalin: Waiting for Hitler, 1929-1941.* New York: Penguin. ISBN 1594203806.; 1184pp; most detailed scholarly biography
- Lee, Stephen J. *Stalin and the Soviet Union* (1999) online edition[97]
- Lewis, Jonathan. *Stalin: A Time for Judgement* (1990)

- McNeal, Robert H. *Stalin: Man and Ruler* (1988)
- Martens, Ludo. *Another view of Stalin* (1994), a highly favorable view from a Maoist historian
- Service, Robert. *Stalin: A Biography* (2004), along with Tucker the standard biography
- Trotsky, Leon. *Stalin: An Appraisal of the Man and His Influence,* (1967), an interpretation by Stalin's worst enemy
- Tucker, Robert C. *Stalin as Revolutionary, 1879–1929* (1973); *Stalin in Power: The Revolution from Above, 1929–1941.* (1990) online edition[98] with Service, a standard biography; at ACLS e-books[99]

World War II

- Barber, John, and Mark Harrison. *The Soviet Home Front: A Social and Economic History of the USSR in World War II,* Longman, 1991.
- Bellamy, Chris. *Absolute War: Soviet Russia in the Second World War* (2008), 880pp excerpt and text search[100]
- Berkhoff, Karel C. *Harvest of Despair: Life and Death in Ukraine Under Nazi Rule.* Harvard U. Press, 2004. 448 pp.
- Berkhoff, Karel C. *Motherland in Danger: Soviet Propaganda during World War II* (2012) excerpt and text search[101] covers both propaganda and reality of homefront conditions
- Braithwaite, Rodric. *Moscow 1941: A City and Its People at War* (2006)
- Broekmeyer, Marius. *Stalin, the Russians, and Their War, 1941–1945.* 2004. 315 pp.
- Dallin, Alexander. *Odessa, 1941–1944: A Case Study of Soviet Territory under Foreign Rule.* Portland: Int. Specialized Book Service, 1998. 296 pp.
- Kucherenko, Olga. *Little Soldiers: How Soviet Children Went to War, 1941–1945* (2011) excerpt and text search[102]
- Overy, Richard. *Russia's War: A History of the Soviet Effort: 1941–1945* (1998) 432pp excerpt and txt search[103]
- Overy, Richard. *Russia's War: A History of the Soviet Effort: 1941–1945* (1998) excerpt and text search[104]
- Roberts, Geoffrey. *Stalin's Wars: From World War to Cold War, 1939–1953* (2006).
- Schofield, Carey, ed. *Russian at War, 1941–1945.* Text by Georgii Drozdov and Evgenii Ryabko, [with] introd. by Vladimir Karpov [and] pref. by Harrison E. Salisbury, ed. by Carey Schofield. New York: Vendome Press, 1987. 256 p., copiously ill. with b&2 photos and occasional maps. *N.B.*: This is mostly a photo-history, with connecting texts. ISBN 978-0-86565-077-0
- Seaton, Albert. *Stalin as Military Commander,* (1998) online edition[105]

- Thurston, Robert W., and Bernd Bonwetsch, eds. *The People's War: Responses to World War II in the Soviet Union* (2000)
- Vallin, Jacques; Meslé, France; Adamets, Serguei; and Pyrozhkov, Serhii. "A New Estimate of Ukrainian Population Losses During the Crises of the 1930s and 1940s." *Population Studies* (2002) 56(3): 249–264. in JSTOR[106] Reports life expectancy at birth fell to a level as low as ten years for females and seven for males in 1933 and plateaued around 25 for females and 15 for males in the period 1941–44.

Cold War

- Brzezinski, Zbigniew. *The Grand Failure: The Birth and Death of Communism in the Twentieth Century* (1989)
- Edmonds, Robin. *Soviet Foreign Policy: The Brezhnev Years* (1983)
- Goncharov, Sergei, John Lewis and Litai Xue, *Uncertain Partners: Stalin, Mao and the Korean War* (1993) excerpt and text search[107]
- Gorlizki, Yoram, and Oleg Khlevniuk. *Cold Peace: Stalin and the Soviet Ruling Circle, 1945–1953* (2004) online edition[108]
- Holloway, David. *Stalin and the Bomb: The Soviet Union and Atomic Energy, 1939–1956* (1996) excerpt and text search[109]
- Mastny, Vojtech. *Russia's Road to the Cold War: Diplomacy, Warfare, and the Politics of Communism, 1941–1945* (1979)
- Mastny, Vojtech. *The Cold War and Soviet Insecurity: The Stalin Years* (1998) excerpt and text search[110]; online complete edition[111]
- Nation, R. Craig. *Black Earth, Red Star: A History of Soviet Security Policy, 1917–1991* (1992)
- Sivachev, Nikolai and Nikolai Yakolev, *Russia and the United States* (1979), by Soviet historians
- Taubman, William. *Khrushchev: The Man and His Era* (2004), Pulitzer Prize; excerpt and text search[112]
- Ulam, Adam B. *Expansion and Coexistence: Soviet Foreign Policy, 1917–1973*, 2nd ed. (1974)
- Zubok, Vladislav M. *Inside the Kremlin's Cold War* (1996) 20% excerpt and online search[113]
- Zubok, Vladislav M. *A Failed Empire: The Soviet Union in the Cold War from Stalin to Gorbachev* (2007)

Collapse

- Beschloss, Michael, and Strobe Talbott. *At the Highest Levels:The Inside Story of the End of the Cold War* (1993)
- Bialer, Seweryn and Michael Mandelbaum, eds. *Gorbachev's Russia and American Foreign Policy* (1988).

- Carrère d'Encausse, Hélène. *Decline of an Empire: the Soviet Socialist Republics in Revolt*. First English language ed. New York: Newsweek Books (1979). 304 p. *N.B.*: Trans. of the author's *L'Empire éclaté*. ISBN 0-88225-280-1
- Garthoff, Raymond. *The Great Transition: American–Soviet Relations and the End of the Cold War* (1994), detailed narrative
- Grachev, A.S. *Gorbachev's Gamble: Soviet Foreign Policy and the End of the Cold War* (2008) excerpt and text search[114]
- Hogan, Michael ed. *The End of the Cold War. Its Meaning and Implications* (1992) articles from *Diplomatic History*
- Roger Keeran and Thomas Keeny. *Socialism Betrayed: Behind the Collapse of the Soviet Union*, International Publishers Co Inc., U.S. 2004
- Kotkin, Stephen. *Armageddon Averted: The Soviet Collapse, 1970–2000* (2008) excerpt and text search[115]
- Matlock, Jack. *Autopsy on an Empire: The American Ambassador's Account of the Collapse of the Soviet Union* (1995)
- Pons, S., Romero, F., *Reinterpreting the End of the Cold War: Issues, Interpretations, Periodizations*, (2005) ISBN 0-7146-5695-X
- Remnick, David. *Lenin's Tomb: The Last Days of the Soviet Empire*, (1994), ISBN 0-679-75125-4
- Solzhenitsyn, Aleksandr. *Rebuilding Russia: Reflections and Tentative Proposals*, trans. and annotated by Alexis Klimoff. First ed. New York: Farrar, Straus and Giroux, 1991. *N.B.*: Also discusses the other national constituents of the U.S.S.R. ISBN 0-374-17342-7

Specialty studies

- Armstrong, John A. *The Politics of Totalitarianism: The Communist Party of the Soviet Union from 1934 to the Present*. New York: Random House, 1961.
- Katz, Zev, ed.: *Handbook of Major Soviet Nationalities* (New York: Free Press, 1975).
- Moore, Jr., Barrington. *Soviet politics: the dilemma of power*. Cambridge, MA: Harvard University Press, 1950.
- Rizzi, Bruno: *The Bureaucratization of the World: The First English edition of the Underground Marxist Classic That Analyzed Class Exploitation in the USSR*, New York, NY: Free Press, 1985.
- Schapiro, Leonard B. *The Origin of the Communist Autocracy: Political Opposition in the Soviet State, First Phase 1917–1922*. Cambridge, MA: Harvard University Press, 1955, 1966.

External links

- ⊛ Wikimedia Atlas of the Soviet Union
- Impressions of Soviet Russia[117], by John Dewey.
- A Country Study: Soviet Union (Former)[118]
- Majority in former Soviet states believe breakup was harmful mistake – poll[119]. *RT*, 21 December 2013.

1917–1927

History of Soviet Russia and the Soviet Union (1917–27)

Part of a series on the
History of the Union of Soviet Socialist Republics (Soviet Union)
1917–1927 Revolutionary Beginnings
• Revolution • Civil War • New Economic Policy • 1922 Treaty • National delimitation

Figure 43:
Lenin and Stalin

1927–1953

Stalinist rule

- Socialism in One Country
- Great Purge

Soviet famine of 1932–33

- (Holodomor
- Kazakhstan famine of 1932-1933)

World War II

- (Molotov–Ribbentrop Pact
- Great Patriotic War
- Operation Barbarossa
- Occupation of the Baltic states
- Soviet occupation of Bessarabia and Northern Bukovina
- Battle of Berlin
- Soviet invasion of Manchuria)

- Soviet deportations
- Soviet famine of 1946–47
- Cold War
- Korean War

1953–1964

Post-Stalin era

- Berlin blockade
- 1954 transfer of Crimea
- Khrushchev Thaw
- On the Cult of Personality and Its Consequences
- We will bury you
- 9 March riots
- Wage reforms
- Cuban Revolution
- Sino-Soviet split
- Space program
- Cuban Missile Crisis

1964–1982

Brezhnev era

- Brezhnev Doctrine
- Era of Stagnation
- 50th anniversary of the Armenian Genocide protests
- Prague Spring

Vietnam War

- (Laotian Civil War
- Operation Menu
- Cambodian Civil War
- Fall of Saigon)

- Six-Day War
- Détente
- Yom Kippur War
- Dirty War

Wars in Africa

- (Angolan War of Independence
- Angolan Civil War
- Mozambican War of Independence
- Mozambican Civil War
- South African Border War
- Rhodesian Bush War)

- Cambodian-Vietnamese War
- Soviet–Afghan War
- 1980 Summer Olympics

Olympic boycotts

- (1980 Olympic boycott
- 1984 Olympic boycott)

- Polish strike
- Death and funeral of Brezhnev

1982–1991

Leadership changes and collapse

- Invasion of Grenada
- Glasnost
- Perestroika
- Soviet withdrawal from Afghanistan

Singing Revolution

- (Estonian Sovereignty Declaration
- Baltic Way
- Act of the Re-Establishment of the State of Lithuania
- On the Restoration of Independence of the Republic of Latvia)

Revolutions of 1989

- (Pan-European picnic
- Die Wende
- Peaceful Revolution
- Fall of the Berlin Wall
- Velvet Revolution
- End of communist rule in Hungary
- Romanian Revolution
- German reunification)

Dissolution

- (Jeltoqsan
- Nagorno-Karabakh War
- 9 April tragedy
- Black January
- Osh riots
- War of Laws
- Dushanbe riots
- January Events
- The Barricades
- Referendum
- Union of Sovereign States
- August Coup
- Ukrainian independence (referendum)
- Belavezha Accords
- Alma-Ata Protocol)

History of

- Russia
- Moscow
- Kiev
- Minsk
- Former Soviet Republics

Soviet leadership

- 1. Lenin
- 2. Stalin
- 3. Malenkov
- 4. Khrushchev
- 5. Brezhnev
- 6. Andropov
- 7. Chernenko
- 8. Gorbachev

- Culture
- Economy
- Education

- Geography
- Politics

■ Soviet Union portal

- $\underline{v}$
- $\underline{t}$
- $\underline{e}$[120]

The history of Soviet Russia and the Soviet Union reflects a period of change for both Russia and the world. Though the terms Soviet Russia and Soviet Union are synonymous in everyday vocabulary, Soviet Russia, in the context of the foundation of the Soviet Union, refers to the few years after the abdication of the crown of the Russian Empire by Tsar Nicholas II (in 1917), but before the creation of the Soviet Union in 1922. Early in its conception, the Soviet Union strived to achieve harmony among all peoples of all countries. The original ideology of the state was primarily based on the works of Karl Marx and Friedrich Engels. In its essence, Marx's theory stated that economic and political systems went through an inevitable evolution in form, by which the current capitalist system would be replaced by a socialist state before achieving international cooperation and peace in a "Workers' Paradise," creating a system directed by what Marx called "Pure Communism."

Displeased by the relatively few changes made by the Tsar after the Revolution of 1905, Russia became a hotbed of anarchism, socialism and other radical political systems. The dominant socialist party, the Russian Social Democratic Labour Party (RSDLP), subscribed to Marxist ideology. Starting in 1903, a series of splits in the party between two main leaders was escalating: the Bolsheviks (meaning "majority") led by Vladimir Lenin, and the Mensheviks (meaning "minority") led by Julius Martov. Up until 1912, both groups continued to stay united under the name "RSDLP," but significant and irreconcilable differences between Lenin and Martov led the party to eventually split. A struggle for political dominance subsequently began between the Mensheviks and the Bolsheviks. Not only did these groups fight with each other, but they also had common enemies, notably, those trying to bring the Tsar back to power. Following the February Revolution in 1917, the Mensheviks gained control of Russia and established a provisional government, but this lasted only until the Bolsheviks took power in the October Revolution (also called the Bolshevik Revolution) later in the year. To distinguish themselves from other socialist parties, the Bolshevik party was renamed the Russian Communist Party (RCP).

Under the control of the party, all politics and attitudes that were not strictly RCP were suppressed, under the premise that the RCP represented the proletariat and all activities contrary to the party's beliefs were "counterrevolutionary" or "anti-socialist." During the years between 1917 and 1923, the Soviet Union achieved peace with the Central Powers, their enemies in World War I, but also fought the Russian Civil War against the White Army and foreign armies from the United States, the United Kingdom, and France, among others. This resulted in large territorial changes, albeit temporarily for some of these. Eventually crushing all opponents, the RCP spread Soviet style rule quickly and established itself through all of Russia. Following Lenin's death in 1924, Joseph Stalin, General Secretary of the RCP, became the de facto leader of the USSR.

The Russian Revolution of 1917

During World War I, Tsarist Russia experienced famine and economic collapse. The demoralized Russian Army suffered severe military setbacks, and many captured soldiers deserted the front lines. Dissatisfaction with the monarchy and its policy of continuing the war grew among the Russian people. Tsar Nicholas II abdicated the throne following the February Revolution of 1917 (March 1917 N.S. See: Soviet calendar.), causing widespread rioting in Petrograd and other major Russian cities.

The Russian Provisional Government was installed immediately following the fall of the Tsar by the Provisional Committee of the State Duma in early March 1917 and received conditional support of the Mensheviks. Led first by Prince Georgy Lvov, then Alexander Kerensky the Provisional Government consisted mainly of the parliamentarians most recently elected to the State Duma of the Russian Empire, which had been overthrown alongside Tsar Nicholas II. The new Provisional Government maintained its commitment to the war, joining the Triple Entente which the Bolsheviks opposed. The Provisional Government also postponed the land reforms demanded by the Bolsheviks.

Lenin, embodying the Bolshevik ideology, viewed alliance with the capitalist countries of Western Europe and the United States as involuntary servitude of the proletariat, who was forced to fight the imperialists' war. As seen by Lenin, Russia was reverting to the rule of the Tsar, and it was the job of Marxist revolutionaries, who truly represented socialism and the proletariat, to oppose such counter-socialistic ideas and support socialist revolutions in other countries.

Within the military, mutiny and desertion were pervasive among conscripts, though being AWOL (Absent Without Leave) was not uncommon throughout all ranks. The intelligentsia was dissatisfied over the slow pace of social reforms; poverty was worsening, income disparities and inequality were becoming out of control while the Provisional Government grew increasingly autocratic and inefficient. The government appeared to be on the verge of succumbing to a military *junta*. Deserting soldiers returned to the cities and gave their weapons to angry, and extremely hostile, socialist factory workers. The deplorable and inhumane poverty and starvation of major Russian centers produced optimum conditions for revolutionaries.

During the months between February and October 1917, the power of the Provisional Government was consistently questioned by nearly all political parties. A system of 'dual power' emerged, in which the Provisional Government held nominal power, though increasingly opposed by the Petrograd Soviet, their chief adversary, controlled by the Mensheviks and Socialist Revolutionaries (both democratic socialist parties politically to the right of the Bolsheviks). The Soviet chose not to force further changes in government due to the belief that the February Revolution was Russia's "crowing" overthrow of the bourgeois. The Soviet also believed that the new Provisional Government would be tasked with implementing democratic reforms and pave the way for a proletarian revolution. Though the creation of a government not based on the dictatorship of the proletariat in any form, was viewed as a "retrograde step" in Vladmir Lenin's April Theses. However, the Provisional Government still remained an overwhelmingly powerful governing body.

Failed military offensives in summer 1917 and large scale protesting and riots in major Russian cities (as advocated by Lenin in his Theses, known as the July Days) led to the deployment of troops in late August to restore order. The July Days were suppressed and blamed on the Bolsheviks, forcing Lenin into hiding. Still, rather than use force, many of the deployed soldiers and military personnel joined the rioters, disgracing the government and military at-large. It was during this time that support for the Bolsheviks grew and another of its leading figures, Leon Trotsky, was elected chair of the Petrograd Soviet, which had complete control over the defenses of the city, mainly, the city's military force. On 24 October, in early days of the October Revolution, the Provisional Government moved against the Bolsheviks, arresting activists and destroying pro-Communist propaganda. The Bolsheviks were able to portray this as an attack against the People's Soviet and garnered support for the Red Guard of Petrograd to take over the Provisional Government. The administrative offices and government buildings were taken with little opposition or bloodshed. The generally accepted end of this transitional revolutionary period, which will lead to the creation of the Union of Soviet Socialist Republics (USSR) lies with the assault and capture of the poorly defended Winter Palace (the traditional home and symbol of power of the Tsar) on the evening of 26 October 1917.

Figure 44: *1919 poster, "Mount your horses, workers and peasants! The Red Cavalry is the pledge of victory."*

The Mensheviks and the right-wing of the Socialist Revolutionaries, outraged by the abusive and coercive acts carried out by the Red Guard and Bolsheviks, fled Petrograd, leaving control in the hands of the Bolsheviks and remaining Left Socialist Revolutionaries. On 25 October 1917, the Sovnarkom was established by the Russian Constitution of 1918 as the administrative arm of the All-Russian Congress of Soviets. By 6 January 1918, the VTsIK, supported by the Bolsheviks, ratified the dissolution of the Russian Constituent Assembly, which intended to establish the non-Bolshevik Russian Democratic Federative Republic as the permanent form of government established at its Petrograd session held 5 and 6 January 1918. At the third meeting of the All-Russian Congress of Soviets on 25 January 1918, the unrecognised state was renamed the Russian Soviet Republic.

The Russian Civil War

Prior to the revolution, the Bolshevik doctrine of democratic centralism argued that only a tightly knit and secretive organization could successfully overthrow the government; after the revolution, they argued that only such an organization could prevail against foreign and domestic enemies. Fighting the civil war would actually force the party to put these principles into practice.

Arguing that the revolution needed not a mere parliamentary organization but a party of action which would function as a scientific body of direction, a vanguard of activists, and a central control organ, the Tenth Party Congress banned factions within the party, initially intending it only to be a temporary measure after the shock of the Kronstadt rebellion. It was also argued that the party should be an elite body of professional revolutionaries dedicating their lives to the cause and carrying out their decisions with iron discipline, thus moving toward putting loyal party activists in charge of new and old political institutions, army units, factories, hospitals, universities, and food suppliers. Against this backdrop, the *nomenklatura* system would evolve and become standard practice.

In theory, this system was to be democratic since all leading party organs would be elected from below, but also centralized since lower bodies would be accountable to higher organizations. In practice, "democratic centralism" was centralist, with decisions of higher organs binding on lower ones, and the composition of lower bodies largely determined by the members of higher ones. Over time, party cadres would grow increasingly careerist and professional. Party membership required exams, special courses, special camps, schools, and nominations by three existing members.

In December 1917, the Cheka was founded as the Bolshevik's first internal security force following the failed assassination attempt on Lenin's life. Later it changed names to GPU, OGPU, MVD, NKVD and finally KGB.

The Polish–Soviet War

The frontiers between Poland, which had established an unstable independent government following World War I, and the former Tsarist empire, were rendered chaotic by the repercussions of the Russian revolutions, the civil war and the winding down World War I. Poland's Józef Piłsudski envisioned a new federation (Międzymorze), forming a Polish-led East European bloc to form a bulwark against Russia and Germany, while the Russian SFSR considered carrying the revolution westward by force. When Piłsudski carried out a military thrust into Ukraine in 1920, he was met by a Red Army offensive that drove into Polish territory almost to Warsaw. However, Piłsudski halted the Soviet advance at the Battle of Warsaw and resumed the offensive. The "Peace of Riga" signed in early 1921 split the territory of Belarus and Ukraine between Poland and Soviet Russia.

Figure 45: *Silver Rubel 1924*

Creation of the USSR

On 29 December 1922 a conference of plenipotentiary delegations from the Russian SFSR, the Transcaucasian SFSR, the Ukrainian SSR and the Byelorussian SSR approved the Treaty on the Creation of the USSR and the Declaration of the Creation of the USSR, forming the Union of Soviet Socialist Republics. These two documents were confirmed by the 1st Congress of Soviets of the USSR and signed by heads of delegations[121] – Mikhail Kalinin, Mikhail Tskhakaya, Mikhail Frunze and Grigory Petrovsky, Alexander Chervyakov[122] respectively on 30 December 1922.

The New Economic Policy

During the Civil War (1917–21), the Bolsheviks adopted War communism, which entailed the breakup of the landed estates and the forcible seizure of agricultural surpluses. In the cities there were intense food shortages and a breakdown in the money system (at the time many Bolsheviks argued that ending money's role as a transmitter of "value" was a sign of the rapidly approaching communist epoch). Many city dwellers fled to the countryside – often to tend the land that the Bolshevik breakup of the landed estates had

Figure 46: *Gold Chervonetz (1979)*

transferred to the peasants. Even small scale "capitalist" production was suppressed.

The Kronstadt rebellion signaled the growing unpopularity of War Communism in the countryside: in March 1921, at the end of the civil war, disillusioned sailors, primarily peasants who initially had been stalwart supporters of the Bolsheviks under the provisional government, revolted against the new regime. Although the Red Army, commanded by Trotsky, crossed the ice over the frozen Baltic Sea to quickly crush the rebellion, this sign of growing discontent forced the party to foster a broad alliance of the working class and peasantry (80% of the population), despite left factions of the party which favored a regime solely representative of the interests of the revolutionary proletariat. At the Tenth Party Congress, it was decided to end War Communism and institute the New Economic Policy (NEP), in which the state allowed a limited market to exist. Small private businesses were allowed and restrictions on political activity were somewhat eased.

However, the key shift involved the status of agricultural surpluses. Rather than simply requisitioning agricultural surpluses in order to feed the urban population (the hallmark of War Communism), the NEP allowed peasants to sell their surplus yields on the open market. Meanwhile, the state still maintained state ownership of what Lenin deemed the "commanding heights" of the economy:

heavy industry such as the coal, iron, and metallurgical sectors along with the banking and financial components of the economy. The "commanding heights" employed the majority of the workers in the urban areas. Under the NEP, such state industries would be largely free to make their own economic decisions.

In the cities and between the cities and the countryside, the NEP period saw a huge expansion of trade in the hands of full-time merchants – who were typically denounced as "speculators" by the leftists and also often resented by the public. The growth in trade, though, did generally coincide with rising living standards in both the city and the countryside (around 80% of Soviet citizens were in the countryside at this point).

The Soviet NEP (1921–29) was essentially a period of "market socialism" similar to the economic reform in China in 1978 in that both foresaw a role for private entrepreneurs and limited markets based on trade and pricing rather than fully centralized planning. As an interesting aside, during the first meeting in the early 1980s between Deng Xiaoping and Armand Hammer, a U.S. industrialist and prominent investor in Lenin's Soviet Union, Deng pressed Hammer for as much information on the NEP as possible.

During the NEP period, agricultural yields not only recovered to the levels attained before the Bolshevik Revolution, but greatly improved. The break-up of the quasi-feudal landed estates of the Tsarist-era countryside gave peasants their greatest incentives ever to maximize production. Now able to sell their surpluses on the open market, peasant spending gave a boost to the manufacturing sectors in the urban areas. As a result of the NEP, and the break-up of the landed estates while the Communist Party was strengthening power between 1917–1921, the Soviet Union became the world's greatest producer of grain.Wikipedia:Citation needed

Agriculture, however, would recover from civil war more rapidly than heavy industry. Factories, badly damaged by civil war and capital depreciation, were far less productive. In addition, the organization of enterprises into trusts or syndicates representing one particular sector of the economy would contribute to imbalances between supply and demand associated with monopolies. Due to the lack of incentives brought by market competition, and with little or no state controls on their internal policies, trusts were likely to sell their products at higher prices.

The slower recovery of industry would pose some problems for the peasantry, who accounted for 80% of the population. Since agriculture was relatively more productive, relative price indexes for industrial goods were higher than those of agricultural products. The outcome of this was what Trotsky deemed the "Scissors Crisis" because of the scissors-like shape of the graph representing shifts in relative price indexes. Simply put, peasants would have to produce more grain to purchase consumer goods from the urban areas. As a result, some peasants withheld agricultural surpluses in anticipation of higher prices, thus contributing to mild shortages in the cities. This, of course, is speculative market behavior, which was frowned upon by many Communist Party cadres, who considered it to be exploitative of urban consumers.

In the meantime, the party took constructive steps to offset the crisis, attempting to bring down prices for manufactured goods and stabilize inflation, by imposing price controls on essential industrial goods and breaking-up the trusts in order to increase economic efficiency.

The death of Lenin and the fate of the NEP

Following Lenin's third stroke, a troika made up of Stalin, Zinoviev and Kamenev emerged to take day to day leadership of the party and the country and try to block Trotsky from taking power. Lenin, however, had become increasingly anxious about Stalin and, following his December 1922 stroke, dictated a letter (known as Lenin's Testament) to the party criticizing him and urging his removal as general secretary, a position which was starting to arise as the most powerful in the party. Stalin was aware of Lenin's Testament and acted to keep Lenin in isolation for health reasons and increase his control over the party apparatus.

Zinoviev and Bukharin became concerned about Stalin's increasing power and proposed that the Orgburo which Stalin headed be abolished and that Zinoviev and Trotsky be added to the party secretariat thus diminishing Stalin's role as general secretary. Stalin reacted furiously and the Orgburo was retained but Bukharin, Trotsky and Zinoviev were added to the body.

Due to growing political differences with Trotsky and his Left Opposition in the fall of 1923, the troika of Stalin, Zinoviev and Kamenev reunited. At the Twelfth Party Congress in 1923, Trotsky failed to use Lenin's Testament as a tool against Stalin for fear of endangering the stability of the party.

Lenin died in January 1924 and in May his Testament was read aloud at the Central Committee but Zinoviev and Kamenev argued that Lenin's objections had proven groundless and that Stalin should remain General Secretary. The Central Committee decided not to publish the testament.

Meanwhile, the campaign against Trotsky intensified and he was removed from the position of People's Commissar of War before the end of the year. In 1925, Trotsky was denounced for his essay *Lessons of October,* which criticized Zinoviev and Kamenev for initially opposing Lenin's plans for an insurrection in 1917. Trotsky was also denounced for his theory of permanent revolution which contradicted Stalin's position that socialism could be built in one country, Russia, without a worldwide revolution. As the prospects for a revolution in Europe, particularly Germany, became increasingly dim through the 1920s, Trotsky's theoretical position began to look increasingly pessimistic as far as the success of Russian socialism was concerned.

With the resignation of Trotsky as War Commissar, the unity of the troika began to unravel. Zinoviev and Kamenev again began to fear Stalin's power and felt that their positions were threatened. Stalin moved to form an alliance with Bukharin and his allies on the right of the party who supported the New Economic Policy and encouraged a slowdown in industrialization efforts and a move towards encouraging the peasants to increase production via market incentives. Zinoviev and Kamenev criticized this policy as a return to capitalism. The conflict erupted at the Fourteenth Party Congress held in December 1925 with Zinoviev and Kamenev now protesting against the dictatorial policies of Stalin and trying to revive the issue of Lenin's Testament which they had previously buried. Stalin now used Trotsky's previous criticisms of Zinoviev and Kamenev to defeat and demote them and bring in allies like Vyacheslav Molotov, Kliment Voroshilov and Mikhail Kalinin. Trotsky was dropped from the politburo entirely in 1926. The Fourteenth Congress also saw the first developments of the Stalin's cult of personality with him being referred to as "leader" for the first time and becoming the subject of effusive praise from delegates.

Trotsky, Zinoviev and Kamenev formed a United Opposition against the policies of Stalin and Bukharin, but they had lost influence as a result of the inner party disputes and in October 1927, Trotsky, Zinoviev and Kamenev were expelled from the Central Committee. In November, prior to the Fifteenth Party Congress, Trotsky and Zinoviev were expelled from the Communist Party itself as Stalin sought to deny the Opposition any opportunity to make their struggle public. By the time, the Congress finally convened in December 1927. Zinoviev had capitulated to Stalin and denounced his previous adherence to the opposition as "anti-Leninist" and the few remaining members still loyal to the opposition were subjected to insults and humiliations. By early 1928, Trotsky and other leading members of the Left Opposition had been sentenced to internal exile.

Stalin now moved against Bukharin by appropriating Trotsky's criticisms of his right wing policies and he promoted a new general line of the party favoring collectivization of the peasantry and rapid industrialization of industry, forcing Bukharin and his supporters into a Right Opposition.

At the Central Committee meeting held in July 1928, Bukharin and his supporters argued that Stalin's new policies would cause a breach with the peasantry. Bukharin also alluded to Lenin's Testament. While he had support from the party organization in Moscow and the leadership of several commissariats, Stalin's control of the secretariat was decisive in that it allowed Stalin to manipulate elections to party posts throughout the country, giving him control over a large section of the Central Committee. The Right Opposition was defeated and Bukharin attempted to form an alliance with Kamenev and Zinoviev but it was too late.

Further reading

- Acton, Edward, V. IU Cherniâev, and William G. Rosenberg, eds. *Critical companion to the Russian Revolution, 1914–1921* (Indiana University Press, 1997), emphasis on historiography
- Cohen, Stephen F. *Rethinking the Soviet Experience: Politics and History since 1917.* New York: Oxford University Press, 1985.
- Daniels, Robert V. "The Soviet Union in Post-Soviet Perspective" *Journal of Modern History* (2002) 74#2 pp: 381–391. in JSTOR[123]
- Fitzpatrick, Sheila. *The Russian Revolution.* New York: Oxford University Press, 1982, 208 pages. ISBN 0-19-280204-6
- Hosking, Geoffrey. *The First Socialist Society: A History of the Soviet Union from Within* (2nd ed. Harvard UP 1992) 570pp
- Gregory, Paul R. and Robert C. Stuart, *Russian and Soviet Economic Performance and Structure* (7th ed. 2001)
- Kort, Michael. *The Soviet Colossus: History and Aftermath* (7th ed. 2010) 502pp
- Kotkin, Stephen. *Stalin: Paradoxes of Power, 1878–1928* (2014)
- Lincoln, W. Bruce. *Passage Through Armageddon: The Russians in War and Revolution, 1914–1918* (1986)
- Lewin, Moshe. *Russian Peasants and Soviet Power.* (Northwestern University Press, 1968)
- McCauley, Martin. *The Rise and Fall of the Soviet Union* (2007), 522 pages.
- Moss, Walter G. *A History of Russia.* Vol. 2: Since 1855. 2d ed. Anthem Press, 2005.
- Nove, Alec. *An Economic History of the USSR, 1917–1991.* 3rd ed. London: Penguin Books, 1993. ISBN 0-14-015774-3.
- Pipes, Richard. *A Concise History of the Russian Revolution* (1996)
- Remington, Thomas. *Building Socialism in Bolshevik Russia.* Pittsburgh: University of Pittsburgh Press, 1984.
- Service, Robert. *A History of Twentieth-Century Russia.* 2nd ed. Cambridge, MA: Harvard University Press, 1999. ISBN 0-674-40348-7.
- Service, Robert, *Lenin: A Biography* (2000)

- Service, Robert. *Stalin: A Biography* (2004), along with Tucker the standard biography
- Tucker, Robert C. *Stalin as Revolutionary, 1879–1929* (1973); *Stalin in Power: The Revolution from Above, 1929–1941.* (1990) online edition[124] with Service, a standard biography; online at ACLS e-books[125]

1927–1953

History of the Soviet Union (1927–1953)

Part of a series on the
History of the Union of Soviet Socialist Republics (Soviet Union)
1917–1927 Revolutionary Beginnings
• Revolution • Civil War • New Economic Policy • 1922 Treaty • National delimitation
1927–1953 Stalinist rule

- Socialism in One Country
- Great Purge

Soviet famine of 1932–33

- (Holodomor
- Kazakhstan famine of 1932-1933)

World War II

- (Molotov–Ribbentrop Pact
- Great Patriotic War
- Operation Barbarossa
- Occupation of the Baltic states
- Soviet occupation of Bessarabia and Northern Bukovina
- Battle of Berlin
- Soviet invasion of Manchuria)

- Soviet deportations
- Soviet famine of 1946–47
- Cold War
- Korean War

1953–1964

Post-Stalin era

- Berlin blockade
- 1954 transfer of Crimea
- Khrushchev Thaw
- On the Cult of Personality and Its Consequences
- We will bury you
- 9 March riots
- Wage reforms
- Cuban Revolution
- Sino-Soviet split
- Space program
- Cuban Missile Crisis

1964–1982

Brezhnev era

- Brezhnev Doctrine
- Era of Stagnation
- 50th anniversary of the Armenian Genocide protests
- Prague Spring

Vietnam War

- (Laotian Civil War
- Operation Menu
- Cambodian Civil War
- Fall of Saigon)

- Six-Day War
- Détente
- Yom Kippur War
- Dirty War

Wars in Africa

- (Angolan War of Independence
- Angolan Civil War
- Mozambican War of Independence
- Mozambican Civil War
- South African Border War
- Rhodesian Bush War)

- Cambodian-Vietnamese War
- Soviet–Afghan War
- 1980 Summer Olympics

Olympic boycotts

- (1980 Olympic boycott
- 1984 Olympic boycott)

- Polish strike
- Death and funeral of Brezhnev

1982–1991

Leadership changes and collapse

- Invasion of Grenada
- Glasnost
- Perestroika
- Soviet withdrawal from Afghanistan

Singing Revolution

- (Estonian Sovereignty Declaration
- Baltic Way
- Act of the Re-Establishment of the State of Lithuania
- On the Restoration of Independence of the Republic of Latvia)

Revolutions of 1989

- (Pan-European picnic
- Die Wende
- Peaceful Revolution
- Fall of the Berlin Wall
- Velvet Revolution
- End of communist rule in Hungary
- Romanian Revolution
- German reunification)

Dissolution

- (Jeltoqsan
- Nagorno-Karabakh War
- 9 April tragedy
- Black January
- Osh riots
- War of Laws
- Dushanbe riots
- January Events
- The Barricades
- Referendum
- Union of Sovereign States
- August Coup
- Ukrainian independence (referendum)
- Belavezha Accords
- Alma-Ata Protocol)

History of

- Russia
- Moscow
- Kiev
- Minsk
- Former Soviet Republics

Soviet leadership

- 1. Lenin
- 2. Stalin
- 3. Malenkov
- 4. Khrushchev
- 5. Brezhnev
- 6. Andropov
- 7. Chernenko
- 8. Gorbachev

- Culture
- Economy
- Education
- Geography
- Politics

■ Soviet Union portal

- $\underline{v}$
- $\underline{t}$
- $\underline{e}^{126}$

The **history of the Soviet Union between 1927 and 1953** covers the period in Soviet history from establishment of Stalinism through victory in the Second World War and down to the death of Joseph Stalin in 1953. He sought to destroy his enemies while transforming Soviet society with aggressive economic planning, in particular a sweeping collectivization of agriculture and rapid development of heavy industry. Stalin consolidated his power within the party and the state and fostered an extensive cult of personality. Soviet secret-police and the mass-mobilization Communist party served as Stalin's major tools in molding Soviet society. Stalin's brutal methods in achieving his goals, which included party purges, political repression of the general population, and forced collectivization, led to millions of deaths: in Gulag labor camps and during man-made famine.

World War II, known as "the Great Patriotic War" in the Soviet Union, devastated much of the USSR, with about one out of every three World War II deaths representing a citizen of the Soviet Union. After World War II, the Soviet Union's armies occupied Eastern Europe, where they established or supported puppet Communist regimes. By 1949, the Cold War had started between the Western Bloc and the Eastern (Soviet) Bloc, with the Warsaw Pact (created 1955) pitched against NATO (created 1949) in Europe. After 1945, Stalin did not directly engage in any wars. He continued his totalitarian rule until his death in 1953.

Soviet state's development

Industrialisation in practice

The mobilization of resources by state planning expanded the country's industrial base. From 1928 to 1932, pig iron output, necessary for further development of the industrial infrastructure rose from 3.3 million to 6.2 million tons per year. Coal production, a basic fuel of modern economies and Stalinist industrialization, rose from 35.4 million to 64 million tons, and the output of iron ore rose from 5.7 million to 19 million tons. A number of industrial complexes such as Magnitogorsk and Kuznetsk, the Moscow and Gorky automobile plants, the Ural Mountains and Kramatorsk heavy machinery plants, and Kharkov, Stalingrad and Chelyabinsk tractor plants had been built or were under construction.[127]

In real terms, the workers' standards of living tended to drop, rather than rise during the industrialization. Stalin's laws to "tighten work discipline" made the situation worse: e.g., a 1932 change to the RSFSR labor law code enabled firing workers who had been absent without a reason from the work place for just one day. Being fired accordingly meant losing "the right to use ration and commodity cards" as well as the "loss of the right to use an apartment" and even blacklisted for new employment which altogether meant a threat of starving. Those measures, however, were not fully enforced, as managers were hard pressed to replace these workers. In contrast, the 1938 legislation, which introduced labor books, followed by major revisions of the labor law, were enforced. For example, being absent or even 20 minutes late were grounds for becoming fired; managers who failed to enforce these laws faced criminal prosecution. Later, the Decree of the Presidium of the Supreme Soviet, 26 June 1940 "On the Transfer to the Eight-Hour Working Day, the Seven-day Work Week, and on the Prohibition of Unauthorized Departure by Laborers and Office Workers from Factories and Offices" replaced the 1938 revisions with obligatory criminal penalties for quitting a job (2–4 months imprisonment), for being late 20 minutes (6 months of probation and pay confiscation of 25 per cent), etc.

Based on these figures, the Soviet government declared that Five Year Industrial Production Plan had been fulfilled by 93.7% in only four years, while parts devoted to heavy-industry part were fulfilled by 108%. Stalin in December 1932 declared the plan a success to the Central Committee, since increases in the output of coal and iron would fuel future development.[128]

During the second five-year plan (1933–37), on the basis of the huge investment during the first plan, industry expanded extremely rapidly, and nearly reached the plan's targets. By 1937, coal output was 127 million tons, pig iron 14.5 million tons, and there had been very rapid development of the armaments industry.[129]

While making a massive leap in industrial capacity, the first Five Year Plan was extremely harsh on industrial workers; quotas were difficult to fulfill, requiring that miners put in 16- to 18-hour workdays.[130] Failure to fulfill quotas could result in treason charges.[131] Working conditions were poor, even hazardous. Due to the allocation of resources for industry along with decreasing productivity since collectivization, a famine occurred. In the construction of the industrial complexes, inmates of Gulag camps were used as expendable resources. But conditions improved rapidly during the second plan. Throughout the 1930s, industrialization was combined with a rapid expansion of technical and engineering education as well as increasing emphasis on munitions.[132]

From 1921 until 1954, the police state operated at high intensity, seeking out anyone accused of sabotaging the system. The estimated numbers vary greatly. Perhaps, 3.7 million people were sentenced for alleged counter-revolutionary crimes, including 600,000 sentenced to death, 2.4 million sentenced to labor camps, and 700,000 sentenced to expatriation. Stalinist repression reached its peak during the Great Purge of 1937–38, which removed many skilled managers and experts and considerably slowed industrial production in 1937[133]

Collectivization of agriculture

Under the NEP, Lenin had to tolerate the continued existence of privately owned agriculture. He decided to wait at least 20 years before attempting to place it under state control and in the meantime concentrate on industrial development. However, after Stalin's rise to power, the timetable for collectivization was shortened to just five years. Demand for food intensified, especially in the USSR's primary grain producing regions, with new, forced approaches implemented. Upon joining kolkhozes (collective farms), peasants had to give up their private plots of land and property. Every harvest, Kolkhoz production was sold to the state for a low price set by the state itself. However, the natural progress of collectivization was slow, and the November 1929 Plenum of the Central Committee decided to accelerate collectivization through force. In any case, Russian peasant culture formed a bulwark of traditionalism that stood in the way of the Soviet state's goals.

Figure 47: *Propaganda shows the use of tractors (in this case McCormick-Deering 15-30) as a backbone of collectivization. Ukrainian SSR 1931*

Given the goals of the first Five Year Plan, the state sought increased political control of agriculture in order to feed the rapidly growing urban population and to obtain a source of foreign currency through increased cereal exports. Given its late start, the USSR needed to import a substantial number of the expensive technologies necessary for heavy industrialization.

By 1936, about 90% of Soviet agriculture had been collectivized. In many cases, peasants bitterly opposed this process and often slaughtered their animals rather than give them to collective farms, even though the government only wanted the grain. Kulaks, prosperous peasants, were forcibly resettled to Kazakhstan, Siberia and the Russian Far North (a large portion of the kulaks served at forced labor camps). However, just about anyone opposing collectivization was deemed a "kulak". The policy of liquidation of kulaks as a class—formulated by Stalin at the end of 1929—meant some executions, and even more deportation to special settlements and, sometimes, to forced labor camps.Wikipedia:Citation needed

Despite the expectations, collectivization led to a catastrophic drop in farm productivity, which did not return to the levels achieved under the NEP until 1940. The upheaval associated with collectivization was particularly severe in Ukraine and the heavily Ukrainian Volga region. Peasants slaughtered their

Figure 48: *Early Soviet poster: The Smoke of chimneys is the breath of Soviet Russia*

livestock en masse rather than give them up. In 1930 alone, 25% of the nation's cattle, sheep, and goats, and one-third of all pigs were killed. It was not until the 1980s that the Soviet livestock numbers would return to their 1928 level. Government bureaucrats, who had been given a rudimentary education on farming techniques, were dispatched to the countryside to "teach" peasants the new ways of socialist agriculture, relying largely on Marxist theoretical ideas that had little basis in reality. Wikipedia:Citation needed Those farmers who did know agriculture well, who were familiar with the local climates, soil types, and other factors, had all been sent off to the gulags or shot for being enemies of the state.Wikipedia:Citation needed Even after the state inevitably won and succeeding in imposing collectivization, the peasants did everything they could in the way of sabotage. They cultivated far smaller portions of their land and worked much less. The scale of the Ukrainian famine has led many Ukrainian scholars to argue that there was a deliberate policy of genocide against the Ukrainian people. Other scholars argue that the massive death totals were an inevitable result of a very poorly planned operation against all peasants, who had given little support to Lenin or Stalin. British historian Robert Service says,

Almost 99% of all cultivated land had been pulled into collective farms by the end of 1937. The ghastly price paid by the peasantry has yet to be estab-

Figure 49: *Endorsed by the Constitution of the USSR in 1924, the State Emblem of the Soviet Union (above) was a hammer and sickle symbolizing the alliance of the working class and the peasantry. Ears of wheat were entwined in a scarlet band with the inscription in the languages of all the 15 union republics: "Workers of All Countries, Unite!" The grain represented Soviet agriculture. A five-pointed star, symbolizing the Soviet Union's solidarity with socialist revolutionaries on five continents, was drawn on the upper part of the Emblem.*

lished with precision, but probably up to 5 million people died of persecution or starvation in these years. Ukrainians and Kazakhs suffered worse than most nations.[134]

In Ukraine alone, the number of people who died in the famines is now estimated to be 3.5 million.[135]

The USSR took over Estonia, Latvia and Lithuania in 1940, which were lost to Germany in 1941, and then recovered in 1944. The collectivization of their farms began in 1948. Using terror, mass killings and deportations, most of the peasantry was collectivized by 1952. Agricultural production fell dramatically in all the other Soviet Republics.

Changes in Soviet society

In the period of rapid industrialization and mass collectivization preceding World War II, Soviet employment figures experienced exponential growth.

3.9 million jobs per annum were expected by 1923, but the number actually climbed to an astounding 6.4 million. By 1937, the number rose yet again, to about 7.9 million. Finally, in 1940 it reached 8.3 million. Between 1926 and 1930, the urban population increased by 30 million. Unemployment had been a problem in late Imperial Russia and even under the NEP, but it ceased being a major factor after the implementation of Stalin's massive industrialization program. The sharp mobilization of resources used in order to industrialize the heretofore agrarian society created a massive need for labor; unemployment virtually dropped to zero. Wage setting by Soviet planners also contributed to the sharp decrease in unemployment, which dropped in real terms by 50% from 1928 to 1940. With wages artificially depressed, the state could afford to employ far more workers than would be financially viable in a market economy. Several ambitious extraction projects were begun that endeavored to supply raw materials for both military hardware and consumer goods.

The Moscow and Gorky automobile plants produced automobiles for the public—despite few Soviet citizens affording to buy a car—and the expansion of steel production and other industrial materials made the manufacture of a greater number of cars possible. Car and truck production, for example, reached 200,000 in 1931.[136]

The Soviet leadership believed that industrial workers needed to be educated in order to be competitive and so embarked on a program contemporaneous with industrialization to greatly increase the number of schools and the general quality of education. In 1927, 7.9 million students attended 118,558 schools. By 1933, the number rose to 9.7 million students in 166,275 schools. In addition, 900 specialist departments and 566 institutions were built and fully operational by 1933. Literacy rates increased substantially as a result, especially in the Central Asian republics.[137]

The Soviet people also benefited from a type of social liberalization. Women were to be given the same education as men and, at least legally speaking, obtained the same rights as men in the workplace. Although in practice these goals were not reached, the efforts to achieve them and the statement of theoretical equality led to a general improvement in the socio-economic status of women. Stalinist development also contributed to advances in health care, which marked a massive improvement over the Imperial era. Stalin's policies granted the Soviet people access to free health care and education. Widespread immunization programs created the first generation free from the fear of typhus and cholera. The occurrences of these diseases dropped to record-low numbers and infant mortality rates were substantially reduced, resulting in the life expectancy for both men and women to increase by over 20 years by the mid-to-late 1950s. Many of the more extreme social and political ideas that were fashionable in the 1920s such as anarchism, internationalism, and

the belief that the nuclear family was a bourgeois concept, were abandoned-
Wikipedia:Citation needed. Schools began to teach a more nationalistic course
with emphasis on Russian history and leaders, though Marxist underpinnings
necessarily remained. Stalin also began to create a Lenin cult. During the
1930s, Soviet society assumed the basic form it would maintain until its collapse in 1991.

Urban women under Stalin, paralleling the western countries, were also the first
generation of women able to give birth in a hospital with access to prenatal care.
Education was another area in which there was improvement after economic
development, also paralleling other western countries. The generation born
during Stalin's rule was the first near-universally literate generation. Some
engineers were sent abroad to learn industrial technology, and hundreds of
foreign engineers were brought to Russia on contract. Transport links were
also improved, as many new railways were built, although with forced labour,
costing thousands of lives. Workers who exceeded their quotas, *Stakhanovites*,
received many incentives for their work, although many such workers were in
fact "arranged" to succeed by receiving extreme help in their work, and then
their achievements were used for propaganda.

Starting in the early 1930s, the Soviet government began an all-out war on organized religion in the country. Many churches and monasteries were closed
and scores of clergymen were imprisoned or executed. The state propaganda
machine vigorously promoted atheism and denounced religion as being an
artifact of capitalist society. In 1937, Pope Pius XI decried the attacks on religion in the Soviet Union. By 1940, only a small number of churches remained
open. It should be noted that the early anti-religious campaigns under Lenin
were mostly directed at the Russian Orthodox Church, as it was a symbol of the
czarist government. In the 1930s however, all faiths were targeted: minority
Christian denominations, Islam, Judaism, and Buddhism.

The Great Purges

As this process unfolded, Stalin consolidated near-absolute power using the
1934 assassination of Sergey Kirov (which many suspect Stalin of having
planned, although there is no evidence for this) as a pretext to launch the Great
Purges against his suspected political and ideological opponents, most notably
the old cadres and the rank and file of the Bolshevik Party. Trotsky had already been expelled from the party in 1927, exiled to Kazakhstan in 1928
and then expelled from the USSR entirely in 1929. Stalin used the purges to
politically and physically destroy his other formal rivals (and former allies) accusing Grigory Zinoviev and Lev Kamenev of being behind Kirov's assassination and planning to overthrow Stalin. Ultimately, those supposedly involved

in this and other conspiracies numbered in the tens of thousands with various Old Bolsheviks and senior party members blamed with conspiracy and sabotage which were used to explain industrial accidents, production shortfalls and other failures of Stalin's regime. Measures used against opposition and suspected opposition ranged from imprisonment in work camps (Gulags) to execution to assassination (of Trotsky's son Lev Sedov and likely of Sergey Kirov—Trotsky himself was to die at the hands of one of Stalin's assassins in 1940).

Several show trials were held in Moscow, to serve as examples for the trials that local courts were expected to carry out elsewhere in the country. There were four key trials from 1936 to 1938, The Trial of the Sixteen was the first (December 1936); then the Trial of the Seventeen (January 1937); then the trial of Red Army generals, including Marshal Tukhachevsky (June 1937); and finally the Trial of the Twenty One (including Bukharin) in March 1938. During these, the defendants were typically accused of things such as sabotage, spying, counter-revolution, and conspiring with Germany and Japan to invade and partition the Soviet Union. Most confessed to the charges. The initial trials in 1935–36 were carried out by the OGPU under Genrikh Yagoda. The following year, he and his associates were removed from office and arrested. They were later tried and executed in 1938–39. The secret police were renamed the NKVD and control given to Nikolai Yezhov, known as the "Bloody Dwarf".

The "Great Purge" swept the Soviet Union in 1937. It was widely known as the "Yezhovschina", the "Reign of Yezhov". The rate of arrests was staggering. In the armed forces alone, 34,000 officers were purged including many at the higher ranks. The entire Politburo and most of the Central Committee were purged, along with foreign communists who were living in the Soviet Union, and numerous intellectuals, bureaucrats, and factory managers. The total of people imprisoned or executed during the Yezhovschina numbered about two million. By 1938, the mass purges were starting to disrupt the country's infrastructure, and Stalin began winding them down. Yezhov was gradually relieved of power. Yezhov was relieved of all powers in 1939, then tried and executed in 1940. His successor as head of the NKVD (from 1938 to 1945) was Lavrentiy Beria, a Georgian friend of Stalin's. Arrests and executions continued into 1952, although nothing on the scale of the Yezhovschina ever happened again.

During this period, the practice of mass arrest, torture, and imprisonment or execution without trial, of anyone suspected by the secret police of opposing Stalin's regime became commonplace. By the NKVD's own count, 681,692 people were shot during 1937–38 alone, and hundreds of thousands of political prisoners were transported to Gulag work camps. The mass terror and purges were little known to the outside world, and many western intellectuals continued to believe that the Soviets had created a successful alternative to a capitalist world that was suffering from the effects of the Great Depression. In 1936, the country adopted its first formal constitution, which on paper at least granted freedom of speech, religion, and assembly.

In March 1939, the 18th congress of the Communist Party was held in Moscow. Most of the delegates present at the 17th congress in 1934 were gone, and Stalin was heavily praised by Litvinov and the western democracies criticized for failing to adopt the principles of "collective security" against Nazi Germany.

World War II

Foreign relations before 1941

The young Soviet Union initially struggled with foreign relations, being the first socialist-run country in the world. The old great powers were not pleased to see the established world order rocked by an ideology claiming to be the harbinger of a world revolution. Indeed, many had actively opposed the very establishment of Soviet rule by meddling in the Russian Civil War. Slowly the international community had to accept, however, that the Soviet Union was there to stay. By 1933, France, Germany, the United Kingdom and Japan, along with many other countries had recognized the Soviet government and established diplomatic ties. On November 16, 1933, the United States joined the list. Thus, by the 1930s, Soviet Russia was no longer an international pariah.

Franco-Soviet relations were initially hostile because the USSR officially opposed the World War I peace settlement of 1919 that France emphatically championed. While the Soviet Union was interested in conquering territories in Eastern Europe, France was determined to protect the fledgling nations there. This led to a rosy German–Soviet relationship in the 1920s. However, Adolf Hitler's foreign policy centered on a massive seizure of Eastern European and Russian lands for Germany's own ends, and when Hitler pulled out of the World Disarmament Conference in Geneva in 1933, the threat hit home. Soviet Foreign Minister Maxim Litvinov reversed Soviet policy regarding the Paris Peace Settlement, leading to a Franco-Soviet rapprochement. In May 1935, the USSR concluded pacts of mutual assistance with France and Czechoslovakia; the Comintern was also instructed to form a united front with leftist parties against the forces of Fascism. The pact was undermined, however, by strong ideological hostility to the Soviet Union and the Comintern's new front in France, Poland's refusal to permit the Red Army on its soil, France's defensive military strategy, and a continuing Soviet interest in patching up relations with Germany.

Figure 50: *Common parade of Wehrmacht and Red Army in Brest at the end of the Invasion of Poland. At the center Major General Heinz Guderian and Brigadier Semyon Krivoshein*

The Soviet Union also supplied military aid to the Republicans in Spain, but held back somewhat. Its support of the government also gave the Republicans a Communist taint in the eyes of anti-Bolsheviks in the UK and France, weakening the calls for Anglo-French intervention in the war.Wikipedia:Citation needed

In response to all of this the Nazi government promulgated an Anti-Comintern Pact with Japan and later Italy and various Eastern European countries (such as Hungary), ostensibly to suppress Communist activity but more realistically to forge an alliance against the USSR.

When Nazi Germany entered Czechoslovakia, the Soviet Union's agreement with Czechoslovakia failed to amount to anything because of Poland and Romania's refusals to permit a Soviet intervention.Wikipedia:Citation needed On April 17, 1939, Stalin suggested a revived military alliance with the UK and France. The Anglo-French military mission sent in August, however, failed to impress Soviet officials; it was sent by a slow ocean-going ship and consisted of low-ranking officers who gave only vague details about their militaries. Stalin favoured Germany.Wikipedia:Citation needed

Stalin arranged the Molotov–Ribbentrop Pact, a non-aggression pact with Nazi Germany on August 23, along with the German-Soviet Commercial Agreement to open economic relations. A secret appendix to the pact gave Eastern Poland, Latvia, Estonia, Bessarabia and Finland to the USSR, and Western Poland and Lithuania to Nazi Germany. This reflected the Soviet desire of territorial gains.

Propaganda was also considered an important foreign relations tool. International exhibitions, the distribution of media such as films, e.g.: *Alexander Nevski*, and journals like *USSR in Construction*, as well as inviting prominent foreign individuals to tour the Soviet Union, were used as a method of gaining international influence.

Start of World War II

Germany invaded Poland on September 1; the USSR followed on September 17. The Soviets quelled opposition by executing and arresting thousands. They sent hundreds of thousands to Siberia and other remote parts of the USSR. Estimates varying from the figure over 1.5 million.[138,139,140,141,142,143] to the most conservative figures[144] using recently found NKVD documents showing 309,000[145,146,147] to 381,220. in four major waves of deportations between 1939 and 1941.

With Poland, including part of the old Prussian state, being divided between two powers, the Soviet Union put forth its territorial demands to Finland for a minor part of the Karelian Isthmus, a naval base at Hanko (Hangö) peninsula and some islands in the Gulf of Finland. Finland rejected the demands and on November 30, the Soviet Union invaded Finland, thus triggering the Winter War. Despite outnumbering Finnish troops by over 2.5:1, the war proved embarrassingly difficult for the Red Army, which was ill-equipped for the winter weather and lacking competent commanders since the purge of the Soviet high command. The Finns resisted fiercely, and received some support and considerable sympathy from the Allies.Wikipedia:Citation needed But in the spring of 1940, the snows melted, and a renewed Soviet offensive compelled them to surrender and relinquish the Karelian Isthmus and some smaller territories.

In 1940, the USSR occupied and illegally annexed Lithuania, Latvia, and Estonia. On June 14, 1941, the USSR performed first mass deportations from Lithuania, Latvia, and Estonia.

On June 26, 1940 the Soviet government issued an ultimatum to the Romanian minister in Moscow, demanding Romania immediately cede Bessarabia and Northern Bukovina. Italy and Germany, which needed a stable Romania and access to its oil fields urged King Carol II to do so. Under duress, with no prospect of aid from France or Britain, Carol complied. On June 28, Soviet

Figure 51: *Soviet children celebrating the school year end on the eve of the Great Patriotic War, June 22, 1941.*

troops crossed the Dniester and occupied Bessarabia, Northern Bukovina, and the Hertza region.

Great Patriotic War

On June 22, 1941, Adolf Hitler abruptly broke the non-aggression pact and invaded the Soviet Union. Soviet intelligence was fooled by German disinformation and sent to Moscow false alarms about German invasion in April, May and the beginning of June. Despite the popular myth there was no warning "Germany will attack on 22 June without declaration of war", moreover, Soviet intelligence reported that Germany would either invade the USSR after the fall of the British Empire or after an unacceptable ultimatum demanding German occupation of Ukraine during the German invasion of Britain.[148] Like in Sino-Soviet conflict on Chinese Eastern Railway or Soviet–Japanese border conflicts Soviet troops on western border received a directive undersigned by Marshal Semyon Timoshenko and General of the Army Georgy Zhukov that ordered (as demanded by Stalin): "do not answer to any provocations" and "do not undertake any (offensive) actions without specific orders" – which meant that Soviet troops could open fire only on their soil and forbade counter-attack on German soil.

The Nazi invasion caught the Soviet military unprepared. In the larger sense, Stalin expected invasion but not so soon. The Army had been decimated by the Purges; time was needed for a recovery of competence. As such, mobilization did not occur and the Soviet Army was tactically unprepared as of the invasion. The initial weeks of the war were a disaster, with tens of thousands of men being killed, wounded, or captured. Whole divisions disintegrated against the German onslaught.

It is said that Stalin, at first, refused to believe Nazi Germany had broken the treaty. However, new evidence shows Stalin held meetings with a variety of senior Soviet government and military figures, including Vyacheslav Molotov (People's Commissar for Foreign Affairs), Semyon Timoshenko (People's Commissar for Defense), Georgy Zhukov (Chief of Staff of the Red Army), Nikolay Kuznetsov (Commander of both North Caucasus and Baltic Military Districts), and Boris Shaposhnikov (Deputy People's Commissar for Defense). All in all, on the very first day of the attack, Stalin held meetings with over 15 individual members of the Soviet government and military apparatus.

German troops reached the outskirts of Moscow in December 1941, but failed to capture it, due to staunch Soviet defence and counterattacks. At the Battle of Stalingrad in 1942–43, the Red Army inflicted a crushing defeat on the German army. Due to the unwillingness of the Japanese to open a second front in Manchuria, the Soviets were able to call dozens of Red Army divisions back from eastern Russia. These units were instrumental in turning the tide, because most of their officer corps had escaped Stalin's purges. The Soviet forces soon launched massive counterattacks along the entire German line. By 1944, the Germans had been pushed out of the Soviet Union onto the banks of the Vistula river, just east of Prussia. With Soviet Marshal Georgy Zhukov attacking from Prussia, and Marshal Ivan Konev slicing Germany in half from the south, the fate of Nazi Germany was sealed. On May 2, 1945 the last German troops surrendered to the overjoyed Soviet troops in Berlin.

Wartime developments

From the end of 1944 to 1949, large sections of eastern Germany came under the Soviet Union's occupation and on 2 May 1945, the capital city Berlin was taken, while over fifteen million Germans were removed from eastern Germany and pushed into central Germany (later called German Democratic Republic) and western Germany (later called Federal Republic of Germany). Russians, Ukrainians, Poles, Czech, etc., were then moved onto German land.

An atmosphere of patriotic emergency took over the Soviet Union during the war, and persecution of the Orthodox Church was halted. The Church was now permitted to operate with a fair degree of freedom, so long as it did not get involved in politics. In 1944, a new Soviet national anthem was written, replacing the Internationale, which had been used as the national anthem since 1918. These changes were made because it was thought that the people would respond better to a fight for their country than for a political ideology.

The Soviets bore the brunt of World War II because the West did not open up a second ground front in Europe until the invasion of Italy and the Battle of Normandy. Approximately 26.6 million Soviets, among them 18 million civilians, were killed in the war. Civilians were rounded up and burned or shot in many cities conquered by the Nazis.Wikipedia:Citation needed The retreating Soviet army was ordered to pursue a 'scorched earth' policy whereby retreating Soviet troops were ordered to destroy civilian infrastructure and food supplies so that the Nazi German troops could not use them.

Stalin's original declaration in March 1946 that there were 7 million war dead was revised in 1956 by Nikita Khrushchev with a round number of 20 million. In the late 1980s, demographers in the State Statistics Committee (Goskomstat) took another look using demographic methods and came up with an estimate of 26–27 million. A variety of other estimates have been made. In most detailed estimates roughly two-thirds of the estimated deaths were civilian losses. However, the breakdown of war losses by nationality is less well known. One study, relying on indirect evidence from the 1959 population census, found that while in terms of the aggregate human losses the major Slavic groups suffered most, the largest losses relative to population size were incurred by minority nationalities mainly from European Russia, among groups from which men were mustered to the front in "nationality battalions" and appear to have suffered disproportionately.

After the war, the Soviet Union occupied and dominated Eastern Europe, in line with their particular Marxist ideology.

Stalin was determined to punish those peoples he saw as collaborating with Germany during the war and to deal with the problem of nationalism, which would tend to pull the Soviet Union apart. Millions of Poles, Latvians, Georgians, Ukrainians and other ethnic minorities were deported to Gulags in Siberia. (Previously, following the 1939 annexation of eastern Poland, thousands of Polish Army officers, including reservists, had been executed in the spring of 1940, in what came to be known as the Katyn massacre.) In addition, in 1941, 1943 and 1944 several whole nationalities had been deported to Siberia, Kazakhstan, and Central Asia, including, among others, the Volga Germans, Chechens, Ingush, Balkars, Crimean Tatars, and Meskhetian Turks. Though these groups were later politically "rehabilitated", some were never given back their former autonomous regions.[149]

At the same time, in a famous Victory Day toast in May 1945, Stalin extolled the role of the Russian people in the defeat of the fascists: "I would like to raise a toast to the health of our Soviet people and, before all, the Russian people. I drink, before all, to the health of the Russian people, because in this war they earned general recognition as the leading force of the Soviet Union among all the nationalities of our country... And this trust of the Russian people in the Soviet Government was the decisive strength, which secured the historic victory over the enemy of humanity – over fascism..."

World War II resulted in enormous destruction of infrastructure and populations throughout Eurasia, from the Atlantic to the Pacific oceans, with almost no country left unscathed. The Soviet Union was especially devastated due to the mass destruction of the industrial base that it had built up in the 1930s. The USSR also experienced a major famine in 1946–48 due to war devastation that cost an estimated 1 to 1.5 million lives as well as secondary population losses due to reduced fertility.[150]</ref> However, the Soviet Union recovered its production capabilities and overcame pre-war capabilities, becoming the country with the most powerful land army in history by the end of the war, and having the most powerful military production capabilities.

War and Stalinist industrial-military development

Although the Soviet Union received aid and weapons from the United States under the Lend-Lease program, the Soviet production of war materials was greater than that of Nazi Germany because of rapid growth of Soviet industrial production during the interwar years (additional supplies from lend-lease accounted for about 10–12% of the Soviet Union's own industrial output).Wikipedia:Citation needed The Second Five Year Plan raised steel production to 18 million tons and coal to 128 million tons.Wikipedia:Citation needed Before it was interrupted, the Third Five Year Plan produced no less than 19 million tons of steel and 150 million tons of coal.Wikipedia:Citation needed

The Soviet Union's industrial output provided an armaments industry which supported their army, helping it resist the Nazi military offensive. According to Robert L. Hutchings, "One can hardly doubt that if there had been a slower buildup of industry, the attack would have been successful and world history would have evolved quite differently."[151] For the laborers involved in industry, however, life was difficult. Workers were encouraged to fulfill and overachieve quotas through propaganda, such as the Stakhanovite movement.

Some historians, however, interpret the lack of preparedness of the Soviet Union to defend itself as a flaw in Stalin's economic planning. David Shearer, for example, argues that there was "a command-administrative economy" but it was not "a planned one". He argues that the Soviet Union was still suffering from the Great Purge, and was completely unprepared for the German invasion.Wikipedia:Citation needed Economist Holland Hunter, in addition,

Figure 52: *Soviet expansion, change of Central-eastern European borders and creation of the Eastern Bloc after World War II*

argues in his *Overambitious First Soviet Five-Year Plan*, that an array "of alternative paths were available, evolving out of the situation existing at the end of the 1920s... that could have been as good as those achieved by, say, 1936 yet with far less turbulence, waste, destruction and sacrifice."Wikipedia:Citation needed

The Cold War

Soviet hegemony over Eastern Europe

In the aftermath of World War II, the Soviet Union extended its political and military influence over Eastern Europe, in a move that was seen by some as a continuation of the older policies of the Russian Empire. Some territories that had been lost by Soviet Russia in the Treaty of Brest-Litovsk (1918) were annexed by the Soviet Union after World War II: the Baltic states and eastern portions of interwar Poland. The Russian SFSR also gained the northern half of East Prussia (Kaliningrad Oblast) from Germany. The Ukrainian SSR gained Transcarpathia (as Zakarpattia Oblast) from Czechoslovakia, and Ukrainian populated Northern Bukovina (as Chernivtsi Oblast) from Romania. Finally, in the late 1940s, pro-Soviet Communist Parties won the elections in five countries of Central and Eastern Europe (Poland, Czechoslovakia, Hungary, Romania and Bulgaria) and subsequently became People's Democracies. These elections are generally regarded as rigged, and the Western powers did not recognize the elections as legitimate. For the duration of the Cold War, the countries of Eastern Europe became Soviet satellite states — they were "independent" nations, which were one-party Communist States whose General Secretary had to be approved by the Kremlin, and so their governments usually kept their policy in line with the wishes of the Soviet Union, although nationalistic forces and pressures within the satellite states played a part in causing some deviation from strict Soviet rule.

Tenor of Soviet–U.S. relations

The wartime alliance between the United States and the Soviet Union was an aberration from the normal tenor of Russian–U.S. relations. Strategic rivalry between the huge, sprawling nations goes back to the 1890s when, after a century of friendship, Americans and Russians became rivals over the development of Manchuria.Wikipedia:Citation needed Tsarist Russia, unable to compete industrially, sought to close off and colonize parts of East Asia, while Americans demanded open competition for markets.Wikipedia:Citation needed

Lasting Russian mistrust arose from the landing of U.S. troops in Soviet Russia in 1918, which became involved, directly and indirectly, in assisting the anti-Bolshevik Whites in the civil war.Wikipedia:Citation needed

In addition, the Soviets requested that the United States and Britain open a second front on the European continent; but the Allied invasion did not occur until June 1944, more than two years later. In the meantime, the Russians suffered horrendous casualties, more than 20 million dead, and the Soviets were forced to withstand the brunt of German strength. The allies claimed that a second front had been opened in 1943 in Italy and were not prepared to immediately assault Nazi-occupied France.Wikipedia:Citation needed

Breakdown of postwar peace

When the war ended in Europe on May 8, 1945, Soviet and Western (US, British, and French) troops were essentially facing each other along a line down the center of Europe ranging from Lübeck to Trieste. Aside from a few minor adjustments, this would be the "Iron Curtain" of the Cold War. In hindsight, Yalta signified the agreement of both sides that they could stay there and that neither side would use force to push the other out. This tacit accord applied to Asia as well, as evinced by U.S. occupation of Japan and the division of Korea. Politically, therefore, Yalta was an agreement on the postwar status quo in which Soviet Union hegemony reigned over about one-third and the Allies over two-thirds.

The Soviets were able to use a well-organized ring of spies in the United States, to gain critical advantages during meetings with representatives of Britain and the United States. Several of President Franklin D. Roosevelt's advisors and cabinet members regularly reported their activities to NKVD handlers.

There were fundamental contrasts between the visions of the United States and the Soviet Union, between capitalism and socialism. Each vindicated in 1945 by previous disasters, those contrasts had been simplified and refined in national ideologies to represent two ways of life. Conflicting models of democratic centralism versus liberal democracy, of state planning against free enterprise, of full or partial employment, of equality versus economic freedom, were to compete for the allegiance of the developing and developed world in the postwar years.

Even so, the basic structures and tensions that marked the cold war were not yet in place in 1945–46. Despite the necessary means of the United States to advance a different vision of postwar Europe, Joseph Stalin viewed the re-emergence of Germany and Japan as the Soviet Union's chief threats, not the United States. At the time, the prospects of an Anglo-American front against the USSR seemed slim from Stalin's standpoint.Wikipedia:Citation needed Economic advisers such as Eugen Varga reinforced this view, predicting a postwar crisis of overproduction in capitalist countries which would culminate by 1947–48 in another great depression.Wikipedia:Citation needed For one, Stalin assumed Wikipedia:Citation needed that the capitalist camp would soon resume its internal rivalry over colonies and trade and not pose a threat to the Soviet Union.

Varga's analysis was partly based on trends in U.S. federal expenditures. Due to the war effort mostly, in the first peacetime year of 1946, federal spending still amounted to $62 billion, or 30% of GDP, up from 3% of GDP in 1929, before the Great Depression, New Deal, and Second World War.Wikipedia:Citation needed Thus, Stalin assumed that the Americans would *need* to look to the Soviet Union, to maintain the same level of exports and state expenditures.Wikipedia:Citation needed

However, there would be no postwar crisis of overproduction. And, as Varga anticipated, the U.S. maintained a roughly comparable level of government spending in the postwar era. It was just maintained in a vastly different way. In the end, the postwar U.S. government would look a lot like the wartime government, with the military establishment, along with military-security, accounting for a significant share of federal expenditures.

Domestic events

The mild political liberalization that took place in the Soviet Union during the war quickly came to an end in 1945. The Orthodox Church was generally left unmolested after the war and was even allowed to print small amounts of religious literature, but persecution of minority religions was resumed.Wikipedia:Citation needed Stalin and the Communist Party were given full credit for the victory over Germany, and generals such as Zhukov were demoted to regional commands (Ukraine in his case). With the onset of the Cold War, anti-Western propaganda was stepped up, with the capitalist world depicted as a decadent place where crime, unemployment, and poverty were rampant.

Things such as the light bulb and the automobile were claimed to have been invented by Russians,Wikipedia:Citation needed and art and science were subjected to rigorous censorship. The former was only allowed to contain themes of socialist realism, and the latter was heavily influenced by the quack biologist Trofim Lysenko, who rejected the concept of Mendelian inheritance. Even the theory of relativity was dismissed as "bourgeoise idealism". Much of this censorship was the work of Andrei Zhdanov, known as Stalin's "ideological hatchet man",Wikipedia:Citation needed until his death from a heart attack in 1948. Stalin's cult of personality reached its height in the postwar period, with his picture displayed in every school, factory, and government office, yet he rarely appeared in public. Postwar reconstruction proceeded rapidly, but as the emphasis was all on heavy industry and energy, living standards remained low, especially outside of the major cities.Wikipedia:Citation needed

In October 1952, the first postwar party congress convened in Moscow. Stalin did not feel up to delivering the main report and for most of the proceedings sat in silence while Nikita Khrushchev and Georgy Malenkov delivered the main speeches. He did suggest however that the party be renamed from "The All-Union Party of Bolsheviks" to "The Communist Party of the Soviet Union" on the grounds that "There was once a time when it was necessary to distinguish ourselves from the Mensheviks, but there are no Mensheviks anymore. We are the entire party now." Stalin also mentioned his advancing age (two months away from 73) and suggested that it might be time to retire. Predictably, no one at the congress would dare agree with it and the delegates instead pleaded for him to stay.

Terror by the secret police continued in the postwar period. Although nothing comparable to 1937 ever happened again, there were many smaller purges, including a mass purge of the Georgian party apparatus in 1951–52. Stalin's health also deteriorated precipitously after WWII. He suffered a stroke in the fall of 1945 and was ill for months. This was followed by another stroke in

1947. Stalin became less active in the day to day running of the state and instead of party meetings, preferred to invite the Politburo members to all-night dinners where he would watch movies and force them to get drunk and embarrass themselves or say something incriminating.

For decades, conspiracy theorists proposed that Stalin had been poisoned by Lavrentia Beria, possibly using warfarin, due to the symptoms he exhibited on his deathbed, including vomiting blood. In 2013, following the 60th anniversary of his death, the Russian State Archives finally made the autopsy findings public, showing conclusively that Stalin had not been poisoned, but died of natural causes, specifically a series of strokes caused by severe high blood pressure as well as gastric bleeding. He also suffered from fatty liver disease. The strokes had affected the part of the brain that controls respiration, which caused him to suffocate.

Two visions of the world

The United States, however, led by President Harry S. Truman since April 1945, was determined to shape the postwar world to America's best interest. He saw the ravaged, war-torn Europe as a place to implant the American system — capitalism, western democracy, constitutional rule — and (according to Soviet thinking) extend American hegemony throughout the world. The Soviet Union was attempting the same thing, extending its own systems as far as it could reach, and with two opposite empires struggling for hegemony, relationships between the United States and the Soviet Union quickly soured.

The United States moved quickly to consolidate its position, as it was the only major industrial power in the world to emerge intact — and even greatly strengthened from an economic perspective. It stood to gain more than any other country from opening up a global market for its exports and access to vital raw materials.

Beginning of the Cold War

Truman could advance these principles with an economic powerhouse that produced 50% of the world's industrial goods and a vast military power that rested on a monopoly of the new atomic bomb (*see also* Soviet atomic bomb project). Such a power could mould and benefit from a recovering Europe, which in turn required a healthy Germany at its center; these aims were at the center of what the Soviet Union strove to avoid as the wartime alliance broke down.

The resolve of the United States to advance a different vision of the postwar world conflicted with Soviet interests. National security had been important to Soviet foreign policy since the 1920s, when the Communist Party adopted Stalin's "Socialism in One Country" and rejected Leon Trotsky's ideas of "world revolution".Wikipedia:Citation needed Before the war, Stalin did not attempt to push Soviet boundaries beyond their full Tsarist extent.

In this sense, the aims of the Soviet Union may not have been aggressive expansionism but rather consolidation, i.e., attempting to secure the war-torn country's western borders. Stalin, assuming that Japan and Germany could menace the Soviet Union once again by the 1960s,Wikipedia:Citation needed thus quickly imposed Moscow-dominated governments in the springboards of the Nazi onslaught: Poland, Romania, and Bulgaria. Much of the rest of the world, however, viewed these moves as an aggressive attempt to expand Soviet influence and communist rule.Wikipedia:Citation needed

Disagreements over postwar plans first centered on Eastern and Central Europe. Having lost more than 20 million in the war, suffered German invasion, and suffered tens of millions of casualties due to onslaughts from the West three times in the preceding 150 years, first with Napoleon, Stalin was determined to destroy Germany's capacity for another war by keeping it under tight control. U.S. aims were quite different.

Winston Churchill, an anti-Communist, condemned Stalin for cordoning off a new Russian empire with an "Iron Curtain."Wikipedia:Citation needed Afterwards, Truman finally refusedWikipedia:Manual of Style/Dates and numbers#Chronological items to give the war-torn Soviet Union "reparations" from West Germany's industrial plants, Stalin retaliated Wikipedia:Manual of Style/Dates and numbers#Chronological items by sealing off East Germany as a Communist state.Wikipedia:Citation needed

The Soviet Union's historic lack of warm water maritime access, a perennial concern of Russian foreign policyWikipedia:Citation needed well before the October Revolution, was yet another area where interests diverged between East and West. Stalin pressed the TurksWikipedia:Manual of Style/Dates and numbers#Chronological items for improved access out of the Black Sea through Turkey's Dardanelles strait, which would allow Soviet passage from the Black Sea to the Mediterranean. Churchill had earlier recognized Stalin's claims,Wikipedia:Citation needed but now the British and Americans forced the Soviet Union to pull back.Wikipedia:Manual of Style/Dates and numbers#Chronological itemsWikipedia:Please clarifyWikipedia:Citation needed

Soviet leadership policies were often more measured, however: the Soviet Union eventually withdrew from Northern Iran,Wikipedia:Manual of Style/Dates and numbers#Chronological items at Anglo-American behest;Wikipedia:Citation needed Stalin did observe his 1944 agreement with Churchill and did not aid the communists in the struggle against government in Greece;Wikipedia:Manual of Style/Dates and numbers#Chronological items in Finland he accepted a friendly, non-communist government;Wikipedia:Manual of Style/Dates and numbers#Chronological itemsWikipedia:Citation needed and Russian troops were withdrawn from Czechoslovakia by the end of 1945. However, a pro-Soviet government seized power in Czechoslovakia three years later.Wikipedia:Citation needed

Containment and the Marshall Plan

An Anglo-American effort was made to support the Greek government in order to protect the free peoples against totalitarian regimes. This was articulated in the Truman Doctrine Speech of March 1947, which declared that the United States would spend as much as $400 million in efforts to "contain" communism.Wikipedia:Citation needed

By successfully aiding Greece in 1947, Truman also set a precedent for the U.S. aid to anti-Communist regimes worldwide, even authoritarian ones at times. U.S. foreign policy moved into alignment with State Department officer George Kennan's argument that the Soviets had to be "contained" using "unalterable counterforce at every point", until the breakdown of Soviet power occurred.Wikipedia:Citation needed

The United States launched massive economic reconstruction efforts, first in Western Europe and then in Japan (as well as in South Korea and Taiwan). The Marshall Plan began to pump $12 billion into Western Europe. The rationale was that economically stable nations were less likely to fall prey to Soviet influence, a view which was vindicated in the long run.

In response, Stalin blockaded Berlin in 1948. The city was within the Soviet zone, although subject to the control of all four major powers. The Soviets cut off all rail and road routes to West Berlin. Convinced that he could starve and freeze West Berlin into submission, no trucks or trains were allowed entry into the city. However, this decision backfired when Truman embarked on a highly visible move that would humiliate the Soviets internationally — supplying the beleaguered city by air. Military confrontation threatened while Truman, with British help, flew supplies over East Germany into West Berlin during the 1948–49 blockade. This costly aerial supplying of West Berlin became known as the Berlin Airlift.

Truman joined eleven other nations in 1949 to form the North Atlantic Treaty Organisation (NATO), the United States' first "entangling" European alliance in 170 years. Stalin replied to these moves by integrating the economies of Eastern Europe in his version of the Marshall Plan, exploding the first Soviet atomic device in 1949, and signing an alliance with Communist China in

February 1950. However, the Warsaw Pact, Eastern Europe's counterpart to NATO, was not created until 1955, two years after Stalin's death.

U.S. officials quickly moved to expand the containment policy. In a secret 1950 document, NSC 68, they proposed to strengthen their alliance systems, quadruple defense spending, and embark on an elaborate propaganda campaign to persuade Americans to fight this costly Cold War. Truman ordered the development of a hydrogen bomb; in early 1950, the U.S. embarked on its first attempt to prop up colonialism in French Indochina in the face of mounting popular, communist-led resistance;Wikipedia:Citation needed and the United States embarked on what the Soviets consideredWikipedia:Citation needed a blatant violation of wartime treaties: plans to form a West German army.

The immediate post-1945 period may have been the historical high point for the popularity of communist ideology. In the late 1940s Communist parties won large shares of the vote in free electionsWikipedia:Citation needed in countries such as Belgium, France, Italy, Czechoslovakia, and Finland; and won significant popular support in Asia (Vietnam, India, and Japan) and throughout Latin America.Wikipedia:Citation needed In addition they won large support in China, Greece, and Iran, where free elections remained absent or constrained but where Communist parties enjoyed widespread appeal.Wikipedia:Citation needed

In response, the United States sustained a massive anti-communist ideological offensive. The United States aimed to contain communism through both aggressive diplomacy and interventionist policies. In retrospect, this initiative appears largely successful: Washington brandished its role as the leader of the "Free World" at least as effectively as the Soviet Union brandished its position as the leader of the "progressive" and "anti-imperialist" camp.

Korean War

In 1950, the Soviet Union protested against the fact that the Chinese seat at the United Nations Security Council was held by the Nationalist government of China, and boycotted the meetings.Wikipedia:Citation needed While the Soviet Union was absent, the UN passed a resolution condemning North Korean actions and offering military support to South Korea.Wikipedia:Citation needed After this incident the Soviet Union was never absent at the meetings of the Security Council.

Further reading

- Brzezinski, Zbigniew. *The Grand Failure: The Birth and Death of Communism in the Twentieth Century* (1989).
- Hosking, Geoffrey. *The First Socialist Society: A History of the Soviet Union from Within* (2nd ed. Harvard UP 1992) 570 pp.
- Kort, Michael. *The Soviet Colossus: History and Aftermath* (7th ed. 2010) 502 pp.
- McCauley, Martin. *The Rise and Fall of the Soviet Union* (2007), 522 pp.
- Moss, Walter G. *A History of Russia. Vol. 2: Since 1855* (2nd ed. 2005).
- Nove, Alec. *An Economic History of the USSR, 1917–1991* (3rd ed. 1993).

Stalin and Stalinism

- Daniels, R. V., ed. *The Stalin Revolution* (1965)
- Davies, Sarah, and James Harris, eds. *Stalin: A New History,* (2006), 310 pp, 14 specialized essays by scholars excerpt and text search[152].
- De Jonge, Alex. *Stalin and the Shaping of the Soviet Union* (1986).
- Fitzpatrick, Sheila, ed. *Stalinism: New Directions,* (1999), 396 pp, excerpts from many scholars on the impact of Stalinism on the people online edition[153].
- Hoffmann, David L. ed. *Stalinism: The Essential Readings,* (2002) essays by 12 scholars.
- Laqueur, Walter. *Stalin: The Glasnost Revelations* (1990).
- Kershaw, Ian, and Moshe Lewin. *Stalinism and Nazism: Dictatorships in Comparison* (2004) excerpt and text search[154].
- Lee, Stephen J. *Stalin and the Soviet Union* (1999) online edition[155].
- Lewis, Jonathan. *Stalin: A Time for Judgement* (1990).
- McNeal, Robert H. *Stalin: Man and Ruler* (1988)
- Martens, Ludo. *Another view of Stalin* (1994), a highly favorable view from a Maoist historian
- Service, Robert. *Stalin: A Biography* (2004), along with Tucker the standard biography
- Tucker, Robert C. *Stalin as Revolutionary, 1879–1929* (1973)
- ——— (1990), *Stalin in Power*[156] (Questia online edition), New York: WW Norton with Service, a standard biography; online at ACLS History e-books[157].

1927–39

- Bendavid-Val, Leah, James H. Billington and Philip Brookman. *Propaganda and Dreams: Photographing the 1930s in the USSR and the US* (1999)
- Clark, Katerina. *Moscow, the Fourth Rome: Stalinism, Cosmopolitanism, and the Evolution of Soviet Culture, 1931–1941* (2011) excerpt and text search[158]
- Fitzpatrick, Sheila. *Stalin's Peasants: Resistance and Survival in the Russian Village after Collectivization* (1996) excerpt and text search[159]
- —— (2000), *Everyday Stalinism: Ordinary Life in Extraordinary Times: Soviet Russia in the 1930s*, ISBN 0195050010.

World War II

- Bellamy, Chris. *Absolute War: Soviet Russia in the Second World War* (2008), 880pp excerpt and text search[160]
- Berkhoff, Karel C. *Motherland in Danger: Soviet Propaganda during World War II* (2012) excerpt and text search[161]
- Broekmeyer, Marius. *Stalin, the Russians, and Their War, 1941–1945.* 2004. 315 pp.
- Hill, Alexander. *The Red Army and the Second World War* (2017), 738 pp.
- Overy, Richard. *Russia's War: A History of the Soviet Effort: 1941–1945* (1998) excerpt and text search[162]
- Roberts, Geoffrey. *Stalin's Wars: From World War to Cold War, 1939–1953* (2006).
- Seaton, Albert. *Stalin as Military Commander,* (1998) online edition[163]

Cold war

- Goncharov, Sergei, John Lewis and Litai Xue, *Uncertain Partners: Stalin, Mao and the Korean War* (1993) excerpt and text search[164]
- Gorlizki, Yoram, and Oleg Khlevniuk. *Cold Peace: Stalin and the Soviet Ruling Circle, 1945–1953* (2004) online edition[165]
- Harrison, Mark. "The Soviet Union after 1945: Economic Recovery and Political Repression," *Past & Present* (2011) Vol. 210 Issue suppl_6, pp 103–120.
- Holloway, David. *Stalin and the Bomb: The Soviet Union and Atomic Energy, 1939–1956* (1996) excerpt and text search[166]
- Mastny, Vojtech. *Russia's Road to the Cold War: Diplomacy, Warfare, and the Politics of Communism, 1941–1945* (1979)
- —— (1998), *The Cold War and Soviet Insecurity: The Stalin Years*[167] (Questia online complete edition);

- Taubman, William. *Khrushchev: The Man and His Era* (2004), Pulitzer Prize; excerpt and text search[168]
- Ulam, Adam B. *Expansion and Coexistence: Soviet Foreign Policy, 1917–1973*, 2nd ed. (1974)
- Zubok, Vladislav M. *A Failed Empire: The Soviet Union in the Cold War from Stalin to Gorbachev* (2007)

External links

- Dewey, John, "Impressions of Soviet Russia", *Dewey texts online*[169], Area 501, archived from the original[170] on 2008-01-21.
- "Moscow: Stalin 2.0"[171] (video), *The Global Post* (report),
- *USSR in Construction*[172] (digital presentation), The University of Saskatchewan – several full issues of the propaganda journal by the USSR government 1930–41.

1953–1964

History of the Soviet Union (1953–64)

Part of a series on the
History of the **Union of Soviet Socialist Republics** (Soviet Union)
1917–1927 **Revolutionary Beginnings**
• Revolution • Civil War • New Economic Policy • 1922 Treaty • National delimitation
1927–1953 **Stalinist rule**

- Socialism in One Country
- Great Purge

Soviet famine of 1932–33

- (Holodomor
- Kazakhstan famine of 1932-1933)

World War II

- (Molotov–Ribbentrop Pact
- Great Patriotic War
- Operation Barbarossa
- Occupation of the Baltic states
- Soviet occupation of Bessarabia and Northern Bukovina
- Battle of Berlin
- Soviet invasion of Manchuria)
- Soviet deportations
- Soviet famine of 1946–47
- Cold War
- Korean War

1953–1964
Post-Stalin era

- Berlin blockade
- 1954 transfer of Crimea
- Khrushchev Thaw
- On the Cult of Personality and Its Consequences
- We will bury you
- 9 March riots
- Wage reforms
- Cuban Revolution
- Sino-Soviet split
- Space program
- Cuban Missile Crisis

1964–1982
Brezhnev era

- Brezhnev Doctrine
- Era of Stagnation
- 50th anniversary of the Armenian Genocide protests
- Prague Spring

                          Vietnam War

- (Laotian Civil War
- Operation Menu
- Cambodian Civil War
- Fall of Saigon)
- Six-Day War
- Détente
- Yom Kippur War
- Dirty War

                          Wars in Africa

- (Angolan War of Independence
- Angolan Civil War
- Mozambican War of Independence
- Mozambican Civil War
- South African Border War
- Rhodesian Bush War)
- Cambodian-Vietnamese War
- Soviet–Afghan War
- 1980 Summer Olympics

                          Olympic boycotts

- (1980 Olympic boycott
- 1984 Olympic boycott)
- Polish strike
- Death and funeral of Brezhnev

1982–1991
Leadership changes and collapse

- Invasion of Grenada
- Glasnost
- Perestroika
- Soviet withdrawal from Afghanistan

Singing Revolution

- (Estonian Sovereignty Declaration
- Baltic Way
- Act of the Re-Establishment of the State of Lithuania
- On the Restoration of Independence of the Republic of Latvia)

Revolutions of 1989

- (Pan-European picnic
- Die Wende
- Peaceful Revolution
- Fall of the Berlin Wall
- Velvet Revolution
- End of communist rule in Hungary
- Romanian Revolution
- German reunification)

Dissolution

- (Jeltoqsan
- Nagorno-Karabakh War
- 9 April tragedy
- Black January
- Osh riots
- War of Laws
- Dushanbe riots
- January Events
- The Barricades
- Referendum
- Union of Sovereign States
- August Coup
- Ukrainian independence (referendum)
- Belavezha Accords
- Alma-Ata Protocol)

History of

- Russia
- Moscow
- Kiev
- Minsk
- Former Soviet Republics

Soviet leadership

- 1. Lenin
- 2. Stalin
- 3. Malenkov
- 4. Khrushchev
- 5. Brezhnev
- 6. Andropov
- 7. Chernenko
- 8. Gorbachev

- **Culture**
- **Economy**
- **Education**
- **Geography**
- **Politics**

■ **Soviet Union portal**

- v
- t
- e[173]

In the USSR, during the eleven-year period from the death of Joseph Stalin (1953) to the political ouster of Nikita Khrushchev (1964), the national politics were dominated by the Cold War, the ideological U.S.–USSR struggle for the planetary domination of their respective socio-economic systems, and the defense of hegemonic spheres of influence. Nonetheless, since the mid-1950s, despite the Communist Party of the Soviet Union (CPSU) having disowned Stalinism, the political culture of Stalinism—a very powerful General Secretary of the CPSU—remained in place, albeit weakened.

De-Stalinization and the Khrushchev era

After Stalin died in March 1953, he was succeeded by Nikita Khrushchev as First Secretary of the Central Committee of the Communist Party of the Soviet Union (CPSU) and Georgi Malenkov as Premier of the Soviet Union. However the central figure in the immediate post-Stalin period was the former head of the state security apparatus, Lavrentiy Beria.

Stalin had left the Soviet Union in an unenviable state when he died. At least 2.5 million people languished in prison and in labor camps, science and the arts had been subjugated to socialist realism, and agriculture productivity on the whole was meager. The country had only one quarter of the livestock it had had in 1928 and in some areas, there were fewer animals than there had been at the start of World War I. Private plots accounted for at least three quarters of meat, dairy, and produce output. Living standards were low and consumer goods scarce. Moscow was also remarkably isolated and friendless on the international stage; Eastern Europe excluding Yugoslavia was held to the Soviet yoke by military occupation and soon after Stalin's death, revolts would break out everywhere. China paid homage to the departed Soviet leader, but held a series of grudges that would soon boil over. The United States had military bases and nuclear-equipped bomber aircraft surrounding the Soviet Union on three sides, and American aircraft regularly overflew Soviet territory on reconnaissance missions and to parachute agents in. Although the Soviet authorities shot down many of these aircraft and captured most of the agents dropped onto their soil, the psychological effect was immense.

American fears of Soviet military and especially nuclear capabilities were strong and heavily exaggerated; Moscow's only heavy bomber, the Tu-4, was a direct clone of the B-29 and had no way to get to the United States except on a one way suicide mission and the Soviet nuclear arsenal contained only a handful of weapons.

Figure 53: *The USSR: the maximum extent of the Soviet sphere of influence,
after the Cuban Revolution (1959) and before the Sino-Soviet split (1961).*

Beria, despite his record as part of Stalin's terror state, initiated a period of relative liberalization, including the release of some political prisoners. Almost
as soon as Stalin was buried, Beria ordered Vyacheslav Molotov's wife freed
from imprisonment and personally delivered her to the Soviet foreign minister. He also directed the Ministry of Internal Affairs (MVD) to reexamine
the Doctors' Plot and other "false" cases. Beria next proposed stripping the
MVD of some of its economic assets and transferring control of them to other
ministries, followed by the proposal to stop using forced labor on construction projects. He then announced that 1.1 million nonpolitical prisoners were
to be freed from captivity, that the Ministry of Justice should assume control
of labor camps from the MVD, and that the Doctors' Plot was false. Finally,
he ordered a halt to physical and psychological abuse of prisoners. Beria also
declared a halt to forced Russification of the Soviet republics.

Next, Beria turned his attention to foreign policy. A secret letter found among
his papers after his death, suggested restoring relations with Tito's Yugoslavia.
He also criticized Soviet handling of Eastern Europe and the numerous "mini-
Stalins" such as Hungary's Matyas Rakosi. East Germany particularly was in
a tenuous situation in 1953 as the attempt by its premier Walter Ulbricht to
impose all-out Stalinism had cause a mass exodus of people to the West. Beria
suggested that East Germany should just be forgotten about entirely and there

was "no purpose" for its existence. He revived the proposal Stalin had made to the Allies in 1946 for the creation of a united, neutral Germany.

The leadership also began allowing some criticism of Stalin, saying that his one-man dictatorship went against the principles laid down by Vladimir Lenin. The war hysteria that characterized his last years was toned down, and government bureaucrats and factory managers were ordered to wear civilian clothing instead of military-style outfits. Estonia, Latvia and Lithuania were given serious prospects of national autonomy, possibly similarly to other Soviet satellite states in Europe.

Some of Beria's moves such as halting Russification of the republics were clearly motivated by personal reasons as he was a non-Russian, but he also displayed a considerable degree of contempt for the rest of the Politburo, letting it be known that they were "complicit" in Stalin's crimes. However, it was not deep-rooted ideological disagreements that turned them against Beria. Khrushchev in particular was appalled at the idea of abandoning East Germany and allowing the restoration of capitalism there, but that alone wasn't enough to plot Beria's downfall and he even supported the new, more enlightened policy towards non-Russian nationalities. The Politburo soon began stonewalling Beria's reforms and trying to prevent them from passing. One proposal, to reduce sentences handed down by the MVD to 10 years max, was later claimed by Khrushchev to be a ruse. "He wants to be able to sentence people to ten years in the camps, and then when they're freed, sentence them to another ten years. This is his way of grinding them down." Molotov was the strongest opponent of abandoning East Germany, and found in Khrushchev an unexpected ally. By late June, it was decided that Beria couldn't simply be ignored or stonewalled, he had to be taken out. They had him arrested on June 26 with the support of the armed forces. At the end of the year, he was shot following a show trial where he was accused of spying for the West, committing sabotage, and plotting to restore capitalism. The secret police were disarmed and reorganized into the KGB, ensuring that they were completely under the control of the party and would never again be able to wage mass terror. In the post-Beria period, Khrushchev rapidly began to emerge as the key figure.

The new leadership declared an amnesty for some serving prison sentences for criminal offenses, announced price cuts, and relaxed the restrictions on private plots. De-Stalinization also spelled an end to the role of large-scale forced labor in the economy.

For a time after Beria's fall, Georgi Malenkov was the seniormost figure in the Politburo. Malenkov, an artistic-minded man who courted intellectuals and artists, had little use for bloodshed or state terror. He called for greater support of private agricultural plots and liberation of the arts from rigid socialist realism and he also criticized the pseudoscience of biologist Trofim Lysenko.

In a November 1953 speech, Malenkov denounced corruption in various government agencies. He also reappraised Soviet views of the outside world and relations with the West, arguing that there were no disputes with the United States and her allies that could not be resolved peacefully, and that nuclear war with the West would simply bring about the destruction of all parties involved.

Khrushchev meanwhile proposed greater agricultural reforms, although he still refused to abandon the concept of collective farming and continued to support Lysenko's pseudoscience. In a 1955 speech, he argued that Soviet agriculture needed a shot in the arm and that it was silly to keep blaming low productivity and failed harvests on Tsar Nicholas II, dead for almost 40 years. He also began allowing ordinary people to stroll the grounds of the Kremlin, which had been closed off except to high ranking state officials for over 20 years.

During a period of collective leadership, Khrushchev gradually rose to power while Malenkov's power waned. The latter was criticized for his economic reform proposals and desire to reduce the CPSU's direct involvement in the day to day running of the state. Molotov called his warning that nuclear war would end all of civilization to be "nonsense" since according to Marx, the collapse of capitalism was a historical inevitability. Khrushchev accused Malenkov of supporting Beria's plan to abandon East Germany, and of being a "capitulationist, social democrat, and a Menshevist".

Khrushchev was also headed for a showdown with Molotov, after having initially respected and left him alone in the immediate aftermath of Stalin's death. Molotov began criticizing all of Khrushchev's ideas and the latter accused him in turn of being an out-of-touch ideologue who never left his dacha or the Kremlin to visit farms or factories. Molotov attacked Khrushchev's suggestions for agricultural reform and also his plans to construct cheap, prefab apartments to alleviate Moscow's severe housing shortages. Khrushchev also endorsed restoring ties with Yugoslavia, the split with Belgrade having been heavily engineered by Molotov, who continued to denounce Tito as a fascist. A 1955 visit by Khrushchev to Yugoslavia patched up relations with that country, but Molotov refused to back down. The near-total isolation of the Soviet Union from the outside world was also blamed by Khrushchev on Molotov's handling of foreign policy and the former admitted in a speech to the Central Committee the obvious Soviet complicity in starting the Korean War.

The late Stalin's reputation meanwhile started diminishing. His 75th birthday in December 1954 had been marked by extensive eulogies and commemorations in the state media as was the second anniversary of his death in March 1955. However, his 76th birthday at the end of the year was hardly mentioned.

At a closed session of the Twentieth Party Congress of the CPSU on 25 February 1956, Khrushchev shocked his listeners by denouncing Stalin's dictatorial rule and cult of personality in a speech entitled *On the Cult of Personality and its Consequences*. He also attacked the crimes committed by Stalin's closest associates. Furthermore, he stated that the orthodox view of war between the capitalist and communist worlds being inevitable was no longer true. He advocated competition with the West rather than outright hostility, stating that capitalism would decay from within and that world socialism would triumph peacefully. But, he added, if the capitalists did desire war, the Soviet Union would respond in kind.

The impact on Soviet politics was immense. The speech stripped the legitimacy of his remaining Stalinist rivals, dramatically boosting his power domestically. Afterwards, Khrushchev eased restrictions and freed over a million prisoners from the Gulag, leaving an estimated 1.5 million prisoners living in a semi-reformed prison system (though a wave of counter-reform followed in the 1960s). Communists around the world were shocked and confused by his condemnation of Stalin, and the speech "...caused a veritable revolution (the word is not too strong) in peoples attitudes throughout the Soviet Union and Eastern Europe. It was the single factor in breaking down the mixture of fear, fanaticism, naivety and 'doublethink' with which everyone...had reacted to Communist rule".

Some of the communist world, in particular China, North Korea, and Albania, stridently rejected de-Stalinization. An editorial in the People's Daily argued that "Stalin made some mistakes, but on the whole he was a good, honest Marxist and his positives outweighed the negatives." Mao Zedong had many quarrels with Stalin, but thought that condemning him undermined the entire legitimacy of world socialism. "Stalin needed to be criticized, not killed." he said and the May Day parade in Beijing featured large Stalin portraits.

By late 1955, thousands of political prisoners had been freed, but Soviet prisons and labor camps still held around 800,000 inmates and no attempt was made to investigate the Moscow Trials or rehabilitate their victims. Meanwhile, many Soviet intellectuals groused that Khrushchev and the rest of the Central Committee had willingly aided and abetted Stalin's crimes and that the late tyrant could not possibly have done everything himself. Furthermore, they asked why it had taken three years to condemn him and noted that Khrushchev mostly criticized what had happened to fellow Party members while completely overlooking far greater atrocities such as the Holodomor and mass deportations from the Baltic States during and after WWII, none of which were allowed to be mentioned in the Soviet press until the end of the 1980s. During the Secret Speech, Khrushchev had tried in an awkward manner to explain why he and his colleagues had not raised their voices against Stalin by saying that they all feared their own destruction if they did not comply with his demands.

In April 1956, there were reports that Stalin busts and portraits around the country had been vandalized or pulled down and some student groups rioted and demanded that Stalin be posthumously expelled from the party and his body taken down from its spot next to Lenin. Party and student meetings called for proper rule of law in the country and even free elections. A 25 year old Mikhail Gorbachev, then a member of the Komsomol in Stavropol reported that reaction to the Secret Speech was explosive and there were strong reactions between people, particularly, young, educated people, who supported it and hated Stalin, others who denounced it and still held the late tyrant in awe, and others who thought it was irrelevant compared to grassroots issues such as food and housing availability. The Presidium responded by issuing a resolution condemning "anti-party" and "anti-Soviet" slanderers and the April 7 Pravda reprinted an editorial from China's *People's Daily* calling on party members to study Stalin's teachings and honor his memory. A Central Committee meeting on June 30 issued a resolution criticizing Stalin merely for "serious errors" and "practicing a cult of personality" but holding the Soviet system itself blameless.

In Stalin's native Georgia, massive crowds of pro-Stalin demonstrators rioted in the streets of Tbilisi and even demanded that Georgia secede from the USSR. Army troops had to be called in to restore order, with 20 deaths, 60 injuries, and scores of arrests.

Eventually several hundred thousand of Stalin's victims were rehabilitated, but the party officials purged in the Moscow Trials remained off the table. Khrushchev ordered an investigation into the trials of Mikhail Tukhachevsky and other army officers. The committee found that the charges leveled against them were baseless and their posthumous rehabilitation was announced in early 1957, but another investigation into the trials of Grigory Zinoviev, Lev Kamenev, and Nikolai Bukharin declared that all three had engaged in "anti-Soviet activity" and would not be rehabilitated. After Khrushchev defeated the "anti-party group" in 1957, he promised to re-open the cases, but ultimately never got around to doing so, in part because of the embarrassing fact that he himself had celebrated the elimination of the Old Bolsheviks during the purges.

Meanwhile, Khrushchev attempted to restore relations with Tito's Yugoslavia with a visit to Belgrade in May 1955, however the Yugoslavian leader was unmoved by an attempt by Khrushchev to blame Beria for the break with Yugoslavia. Khrushchev persisted and began urging the Eastern European bloc to restore ties with Yugoslavia. He also disbanded the Cominform, used as a club to beat Belgrade over the head with. The trip was reciprocated by a visit of Tito to Moscow in May 1956 where he was given a regal welcome and immense crowds dispatched to greet him. The Politburo members attempted to outdo each other in courting Tito and apologizing for Stalin, but the visit had no ultimate effect on Tito's foreign policy stance and he still refused to join the Soviet bloc, abandon his nonaligned stance, or cut off economic and military ties with the West. Worse than that, Tito began offering his nonaligned socialism to other countries, in particular Poland and Hungary.

After Hungarian leader Imre Nagy briefly took refuge in the Yugoslavian embassy in Budapest during the events of October 1956, Tito stayed aloof from the Soviet suppression of the Hungarian revolt and Soviet-Yugoslav relations waned from that point onward. Tito declined to attend the celebrations of the 40th anniversary of the Bolshevik Revolution in November 1957 and continued to actively promote his nonaligned stance at the Yugoslavian Communist Party's congress the following March. Khrushchev refused to send any delegates to the congress and authorized a lengthy denunciation of it in *Pravda*. Accusing Tito of being a traitor similar to Imre Nagy, Khrushchev ordered the execution of the Hungarian leader, who had been incarcerated for the last several months.

In September 1959, Khrushchev became the first Russian head of state to visit the United States. This groundbreaking trip was made on the new Tu-114 long range airliner despite still being an experimental aircraft, since the Soviet Union did not have any other plane capable of nonstop trans-Atlantic travel. The 13 day trip included meetings with American businessmen and labor leaders, Hollywood actors, and Roswell Garst's farm in Iowa. Khrushchev became openly dismayed when he was told he could not visit Disneyland because it was too difficult to guarantee his security there.

During this time, Khrushchev also ran afoul of China when he proposed a joint Sino-Soviet fleet in the Pacific to counter the US Seventh Fleet. Soviet ambassador to China Pavel Yudin was rebuffed by Mao Zedong in a July 1958 meeting. Mao demanded to talk to Khrushchev in person, so the latter obliged and flew to Beijing. The meeting proved no more successful than the previous one with Yudin and Mao continued to reject the idea of a joint fleet, allowing Soviet warships to dock at Chinese ports in peacetime, and operating joint radar stations as an infringement on Chinese sovereignty. Shortly after Khrushchev went home, the Chinese military shelled the islands of Jinmen and Mazu in the Formosa Strait, provoking the US Seventh Fleet to the area in a major show of force. Moscow supported the Chinese shelling of the islands with reluctance and after American threats of force on China, Mao told an appalled Andrei Gromyko that he was more than willing to start a nuclear war with the imperialist powers.

After this, Sino-Soviet relations calmed during the next six months only to worsen again during the summer of 1959 when Khrushchev criticized the Great Leap Forward and remained noncommittal during a Chinese border clash with India. On August 20, Moscow informed Beijing that they would not give them a proposed sample atomic bomb. When Khrushchev headed to Beijing in late September, just after his US trip, he was given an icy reception and further alienated the Chinese with his warm accounts of Americans and of Eisenhower. A suggestion by the Soviet premier to free American pilots captured by China during the Korean War was rejected as well as Beijing's recent actions in the Formosa Strait and the Indian border. The talks ended after only three days and Khrushchev went home despondent.

Khrushchev initiated "The Thaw" better known as Khrushchev Thaw, a complex shift in political, cultural and economic life in the Soviet Union. That included some openness and contact with other countries and new social and economic policies with more emphasis on commodity goods, allowing living standards to rise dramatically while maintaining high levels of economic growth. Censorship was relaxed as well. Some subtle critiques of the Soviet society were tolerated, and artists were not expected to produce only works which had government-approved political context. Still, artists, most of whom were proud of both the country and the Party, were careful not to get into trouble. On the other hand, he reintroduced aggressive anti-religious campaigns, closing down many houses of worship.

Such loosening of controls also caused an enormous impact on other socialist countries in Central Europe, many of which were resentful of Soviet influence in their affairs. Riots broke out in Poland in the summer of 1956, which led to reprisals from national forces there. A political convulsion soon followed, leading to the rise of Władysław Gomułka to power in October. This almost triggered a Soviet invasion when Polish Communists elected him without consulting the Kremlin in advance, but in the end, Khrushchev backed down due to Gomułka's widespread popularity in the country. Poland would still remain a member of the Warsaw Pact (established a year earlier), and in return, the Soviet Union seldom intervened in its neighbors' domestic and external affairs. Khrushchev also began reaching out to newly independent countries in Asia and Africa, which was in sharp contrast to Stalin's Europe-centered foreign policy. And in September 1959, he became the first Soviet leader to visit the US.

In November 1956, the Hungarian Revolution was brutally suppressed by Soviet troops. About 2,500–3,000 Hungarian insurgents and 700 Soviet troops were killed, thousands more were wounded, and nearly a quarter million left the country as refugees. The Hungarian uprising was a blow to Western communists; many who had formerly supported the Soviet Union began to criticize it in the wake of the Soviet suppression of the Hungarian uprising.

The following year Khrushchev defeated a concerted Stalinist attempt to recapture power, decisively defeating the so-called "Anti-Party Group". This event also illustrated the new nature of Soviet politics—the most decisive attack on the Stalinists was delivered by defense minister Georgy Zhukov, and the implied threat to the plotters was clear; however, none of the "anti-party group" were killed or even arrested, and Khrushchev disposed of them quite cleverly: Georgy Malenkov was sent to manage a power station in Kazakhstan, and Vyacheslav Molotov, one of the most die-hard Stalinists, was made ambassador to Mongolia. Eventually however, Molotov was reassigned to be the Soviet representative of the International Atomic Energy Commission in Vienna after the Kremlin decided to put some safe distance between him and China since Molotov was becoming increasingly cozy with the anti-Khrushchev Chinese leadership. Molotov continued to attack Khrushchev every opportunity he got, and in 1960, on the occasion of Lenin's 90th birthday, wrote a piece describing his personal memories of the Soviet founding father and thus implying that he was the keeper of the true faith. In 1961, just prior to the 22nd CPSU Congress, Molotov wrote a vociferous denunciation of Khrushchev's party platform and was rewarded for this action with expulsion from the party. Foreign Minister Dmitri Shepilov also met the chopping block when he was sent to manage the Kirghizia Institute of Economics. Later, when he was appointed as a delegate to the Kirghiz Republic party conference, Khrushchev deputy Leonid Brezhnev intervened and ordered Shepilov dropped from the conference. He and his wife were evicted from their Moscow apartment and then reassigned to a smaller one that lay exposed to the fumes from a nearby food processing plant, and he was dropped from membership in the Soviet Academy of Sciences before being expelled from the party. Kliment Voroshilov held the ceremonial title of head of state despite his advancing age and declining health; he retired in 1960. Nikolai Bulganin ended up managing the Stavropol Economic Council. Also banished was Lazar Kaganovich, sent to manage a potash works in the Urals before being expelled from the party along with Molotov in 1962.

As part of de-Stalinization, Khrushchev set about renaming the numerous towns, cities, factories, natural features, and kholkozes around the country named in honor of Stalin and his aides, most notably Stalingrad, site of the great WWII battle, was renamed to Volgograd. Much like the initial condemnation of Stalin, Khrushchev's attack on the "anti-party group" drew negative reactions from China. The People's Daily remarked "How can [Molotov], one of the founding fathers of the CPSU, be a member of an anti-party group?"

Khrushchev became premier on March 27, 1958, consolidating his power—the tradition followed by all his predecessors and successors. This was the final stage in the transition from the earlier period of post-Stalin collective leadership. He was now the ultimate source of authority in the Soviet Union, but would never possess the absolute power Stalin had.

Aid to developing countries and scientific research, especially into space technology and weaponry, maintained the Soviet Union as one of the world's two major world powers. The Soviet Union launched the first ever artificial Earth satellite in history, Sputnik 1, which orbited the Earth in 1957. The Soviets also sent the first man into space, Yuri Gagarin, in 1961.

Khrushchev outmaneuvered his Stalinist rivals, but he was regarded by his political enemies—especially the emerging caste of professional technocrats—as a boorish peasant who would interrupt speakers to insult them. Incidents such as pounding his shoe on a table at the UN in 1960 and red-faced rants against the West and intellectuals were a source of grave embarrassment to Soviet politicians.Wikipedia:Citation needed

Reforms and Khrushchev's fall

Throughout his years of leadership, Khrushchev attempted to carry out reform in a range of fields. The problems of Soviet agriculture, a major concern of Khrushchev's, had earlier attracted the attention of the collective leadership, which introduced important innovations in this area of the Soviet economy. The state encouraged peasants to grow more on their private plots, increased payments for crops grown on collective farms, and invested more heavily in agriculture.

After Khrushchev had defeated his rivals and secured his power as supreme leader, he set his attention to economic reforms, particularly in the field of agriculture. "If a capitalist farmer required eight kilos of grain to produce one kilo of meat," he told a farmers' council, "he would lose his pants. Yet if a state farm director here does the same, he manages to keep his pants. Why? Because no one will hold him accountable for it." Back in the early 1950s, Khrushchev had defended private plots. Now as supreme leader, he spoke of communal farming as inevitable. In particular, the Soviet leader looked to his country's greatest rival for inspiration. As far back as the 1940s, he had promoted the use of American farming techniques and even obtained seeds from the US, in particular from a cagey Iowa farmer named Roswell Garst, who believed positive trade and business relations with Moscow would ease superpower tensions. This led to Khrushchev's soon to be notorious fascination with growing corn, although most of the Soviet Union outside of Ukraine lacked a suitable climate and much of the infrastructure used by American farmers, including adequate mechanized equipment, knowledge of advanced farming techniques, and proper use of fertilizer and pesticides, was in short supply. Although Khrushchev's corn obsession was exaggerated by popular myth, he did nonetheless advocate any number of unrealistic ideas such as planting corn in Siberia.

Khrushchev also abolished the Machine Tractor Stations, which were rural agencies to provide farming equipment, and had them sell their inventory directly to the farmers, but the latter ended up incurring huge debts buying the farming equipment, which ended up being used less effectively than the MTS had done. Alexsei Larionov, party boss of Ryazan, meanwhile attempted to triple meat production in the province after overall Soviet meat output for 1958 had been lacking (the grain harvest for comparison had been a strong one). The scheme, which was similar in nature to China's contemporary Great Leap Forward, involved setting unrealistic quotas and frantically slaughtering every animal in the province, including dairy cows and breeding stock, in an attempt to meet them. When the quotas still could not be met, Ryazan farmers tried to steal livestock from neighboring provinces, which took measures to protect their own farms such as police roadblocks. The Ryazan farmers resorted to theft of cattle under cover of darkness and Larionov, growing ever more desperate, made taxes payable in meat. In the end, Ryazan produced just 30,000 tons of meat for 1959, when they had promised 180,000 tons. The disgraced Larionov committed suicide shortly thereafter.

Khrushchev continued to believe in the theories of the biologist Trofim Lysenko, a carryover from the Stalin era. In his Virgin Lands Campaign in the mid-1950s, he opened many tracts of land to farming in Kazakhstan and neighboring areas of Russia. These new farmlands turned out to be susceptible to droughts, but in some years they produced excellent harvests. Later agricultural reforms by Khrushchev, however, proved counterproductive. His plans for growing corn and increasing meat and dairy production failed, and his reorganization of collective farms into larger units produced confusion in the countryside.

In a politically motivated move to weaken the central state bureaucracy in 1957, Khrushchev did away with the industrial ministries in Moscow and replaced them with regional economic councils (sovnarkhozes).

Although he intended these economic councils to be more responsive to local needs, the decentralization of industry led to disruption and inefficiency.Wikipedia:Citation needed Connected with this decentralization was Khrushchev's decision in 1962 to recast party organizations along economic, rather than administrative, lines. The resulting bifurcation of the party apparatus into industrial and agricultural sectors at the oblast (province) level and below contributed to the disarray and alienated many party officials at all levels. Symptomatic of the country's economic difficulties was the abandonment in 1963 of Khrushchev's special seven-year economic plan (1959–65) two years short of its completion.

Khrushchev significantly reduced Soviet defense spending and the size of conventional forces, accusing the army of being "metal eaters" and "If you let the army have their way, they will eat up the country's entire resources and still claim it's not enough." Several warships under construction were scrapped as Khrushchev considered them useless, as well as plans for long range bombers.

Orders for fighter planes slowed and several military airfields were converted to civilian use. Although he alienated the Soviet military establishment, he insisted that the country could not match the United States for conventional military capabilities and that the nuclear arsenal was sufficient deterrence. There were also practical reasons for this stance as the low birth rate of the 1940s caused a shortage of military-aged men.

The size of the Soviet military was reduced by nearly 2 million men in 1955-57, and further cuts followed in 1958 and 1960. These cuts in troop strength were not well planned out and many soldiers and officers were left jobless and homeless. Discontent in the military started building up.

Despite Khrushchev's boasts about Soviet missile capabilities, they were mostly bluster. The R-7 ICBM used to launch Sputnik was almost useless as a workable ICBM and Soviet missiles were launched from above-ground surface pads which were completely exposed to enemy attack. When Khrushchev suggested putting them in underground silos, Soviet rocket engineers argued that it couldn't be done until he stumbled across an article in an American technical journal describing the use of silos to house missiles. He admonished the rocket engineers for failing to pay attention to American technical developments and when the first Soviet silo launch took place in September 1959, Khrushchev took it as a personal triumph.

The 22nd Congress of the CPSU, which convened from October 17–21, 1961, marked the apex of Khrushchev's power and prestige, despite there being already mounting doubts about his policies. However, the real opposition to him had yet to come and he glowed in the praise of the CPSU delegates as he read off the general report of the Central Committee and the party program, two monumental speeches that lasted a total of ten hours. Within a decade, Khrushchev declared, the Soviet people would have equal living standards and material comforts with the United States and Western Europe. In addition, the 22nd Congress saw a renewed attack on Stalin, which culminated in the expulsion of remaining Old Bolsheviks like Molotov and Kaganovich from the party. Stalin's embalmed body, which still lay in Red Square next to Lenin, was immediately removed and reburied in the Kremlin Wall.

The harvest for 1961 was disappointing, with agricultural output a mere 0.7% higher than 1960 and meat production actually less than the previous two years. Discontent began building, and in the face of it, Khrushchev continued to offer new proposals to improve farm output and condemnation of inefficient farming practices. Despite complaints from farmers that they lacked enough funding for tools and farm equipment, Khrushchev argued that he had no spare money to allot to agriculture. His only solution was to add yet more bureaucracy to the agricultural sector.

Price increases of meat and dairy in the spring of 1962, combined with attempts to convince industrial workers to work harder for the same or less pay, paved the way for a mounting disaster. The price increases went into effect on June 1 and were immediately greeted by strikes and demonstrations in several cities, the biggest and most cataclysmic in the city of Novocherrkask where workers went on strike to protest rising costs of living and poor workplace conditions. The following day, workers at the Budenny Electric Locomotive Factory marched to the central square of the city where army units fired on them, killing 23. Another 116 demonstrators were arrested, with 14 tried for "anti-Soviet agitation" and seven of them sentenced to death. The other seven received 10–15 years in prison. Smaller riots in other cities were also put down with several fatalities. Khrushchev made a speech the same day half-apologizing for the price increases, but insisted that he had no choice. He never fully came to terms with the Novocherrkask Massacre and did not bring it up in his memoirs.

Khrushchev's boasts about Soviet missile forces provided John F. Kennedy with a key issue to use against Richard Nixon in the 1960 U.S. presidential election—the so-called 'missile gap'. But all Khrushchev's (probably sincere) attempts to build a strong personal relationship with the new president failed, as his typical combination of bluster, miscalculation and mishap resulted in the Cuban fiasco. After the Berlin and Cuba crises, tensions tapered off between the two superpowers. Khrushchev openly wept at the news of Kennedy's assassination in November 1963 and feared that new US president Lyndon Johnson would pursue a more aggressive anti-Soviet stance. Johnson turned out to be more in favor of detente than Khrushchev had assumed, but would end up letting superpower relations take a backseat to his Great Society programs and the Vietnam War.

During 1963, Khrushchev increasingly despaired over his inability to cure the perennial ailments of Soviet agriculture. He accused farmers of needlessly wasting fertilizer, adding that a farmer in the United States would be out of business if he did the same and he also complained about aging *kholkoz* managers who should have retired and made way for younger men, but continued to hold onto their jobs. Drought affected a large portion of the west-central USSR during the fall months and overall the 1963 harvest was an abject failure with a mere 107 million tons of grain produced and there was serious consideration given to rationing. Khrushchev could offer no solutions other than empty sloganeering and criticizing incompetent managers. After initially bristling at the idea of importing grain from overseas, he finally gave in after learning that Soviet grain stocks were almost depleted.

In October 1964, while Khrushchev was on holiday in Crimea, the Presidium unanimously voted him out of office and refused to permit him to take his case to the Central Committee. He retired as a private citizen after an editorial in Pravda denounced him for "hare-brained schemes, half–baked conclusions, hasty decisions, and actions divorced from reality." However, Khrushchev must also be remembered for his public disavowal of Stalinism, significant liberalization in the country, and the greater flexibility he brought to Soviet leadership.

Further reading

* Baradat, Leon P., *Soviet Political Society*, Prentice–Hall, New Jersey, 1986. ISBN 0-13-823592-9
* Nenarokov, Albert P., *Russia in the Twentieth Century: the View of a Soviet Historian*, William Morrow Co, New York, 1968.
* Schapiro, Leonard, *The Communist Party of the Soviet Union*, Vintage Books, New York, 1971. ISBN 0-394-70745-1

1964–1982

History of the Soviet Union (1964–82)

<indicator name="good-star"> ⊕ </indicator>

Part of a series on the
History of the **Union of Soviet Socialist Republics** (Soviet Union)
1917–1927 **Revolutionary Beginnings**
• Revolution • Civil War • New Economic Policy • 1922 Treaty • National delimitation
1927–1953 **Stalinist rule**

- Socialism in One Country
- Great Purge

Soviet famine of 1932–33

- (Holodomor
- Kazakhstan famine of 1932-1933)

World War II

- (Molotov–Ribbentrop Pact
- Great Patriotic War
- Operation Barbarossa
- Occupation of the Baltic states
- Soviet occupation of Bessarabia and Northern Bukovina
- Battle of Berlin
- Soviet invasion of Manchuria)
- Soviet deportations
- Soviet famine of 1946–47
- Cold War
- Korean War

1953–1964
Post-Stalin era

- Berlin blockade
- 1954 transfer of Crimea
- Khrushchev Thaw
- On the Cult of Personality and Its Consequences
- We will bury you
- 9 March riots
- Wage reforms
- Cuban Revolution
- Sino-Soviet split
- Space program
- Cuban Missile Crisis

1964–1982
Brezhnev era

* Brezhnev Doctrine
* Era of Stagnation
* 50th anniversary of the Armenian Genocide protests
* Prague Spring

Vietnam War

* (Laotian Civil War
* Operation Menu
* Cambodian Civil War
* Fall of Saigon)
* Six-Day War
* Détente
* Yom Kippur War
* Dirty War

Wars in Africa

* (Angolan War of Independence
* Angolan Civil War
* Mozambican War of Independence
* Mozambican Civil War
* South African Border War
* Rhodesian Bush War)
* Cambodian-Vietnamese War
* Soviet–Afghan War
* 1980 Summer Olympics

Olympic boycotts

* (1980 Olympic boycott
* 1984 Olympic boycott)
* Polish strike
* Death and funeral of Brezhnev

1982–1991
Leadership changes and collapse

- Invasion of Grenada
- Glasnost
- Perestroika
- Soviet withdrawal from Afghanistan

Singing Revolution

- (Estonian Sovereignty Declaration
- Baltic Way
- Act of the Re-Establishment of the State of Lithuania
- On the Restoration of Independence of the Republic of Latvia)

Revolutions of 1989

- (Pan-European picnic
- Die Wende
- Peaceful Revolution
- Fall of the Berlin Wall
- Velvet Revolution
- End of communist rule in Hungary
- Romanian Revolution
- German reunification)

Dissolution

- (Jeltoqsan
- Nagorno-Karabakh War
- 9 April tragedy
- Black January
- Osh riots
- War of Laws
- Dushanbe riots
- January Events
- The Barricades
- Referendum
- Union of Sovereign States
- August Coup
- Ukrainian independence (referendum)
- Belavezha Accords
- Alma-Ata Protocol)

History of

- Russia
- Moscow
- Kiev
- Minsk
- Former Soviet Republics

Soviet leadership

- 1. Lenin
- 2. Stalin
- 3. Malenkov
- 4. Khrushchev
- 5. Brezhnev
- 6. Andropov
- 7. Chernenko
- 8. Gorbachev

- **Culture**
- **Economy**
- **Education**
- **Geography**
- **Politics**

Soviet Union portal

- $\underline{v}$
- $\underline{t}$
- $\underline{e}$[174]

The **history of the Soviet Union from 1964 to 1982**, referred to as the **Brezhnev Era**, covers the period of Leonid Brezhnev's rule of the Union of Soviet Socialist Republics (USSR). This period began with high economic growth and soaring prosperity, but gradually significant problems in social, political, and economic areas accumulated, so that the period is often described as the Era of Stagnation.

Nikita Khrushchev was ousted as First Secretary of the Central Committee of the Communist Party of the Soviet Union (CPSU) (as well as Chairman of the Council of Ministers) on 14 October 1964, due to his failed reforms and disregard for Party and Government institutions. Brezhnev replaced Khrushchev as First Secretary and Alexei Kosygin replaced him as Chairman of the Council of Ministers. Anastas Mikoyan, and later Nikolai Podgorny, became Chairmen of the Presidium of the Supreme Soviet. Together with Andrei Kirilenko as organizational secretary, and Mikhail Suslov as Chief Ideologue, they made up a reinvigorated collective leadership, which contrasted in form with the autocracy that characterized Khrushchev's rule.

The collective leadership first set out to stabilize the Soviet Union and calm Soviet society, a task which they were able to accomplish. In addition, they attempted to speed up economic growth, which had slowed considerably during Khrushchev's last years as ruler. In 1965, Kosygin initiated several reforms to decentralize the Soviet economy. After initial success in creating economic growth, hard-liners within the Party halted the reforms, fearing that they would weaken the Party's prestige and power. The reforms itself were never officially abolished, they were simply sidelined and stopped having any effect. No other

Figure 54: *Alexei Kosygin, a member of the collective leadership, with Lyndon B. Johnson, President of the United States, at the 1967 Glassboro Summit Conference*

radical economic reforms were carried out during the Brezhnev era, and economic growth began to stagnate in the early-to-mid-1970s. By Brezhnev's death in 1982, Soviet economic growth had, according to several historians, nearly come to a standstill.

The stabilization policy brought about after Khrushchev's removal established a ruling gerontocracy, and political corruption became a normal phenomenon. Brezhnev, however, never initiated any large-scale anti-corruption campaigns. Due to the large military buildup of the 1960s, the Soviet Union was able to consolidate itself as a superpower during Brezhnev's rule. The era ended with Brezhnev's death on 10 November 1982.

Politics

Collectivity of leadership

After a prolonged power struggle,[176] Khrushchev was finally ousted from his post as First Secretary in October 1964, charged with the failure of his reforms, his obsessive re-organizations of the Party and Government apparatus, his disregard for Party and Government institutions, and his one-man domineering leadership style.[177] The Presidium (Politburo), the Central Committee and other important Party–Government bodies had grown tired of Khrushchev's repeated violations of established Party principles. The Soviet leadership also believed that his individualistic leadership style ran contrary to the ideal collective leadership.[176] Leonid Brezhnev and Alexei Kosygin succeeded Khrushchev in his posts as First Secretary and Premier respectively, and Mikhail Suslov, Andrei Kirilenko, and Anastas Mikoyan (replaced in 1965 by Nikolai Podgorny), were also given prominence in the new leadership. Together they formed a functional collective leadership.[178]

The collective leadership was, in its early stages, usually referred to as the "Brezhnev–Kosygin" leadership[179] and the pair began their respective periods in office on a relatively equal footing. After Kosygin initiated the economic reform of 1965, however, his prestige within the Soviet leadership withered and his subsequent loss of power strengthened Brezhnev's position within the Soviet hierarchy.[180] Kosygin's influence was further weakened when Podgorny took his post as the second-most powerful figure in the Soviet Union.[181]

Brezhnev conspired to oust Podgorny from the collective leadership as early as 1970. The reason was simple: Brezhnev was third, while Podgorny was first in the ranking of Soviet diplomatic protocol; Podgorny's removal would have made Brezhnev head of state, and his political power would have increased significantly. For much of the period, however, Brezhnev was unable to have Podgorny removed, because he could not count on enough votes in the Politburo, since the removal of Podgorny would have meant weakening of the power and the prestige of the collective leadership itself. Indeed, Podgorny continued to acquire greater power as the head of state throughout the early 1970s, due to Brezhnev's liberal stance on Yugoslavia and his disarmament talks with some Western powers, policies which many Soviet officials saw as contrary to common communist principles.

This did not remain the case, however. Brezhnev strengthened his position considerably during the early to mid-1970s within the Party leadership and by a further weakening of the "Kosygin faction"; by 1977 he had enough support in the Politburo to oust Podgorny from office and active politics in general.[182] Podgorny's eventual removal in 1977 had the effect of reducing Kosygin's role in day-to-day management of government activities by strengthening the powers of the government apparatus led by Brezhnev. After Podgorny's removal rumours started circulating Soviet society that Kosygin was about to retire due to his deteriorating health condition.[183] Nikolai Tikhonov, a First Deputy Chairman of the Council of Ministers under Kosygin, succeeded the later as premier in 1980 (see Kosygin's resignation).[183]

Podgorny's fall was not seen as the end of the collective leadership, and Suslov continued to write several ideological documents about it. In 1978, one year after Podgorny's retirement, Suslov made several references to the collective leadership in his ideological works. It was around this time that Kirilenko's power and prestige within the Soviet leadership started to wane.[184] Indeed, towards the end of the period, Brezhnev was regarded as too old to simultaneously exercise all of the functions of head of state by his colleagues. With this in mind, the Supreme Soviet, on Brezhnev's orders, established the new post of First Deputy Chairman of the Presidium of the Supreme Soviet, a post akin to a "vice president". The Supreme Soviet unanimously approved Vasili Kuznetsov, at the age of 76, to be First Deputy Chairman of the Presidium in late 1977. As Brezhnev's health worsened, the collective leadership took an even more important role in everyday decision-making. For this reason, Brezhnev's death did not alter the balance of power in any radical fashion, and Yuri Andropov and Konstantin Chernenko were obliged by protocol to rule the country in the same fashion as Brezhnev left it.[185]

Assassination attempt

Viktor Ilyin, a disenfranchised Soviet soldier, attempted to assassinate Brezhnev on 22 January 1969 by firing shots at a motorcade carrying Brezhnev through Moscow. Though Brezhnev was unhurt, the shots killed a driver and lightly injured several celebrated cosmonauts of the Soviet space programme who were also travelling in the motorcade. Brezhnev's attacker was captured, and interrogated personally by Andropov, then KGB chairman and future Soviet leader. Ilyin was not given the death penalty because his desire to kill Brezhnev was considered so absurd that he was sent to the Kazan mental asylum instead for treatment.

Defense policy

The Soviet Union launched a large military build-up in 1965 by expanding both nuclear and conventional arsenals. The Soviet leadership believed a strong military would be useful leverage in negotiating with foreign powers, and increase the Eastern Bloc's security from attacks. In the 1970s, the Soviet leadership concluded that a war with the capitalist countries might not necessarily become nuclear, and therefore they initiated a rapid expansion of the country's conventional forces. Due to the country's weaker infrastructure compared to the United States, the Soviet leadership believed that the only way to beat the First World was by a rapid military conquest of Western Europe, relying on sheer numbers alone. The Soviet Union achieved nuclear parity with the United States by the early 1970s, after which the country consolidated itself as a superpower.[187] The apparent success of the military build-up led the Soviet leadership to believe that the military, and the military alone, according to Willard Frank, "bought the Soviet Union security and influence".[188]

Brezhnev had, according to some of his closest advisers, been concerned for a very long time about the growing military expenditure in the 1960s. Advisers have recounted how Brezhnev came into conflict with several top-level

Figure 55: *Dmitriy Ustinov (depicted in this 1988 Soviet postage stamp), the Minister of Defense from 1976 until his death in 1984, was one of the most influential figures in Soviet security policy-making along with Andrei Gromyko, Yuri Andropov and Brezhnev*[186]

military industrialists, the most notable being Marshal Andrei Grechko, the Minister of Defense. In the early 1970s, according to Anatoly Aleksandrov-Agentov, one of Brezhnev's closest advisers, Brezhnev attended a five-hour meeting to try to convince the Soviet military establishment to reduce military spending.[189] In the meeting an irritated Brezhnev asked why the Soviet Union should, in the words of Matthew Evangelista, "continue to exhaust" the economy if the country could not be promised a military parity with the West; the question was left unanswered.[190] When Grechko died in 1976, Dmitriy Ustinov took his place as Defense Minister. Ustinov, although a close associate and friend of Brezhnev, hindered any attempt made by Brezhnev to reduce national military expenditure. In his later years, Brezhnev lacked the will to reduce defense expenditure, due to his declining health.[191] According to the Soviet diplomat Georgy Arbatov, the military–industrial complex functioned as Brezhnev's power base within the Soviet hierarchy even if he tried to scale-down investments.[192]

At the 23rd Party Congress in 1966, Brezhnev told the delegates that the Soviet military had reached a level fully sufficient to defend the country. The Soviet Union reached ICBM parity with the United States that year.[193] In early 1977,

Brezhnev told the world that the Soviet Union did not seek to become superior to the United States in nuclear weapons, nor to be militarily superior in any sense of the word.[194] In the later years of Brezhnev's reign, it became official defense policy to only invest enough to maintain military deterrence, and by the 1980s, Soviet defense officials were told again that investment would not exceed the level to retain national security.[195] In his last meeting with Soviet military leaders in October 1982, Brezhnev stressed the importance of not over-investing in the Soviet military sector. This policy was retained during the rules of Andropov, Konstantin Chernenko and Mikhail Gorbachev.[196] He also said that the time was opportune to increase the readiness of the armed forces even further. At the anniversary of the 1917 Revolution a few weeks later (Brezhnev's final public appearance), Western observers noted that the annual military parade featured only two new weapons and most of the equipment displayed was obsolete. Two days before his death, Brezhnev stated that any aggression against the Soviet Union "would result in a crushing retaliatory blow".

Stabilization

Though Brezhnev's time in office would later be characterized as one of stability, early on, Brezhnev oversaw the replacement of half of the regional leaders and Politburo members. This was a typical move for a Soviet leader trying to strengthen his power base. Examples of Politburo members who lost their membership during the Brezhnev Era are Gennady Voronov, Dmitry Polyansky, Alexander Shelepin, Petro Shelest and Podgorny.[197] Polyansky and Voronov lost their membership in the Politburo because they were considered to be members of the "Kosygin faction." In their place came Andrei Grechko, the Minister of Defense, Andrei Gromyko the Minister of Foreign Affairs and KGB Chairman Andropov. The removal and replacement of members of the Soviet leadership halted in late 1970s.[198]

Initially, in fact, Brezhnev portrayed himself as a moderate — not as radical as Kosygin but not as conservative as Shelepin. Brezhnev gave the Central Committee formal permission to initiate Kosygin's 1965 economic reform. According to historian Robert Service, Brezhnev did modify some of Kosygin's reform proposals, many of which were unhelpful at best. In his early days, Brezhnev asked for advice from provincial party secretaries, and spent hours each day on such conversations.[199] During the March 1965 Central Committee plenum, Brezhnev took control of Soviet agriculture, another hint that he opposed Kosygin's reform program. Brezhnev believed, in contrast to Khrushchev, that rather than wholesale re-organization, the key to increasing agricultural output was making the existing system work more efficiently.[199]

Figure 56: *Mikhail Gorbachev, as seen in 1985. Along with Grig-ory Romanov he was, in contrast to the norm, one of the young members elected to top positions during the Brezhnev Era*[202]

In the late 1960s, Brezhnev talked of the need to "renew" the party cadres, but according to Robert Service, his "self-interest discouraged him from putting an end to the immobilism he detected. He did not want to risk alienating lower-level officialdom."[200] The Politburo saw the policy of stabilization as the only way to avoid returning to Joseph Stalin's purges and Khrushchev's re-organization of Party-Government institutions. Members acted in optimism, and believed a policy of stabilization would prove to the world, according to Robert Service, the "superiority of communism".[200] The Soviet leadership was not entirely opposed to reform, even if the reform movement had been weakened in the aftermath of the Prague Spring in the Czechoslovakia.[200] The result was a period of overt stabilization at the heart of government, a pol-icy which also had the effect of reducing cultural freedom: several dissident samizdats were shut down.[201]

Gerontocracy

After the reshuffling process of the Politburo ended in the mid-to-late 1970, the Soviet leadership evolved into a *gerontocracy*, a form of rule in which the rulers are significantly older than most of the adult population.[198]

The Brezhnev generation — the people who lived and worked during the Brezhnev Era — owed their rise to prominence to Joseph Stalin's Great Purge in the late 1930s. In the purge, Stalin ordered the execution or exile of nearly all Soviet bureaucrats over the age of 35, thereby opening up posts and offices for a younger generation of Soviets. This generation would rule the country from the aftermath of Stalin's purge up to Mikhail Gorbachev's rise to power in 1985. The majority of these appointees were of either peasant or working class origin. Mikhail Suslov, Alexei Kosygin, and Brezhnev are prime examples of men appointed in the aftermath of Stalin's Great Purge.[203]

The average age of the Politburo's members was 58 years in 1961, and 71 in 1981. A similar greying also took place in the Central Committee, the median age rising from 53 in 1961 to 62 in 1981, with the proportion of members older than 65 increasing from 3 percent in 1961 to 39 percent in 1981. The difference in the median age between Politburo and Central Committee members can be explained by the fact that the Central Committee was consistently enlarged during Brezhnev's leadership; this made it possible to appoint new and younger members to the Central Committee without retiring some of its oldest members. Of the 319-member Central Committee in 1981, 130 were younger than 30 when Stalin died in 1953.[204]

Young politicians, such as Fyodor Kulakov and Grigory Romanov, were seen as potential successors to Brezhnev, but none of them came close. For example, Kulakov, one of the youngest members in the Politburo, was ranked seventh in the prestige order voted by the Supreme Soviet, far behind such notables as Kosygin, Podgorny, Suslov, and Kirilenko.[205] As Edwin Bacon and Mark Sandle note in their book, *Brezhnev Reconsidered*, the Soviet leadership at Brezhnev's deathbed had evolved into "a gerontocracy increasingly lacking of physical and intellectual vigour".[187]

New constitution

During the era, Brezhnev was also the Chairman of the Constitutional Commission of the Supreme Soviet, which worked for the creation of a new constitution. The Commission had 97 members, with Konstantin Chernenko among the more prominent. Brezhnev was not driven by a wish to leave a mark on history, but rather to even further weaken Premier Alexei Kosygin's prestige.[206] The formulation of the constitution kept with Brezhnev's political style and was neither anti-Stalinist nor neo-Stalinist, but stuck to a middle path, following most of the same principles and ideas as the previous constitutions.[207] The most notable difference was that it codified the developmental changes which the Soviet Union had passed through since the formulation of the 1936 Constitution. It described the Soviet Union, for example, as an "advanced industrial society".[208] In this sense, the resulting document can be seen as proof of the

Figure 57: *A souvenir sheet commemorating the 1977*
Soviet Constitution, Brezhnev is depicted in the middle

achievements, as well as the limits, of de-Stalinization. It enhanced the status
of the individual in all matters of life, while at the same time solidifying the
Party's hold on power.[209]

During the drafting process, a debate within the Soviet leadership took place
between the two factions on whether to call Soviet law "State law" or "Constitutional law." Those who supported the thesis of state law believed that the
Constitution was of low importance, and that it could be changed whenever
the socio-economic system changed. Those who supported Constitutional law
believed that the Constitution should "conceptualise" and incorporate some
of the Party's future ideological goals. They also wanted to include information on the status of the Soviet citizen, which had changed drastically in the
post-Stalin years.[210] Constitutional thought prevailed to an extent, and the
1977 Soviet Constitution had a greater effect on conceptualising the Soviet
system.[211]

Later years

In his later years, Brezhnev developed his own cult of personality, and awarded
himself the highest military decorations of the Soviet Union. The media extolled Brezhnev "as a dynamic leader and intellectual colossus".[212] Brezhnev
was awarded a Lenin Prize for Literature for *Brezhnev's trilogy*, three auto-
biographical novels.[213] These awards were given to Brezhnev to bolster his
position within the Party and the Politburo.[214] When Alexei Kosygin died on
18 December 1980, one day before Brezhnev's birthday, *Pravda* and other media outlets postponed the reporting of his death until after Brezhnev's birthday

Figure 58: *A Soviet stamp from 1981 devoted to the 26th Party Congress*

celebration.[212] In reality, however, Brezhnev's physical and intellectual capacities had started to decline in the 1970s from bad health.[215]

Brezhnev approved the Soviet intervention in Afghanistan (see also *Soviet–Afghan relations*) just as he had previously approved the Warsaw Pact invasion of Czechoslovakia. In both cases, Brezhnev was not the one pushing hardest for a possible armed intervention.[215] Several leading members of the Soviet leadership decided to retain Brezhnev as General Secretary so that their careers would not suffer by a possible leadership reshuffling by his successor. Other members, who disliked Brezhnev, among them Dmitriy Ustinov (Minister of Defence), Andrei Gromyko (Minister of Foreign Affairs), and Mikhail Suslov (Central Committee Secretary), feared that Brezhnev's removal would spark a succession crisis, and so they helped to maintain the status quo.[216]

Brezhnev stayed in office under pressure from some of his Politburo associates, though in practice the country was not governed by Brezhnev, but instead by a collective leadership led by Suslov, Ustinov, Gromyko, and Yuri Andropov. Konstantin Chernenko, due to his close relationship with Brezhnev, had also acquired influence. While the Politburo was pondering who would take Brezhnev's place, his health continued to worsen. The choice of a successor would have been influenced by Suslov, but since he died in January 1982, before Brezhnev, Andropov took Suslov's place in the Central Committee Secretariat. With Brezhnev's health worsening, Andropov showed his Politburo colleagues that he was not afraid of Brezhnev's reprisals any more, and launched a major anti-corruption campaign. On 10 November 1982, Brezhnev died and was honored with major state funeral and buried 5 days later at the Kremlin Wall Necropolis.[217]

Economy

1965 reform

The 1965 Soviet economic reform, often referred to as the "Kosygin reform", of economic management and planning was carried out between 1965 and 1971. Announced in September 1965, it contained three main measures: the re-centralization of the Soviet economy by re-establishing several central ministries, a decentralizing overhaul of the enterprise incentive system (including wider usage of capitalist-style material incentives for good performance), and thirdly, a major price reform.[218] The reform was initiated by Alexei Kosygin's First Government and implemented during the Eighth Five-Year Plan, 1968–1970.

Though these measures were established to counter many of the irrationalities in the Soviet economic system, the reform did not try to change the existing system radically; it instead tried to improve it gradually.[219] Success was ultimately mixed, and Soviet analyses on why the reform failed to reach its full potential have never given any definitive answers. The key factors are agreed upon, however, with blame being put on the combination of the recentralisation of the economy with the decentralisation of enterprise autonomy, creating several administrative obstacles. Additionally, instead of creating a market which in turn would establish a pricing system, administrators were given the responsibility for overhauling the pricing system themselves. Because of this, the market-like system failed to materialise. To make matters worse, the reform was contradictory at best.[220] In retrospect, however, the Eighth Five-Year Plan as a whole is considered to be one of the most successful periods for the Soviet economy, and the most successful for consumer production.

The marketization of the economy, in which Kosygin supported, was considered too radical in the light of the Prague Spring in Czechoslovakia. Nikolai Ryzhkov, the future Chairman of the Council of Ministers, referred in a 1987 speech to the Supreme Soviet of the Soviet Union to the "sad experiences of the 1965 reform", and claimed that everything went from bad to worse following the reform's cancellation.

Era of Stagnation

Period	GNP (according to the CIA)	NMP (according to Grigorii Khanin)	NMP (according to the USSR)
1960–1965[221]	4.8	4.4	6.5
1965–1970[221]	4.9	4.1	7.7
1970–1975[221]	3.0	3.2	5.7
1975–1980[221]	1.9	1.0	4.2
1980–1985[221]	1.8	0.6	3.5

[222] Grigorii Khanin published his growth rates in the 1980s as a "translation" of NMP to GNP. His growth rates were (as seen above) much lower than the official figures, and lower than some Western estimates. His estimates were widely publicised by conservative think tanks as, for instance, The Heritage Foundation of Washington, D.C.. After the dissolution of the Soviet Union in 1991, Khanin's estimates led several agencies to criticise the estimates made by the Central Intelligence Agency (CIA). Since then the CIA has often been accused of overestimating Soviet growth. In response to the criticism of CIA's work, a panel led by economist James R. Millar was established to find out if this was in fact true. The panel concluded that the CIA estimates were based on facts, and that "Methodologically, Khanin's approach was naive, and it has not been possible for others to reproduce his results."[223] Michael Boretsky, a US Department of Commerce economist, criticised the CIA estimates for being too low. He used the same CIA methodology to estimate West German and American growth rates. The results were 32 percent below the official GNP growth for West Germany and 13 below the official GNP growth for the United States. In the end, the conclusion is the same, the Soviet Union grew rapidly economically until the mid-1970s, when a system crisis set in.[224]

Growth figures for the Soviet economy vary widely (as seen below):

Eighth Five-Year Plan (1966–1970)
- Gross national product (GNP): 5.2 percent
- GNP: 5.3 percent
- Gross national income (GNI): 7.1 percent
- Capital investments in agriculture: 24 percent

Ninth Five-Year Plan (1971–1975)
- GNP: 3.7 percent
- GNI: 5.1 percent
- Labour productivity: 6 percent
- Capital investments in agriculture: 27 percent

Tenth Five-Year Plan (1976–1980)
- GNP: 2.7 percent
- GNP: 3 percent
- Labour productivity: 3.2 percent

Eleventh Five-Year Plan (1981–1985)
</ref>

The value of all consumer goods manufactured in 1972 in retail prices was about 118 billion rubles ($530 billion).[225] The Era of Stagnation, a term coined by Mikhail Gorbachev, is considered by several economists to be the worst financial crisis in the Soviet Union. It was triggered by the Nixon Shock, over-centralisation and a conservative state bureaucracy. As the economy grew, the volume of decisions facing planners in Moscow became overwhelming. As a result, labour productivity decreased nationwide. The cumbersome procedures of bureaucratic administration did not allow for the free communication and flexible response required at the enterprise level to deal with worker alienation, innovation, customers and suppliers.[226] The late Brezhnev Era also saw an increase in political corruption. Data falsification became common practice among bureaucrats to report satisfied targets and quotas to the government, and this further aggravated the crisis in planning.[227]

With the mounting economic problems, skilled workers were usually paid more than had been intended in the first place, while unskilled labourers tended to turn up late, and were neither conscientious nor, in a number of cases, entirely sober. The state usually moved workers from one job to another which ultimately became an ineradicable feature in Soviet industry;[228] the Government had no effective counter-measure because of the country's lack of unemployment. Government industries such as factories, mines and offices were staffed by undisciplined personnel who put a great effort into not doing their jobs. This ultimately led to, according to Robert Service, a "work-shy workforce" among Soviet workers and administrators.[229]

1973 and 1979 reform

Kosygin initiated the 1973 Soviet economic reform to enhance the powers and functions of the regional planners by establishing associations. The reform was never fully implemented; indeed, members of the Soviet leadership complained that the reform had not even begun by the time of the 1979 reform.[230] The 1979 Soviet economic reform was initiated to improve the then-stagnating Soviet economy. The reform's goal was to increase the powers of the central ministries by centralising the Soviet economy to an even greater extent. This reform was also never fully implemented, and when Kosygin died in 1980 it was practically abandoned by his successor, Nikolai Tikhonov. Tikhonov told the Soviet people at the 26th Party Congress that the reform was to be implemented, or at least parts of it, during the Eleventh Five-Year Plan (1981–1985). Despite this, the reform never came to fruition.[231] The reform is seen by several Sovietologists as the last major pre-*perestroika* reform initiative put forward by the Soviet government.

Kosygin's resignation

Following Nikolai Podgorny's removal from office, rumours started circulating within the top circles, and on the streets, that Kosygin would retire due to bad health. During one of Kosygin's spells on sick leave, Brezhnev appointed Nikolai Tikhonov, a like-minded conservative, to the post of First Deputy Chairman of the Council of Ministers; through this office Tikhonov was able to reduce Kosygin to a backup role. For example, at a Central Committee plenum in June 1980, the Soviet economic development plan was outlined by Tikhonov, not Kosygin.[183] Following Kosygin's resignation in 1980, Tikhonov, at the age of 75, was elected the new Chairman of the Council of Ministers. At the end of his life, Kosygin feared the complete failure of the Eleventh Five-Year

Figure 59: *Soviet Premier Alexei Kosygin (in front) next to U.S. President Lyndon B. Johnson (behind) at the Glassboro Summit Conference*

Plan (1981–1985), believing that the sitting leadership was reluctant to reform the stagnant Soviet economy.

Foreign relations

First World

Alexei Kosygin, the Soviet Premier, tried to challenge Brezhnev on the rights of the General Secretary to represent the country abroad, a function Kosygin believed should fall into the hands of the Premier, as was common in non-communist countries. This was actually implemented for a short period. Later, however, Kosygin, who had been the chief negotiator with the First World during the 1960s, was hardly to be seen outside the Second World[232] after Brezhnev strengthened his position within the Politburo. Kosygin did head the Soviet Glassboro Summit Conference delegation in 1967 with Lyndon B. Johnson, the then-current President of the United States. The summit was dominated by three issues: the Vietnam War, the Six-Day War and the Soviet–American arms race. Immediately following the summit at Glassboro, Kosygin headed the Soviet delegation to Cuba, where he met an angry Fidel Castro who accused the Soviet Union of "capitulationism".

Détente, literally the easing of strained relations, or in Russian "unloading", characterized the early part of the era. It meant "ideological co-existence" in

Figure 60: *Andrei Gromyko, the Soviet Foreign Minister from 1957 to 1985, as seen in 1978 during a visit to the United States*

the context of Soviet foreign policy, but it did not, however, entail an end to competition between capitalist and communist societies.[233] The Soviet leadership's policy did, however, help to ease the Soviet Union's strained relations with the United States. Several arms control and trade agreements were signed and ratified in this time period.[234]

One such success of diplomacy came with Willy Brandt's ascension to the West German chancellorship in 1969, as West German–Soviet tension started to ease. Brandt's Ostpolitik policy, along with Brezhnev's détente, contributed to the signing of the Moscow and Warsaw Treaties in which West Germany recognized the state borders established following World War II, which included West German recognition of East Germany as an independent state. The foreign relations of the two countries continued to improve during Brezhnev's rule, and in the Soviet Union, where the memory of German brutality during World War II was still remembered, these developments contributed to greatly reducing the animosity the Soviet people felt towards Germany, and Germans in general.[234]

Not all efforts were so successful, however. The 1975 Helsinki Accords, a Soviet-led initiative which was hailed as a success for Soviet diplomacy, "backfired", in the words of historian Archie Brown.[235] The U.S. Government retained little interest through the whole process, and Richard Nixon once told a senior British official that the United States "had never wanted the conference".[236] Other notables, such as Nixon's successor President Gerald Ford,

Figure 61: *Carter and Brezhnev sign the*
SALT II treaty on 18 June 1979 in Vienna.

and National Security Advisor Henry Kissinger were also unenthusiastic.[236]
It was Western European negotiators who played a crucial role in creating the
treaty.[236]

The Soviet Union sought an official acceptance of the state borders drawn up
in post-war Europe by the United States and Western Europe. The Soviets
were largely successful; some small differences were that state borders were
"inviolable" rather than "immutable", meaning that borders could be changed
only without military interference, or interference from another country.[236]
Both Brezhnev, Gromyko and the rest of the Soviet leadership were strongly
committed to the creation of such a treaty, even if it meant concessions on such
topics as human rights and transparency. Mikhail Suslov and Gromyko, among
others, were worried about some of the concessions. Yuri Andropov, the KGB
Chairman, believed the greater transparency was weakening the prestige of the
KGB, and strengthening the prestige of the Ministry of Foreign Affairs.[237]

Another blow to Soviet communism in the First World came with the establishment of eurocommunism. Eurocommunists espoused and supported the
ideals of Soviet communism while at the same time supporting rights of the individual.[238] The largest obstacle was that it was the largest communist parties,
those with highest electoral turnout, which became eurocommunists. Origi-
nating with the Prague Spring, this new thinking made the First World more
skeptical of Soviet communism in general.[239] The Italian Communist Party

notably declared that should war break out in Europe, they would rally to the defense of Italy and resist any Soviet incursion on their nation's soil.

In particular, Soviet–First World relations deteriorated when the US President Jimmy Carter, following the advice of his National Security Adviser Zbigniew Brzezinski, denounced the 1979 Soviet intervention in Afghanistan (see Soviet–Afghan relations) and described it as the "most serious danger to peace since 1945". The United States stopped all grain export to the Soviet Union and persuaded US athletes not to enter the 1980 Summer Olympics held in Moscow. The Soviet Union responded by boycotting the next Summer Olympics held in Los Angeles. The détente policy collapsed.[234] When Ronald Reagan succeeded Carter as US president in 1981, he promised a sharp increase in US defense spending and a more aggressively anti-Soviet foreign policy. This caused alarm in Moscow, with the Soviet media accusing him of "warmongering" and "mistakenly believing that stepping up the arms race will bring peace to the world". General Nikolai Ogarkov also commented that too many Soviet citizens had begun believing that any war was bad and peace at any price was good, and that better political education was necessary to inculcate a "class" point of view in world affairs.

An event of grave embarrassment to the Soviet Union came in October 1981 when one of its submarines ran aground near the Swedish naval base at Karlskrona. As this was a militarily sensitive location, Sweden took an aggressive stance on the incident, detaining the Whiskey-class sub for two weeks as they awaited an official explanation from Moscow. Eventually it was released, but Stockholm refused to accept Soviet claims that this was merely an accident, especially since numerous unidentified submarines had been spotted near the Swedish coast. Sweden also announced that radiation had been detected emanating from the submarine and they believed it to be carrying nuclear missiles. Moscow would neither confirm nor deny this and instead merely accused the Swedes of espionage.

People's Republic of China

In the aftermath of Khrushchev's removal and the Sino-Soviet split, Alexei Kosygin was the most optimistic member of the Soviet leadership for a future rapprochement with the People's Republic of China (PRC), while Yuri Andropov remained skeptical and Brezhnev did not even voice his opinion. In many ways, Kosygin even had problems understanding why the two countries were quarreling with each other in the first place.[240] The collective leadership; Anastas Mikoyan, Brezhnev and Kosygin were considered by the PRC to retain the revisionist attitudes of their predecessor, Nikita Khrushchev.[241] At first, the new Soviet leadership blamed the Sino-Soviet split not on the PRC, but on policy errors made by Khrushchev. Both Brezhnev and Kosygin were

Figure 62: *Alexei Kosygin was the most optimistic members of the So-viet leadership regarding the Soviet rapprochement with the PRC*[240]

enthusiastic for rapprochement with the PRC. When Kosygin met his coun-terpart, the Chinese Premier Zhou Enlai, in 1964, Kosygin found him to be in an "excellent mood".[242] The early hints of rapprochement collapsed, how-ever, when Zhou accused Kosygin of Khrushchev-like behavior after Rodion Malinovsky's anti-imperialistic speech against the First World.[243]

When Kosygin told Brezhnev that it was time to reconcile with the PRC, Brezh-nev replied: "If you think this is necessary, then you go by yourself".[244] Kosy-gin was afraid that the PRC would turn down his proposal for a visit, so he decided to stop off in Beijing on his way to Vietnamese Communist leaders in Hanoi on 5 February 1965; there he met with Zhou. The two were able to solve smaller issues, agreeing to increase trade between the countries, as well as celebrate the 15th anniversary of the Sino-Soviet alliance.[245] Kosygin was told that a reconciliation between the two countries might take years, and that rapprochement could occur only gradually.[246] In his report to the Soviet leadership, Kosygin noted Zhou's moderate stance against the USSR, and be-lieved he was open for serious talks about Sino-Soviet relations.[244] After his visit to Hanoi, Kosygin returned to Beijing on 10 February, this time to meet Mao Zedong personally. At first Mao refused to meet Kosygin, but eventu-ally agreed and the two met on 11 February.[247] His meeting with Mao was in an entirely different tone to the previous meeting with Zhou. Mao criticized

Kosygin, and the Soviet leadership, of revisionist behavior. He also continued to criticize Khrushchev's earlier policies.[247] This meeting was to become Mao's last meeting with any Soviet leader.[248]

The Cultural Revolution caused a complete meltdown of Sino-Soviet relations, inasmuch as Moscow (along with every communist state save for Albania) considered that event to be simple-minded insanity. Red Guards denounced the Soviet Union and the entire Eastern Bloc as revisionists who pursued a false socialism and of being in collusion with the forces of imperialism. Brezhnev was referred to as "the new Hitler" and the Soviets as warmongers who neglected their people's living standards in favor of military spending. In 1968 Lin Biao, the Chinese Defence Minister, claimed that the Soviet Union was preparing itself for a war against the PRC. Moscow shot back by accusing China of false socialism and plotting with the US as well as promoting a guns-over-butter economic policy. This tension escalated into small skirmishes alongside the Sino-Soviet border, and both Khrushchev and Brezhnev were derided as "betrayers of [Vladimir] Lenin" by the Chinese.[249] To counter the accusations made by the Chinese Central Government, Brezhnev condemned the PRC's "frenzied anti-Sovietism", and asked Zhou Enlai to follow up on his word to normalize Sino-Soviet relations. In another speech, this time in Tashkent, Uzbek SSR in 1982, Brezhnev warned First World powers of using the Sino-Soviet split against the Soviet Union, saying it would spark "tension and mistrust".[250] Brezhnev had offered a non-aggression pact to China, but its terms included a renunciation of China's territorial claims, and would have left China defenseless against threats from the USSR.[250] In 1972, US president Richard Nixon visited Beijing to restore relations with the PRC, which only seemed to confirm Soviet fears of Sino-US collusion. Relations between Moscow and Beijing remained extremely hostile through the entire decade of the 1970s, the latter deciding that "social" imperialism presented a greater danger than capitalist imperialism, and even after Mao Zedong's death showed no sign of a chill. The Soviet Union had by this time championed an Asian collective security treaty in which the USSR would defend any country against a possible attack from the PRC, but when the latter engaged Vietnam in a border war during early 1979, Moscow contented itself with verbal protests.[251] The Soviet leadership after Brezhnev's death actively pursued a more friendly foreign policy to the PRC, and the normalization of relations which had begun under Brezhnev, continued under his successors.

Figure 63: *Władysław Gomułka (left), the leader of Poland, in East Germany with Brezhnev.*

Eastern Bloc

The Soviet leadership's policy towards the Eastern Bloc did not change much with Khrushchev's replacement, as the states of Eastern Europe were seen as a buffer zone essential to placing distance between NATO and the Soviet Union's borders. The Brezhnev regime inherited a skeptical attitude towards reform policies which became more radical in tone following the Prague Spring in 1968.[252] János Kádár, the leader of Hungary, initiated a couple of reforms similar to Alexei Kosygin's 1965 economic reform. The reform measures, named the New Economic Mechanism, were introduced in Hungary during Khrushchev's rule, and were protected by Kosygin in the post-Khrushchev era.[253] Polish leader Władysław Gomułka, who was removed from all of his posts in 1970, was succeeded by Edward Gierek who tried to revitalize the economy of Poland by borrowing money from the First World. The Soviet leadership approved both countries' respective economic experiments, since it was trying to reduce its large Eastern Bloc subsidy program in the form of cheap oil and gas exports.[254]

Not all reforms were supported by the Soviet leadership, however. Alexander Dubček's political and economic liberalisation in the Czechoslovak Socialist Republic led to a Soviet-led invasion of the country by Warsaw Pact countries in August 1968.[254] Not all in the Soviet leadership were as enthusiastic for a

Figure 64: *Alexei Kosygin (right) shaking hands with Romanian communist leader Nicolae Ceaușescu on 22 August 1974. Ceaușescu was one of the communist leaders who opposed the 1968 Brezhnev Doctrine.*

military intervention; Brezhnev remained wary of any sort of intervention and Kosygin reminded leaders of the consequences of the Soviet suppression of the 1956 Hungarian revolution. In the aftermath of the invasion the Brezhnev Doctrine was introduced; it stated that the Soviet Union had the right to intervene in any socialist country on the road to communism which was deviating from the communist norm of development.[255] The doctrine was condemned by Romania, Albania and Yugoslavia. As a result, the worldwide communist movement became poly-centric, meaning that the Soviet Union lost its role as 'leader' of the world communist movement.[256] In the aftermath of the invasion, Brezhnev reiterated this doctrine in a speech at the Fifth Congress of the Polish United Workers' Party (PUWP) on 13 November 1968:

> *When forces that are hostile to socialism try to turn the development of some socialist country towards capitalism, it becomes not only a problem of the country concerned, but a common problem and concern of all socialist countries.*

> —*Brezhnev, Speech to the Fifth Congress of the Polish United Workers' Party in November 1968*

Figure 65: *A stamp showing Brezhnev and Erich Honecker, the leader of East Germany, shaking hands. Honecker was supportive of Soviet policy in Poland.*

On 25 August 1980 the Soviet Politburo established a commission chaired by Mikhail Suslov to examine the political crisis in Poland that was beginning to gain speed. The importance of the commission was demonstrated by its composition: Dmitriy Ustinov (Minister of Defence), Andrei Gromyko (Minister of Foreign Affairs), Yuri Andropov (KGB Chairman) and Konstantin Chernenko, the Head of the General Department of the Central Committee and Brezhnev's closest associate. After just three days, the commission proposed the possibility of a Soviet military intervention, among other concrete measures. Troops and tank divisions were moved to the Soviet–Polish border. Later, however, the Soviet leadership came to the conclusion that they should not intervene in Poland.[257] Stanisław Kania, the First Secretary of the PUWP, mooted the Soviet proposal for introducing martial law in Poland.[257] Erich Honecker, the First Secretary of the East German Socialist Unity Party, supported the decision of the Soviet leadership, and sent a letter to Brezhnev and called for a meeting of the Eastern Bloc leaders to discuss the situation in Poland.[258] When the leaders met at the Kremlin later that year, Brezhnev had concluded that it would be better to leave the domestic matters of Poland alone for the time being, reassuring the Polish delegation, headed by Kania, that the USSR would intervene only if asked to.[258]

As Archie Brown notes in his book *The Rise and Fall of Communism*, "Poland was a special case".[259] The Soviet Union had intervened in the Democratic Republic of Afghanistan the previous year, and the increasingly hard-line policies of the Reagan administration along with the vast organisational network of the opposition, were among the major reasons why the Politburo Commission pushed for martial law instead of an intervention.[259] When Wojciech Jaruzelski became Prime Minister of Poland in February 1980, the Soviet leadership, but also Poles in general, supported his appointment. As time went by, however, Jaruzelski tried, and failed, according to Archie Brown, "to walk a tightrope" between the demands made by the USSR and the Poles.[260] Martial law was initiated on 13 December 1981 by the Jaruzelski Government.[261]

During the final years of Brezhnev's rule, and in the aftermath of his death, the Soviet leadership was forced by domestic difficulties to allow the Eastern Bloc governments to introduce more nationalistic communist policies to head off similar unrest to the turmoil in Poland and hence preventing it spreading to other communist countries. In a similar vein, Yuri Andropov, Brezhnev's successor, claimed in a report to the Politburo that maintaining good relations with the Eastern Bloc "took precedence in Soviet foreign policy".

Third World

"   **"**
> "You see, even in the jungles they
> want to live in Lenin's way!"
>
> — Leonid Brezhnev, the General Secretary of the Soviet Communist Party, in a close-knit discussion with his Politburo colleagues.[262]

All self-proclaimed African socialist states and the Middle Eastern country of South Yemen were labelled by Soviet ideologists as "States of Socialist Orientation".[263] Numerous African leaders were influenced by Marxism, and even Leninism.[262] Several Soviet think tanks were opposed to the Soviet leadership's policy towards Third World self-proclaimed socialist states, claiming that none of them had built a strong enough capitalist base of development as to be labelled as any kind of socialist. According to historian Archie Brown, these Soviet ideologists were correct, and, as a result no true socialist states were ever established in Africa, though Mozambique certainly came close.[263]

When the Ba'ath Party nationalised the Iraq Petroleum Company, the Iraqi Government sent Saddam Hussein, the Vice President of Iraq, to negotiate a trade agreement with the Soviet Union to soften the anticipated loss of revenue. When Hussein visited the Soviet Union, he managed to get a trade agreement and a treaty of friendship. When Kosygin visited Iraq in 1972, he and Ahmed Hassan al-Bakr, the President of Iraq signed and ratified the Iraqi–Soviet Treaty of Friendship and Co-operation. The alliance also forced the Iraqi Ba'athist government to temporarily stop their prosecution of the Iraqi Communist Party (ICP). The ICP was even given two ministerships following

Figure 66: *Kosygin (left) and Ahmed Hassan al-Bakr (right) signing the Iraqi–Soviet Treaty of Friendship and Co-operation in 1972*

the establishment of an alliance between the Soviet Union and Iraq. The following year, in 1973, al-Bakr went on a state visit to the Soviet Union, and met Brezhnev personally. Relations between the two countries only soured in 1976 when the Iraq Ba'athist regime started a mass campaign against the ICP and other communists. Despite pleas from Brezhnev for clemency, several Iraqi communists were executed publicy.

After the Angolan War of Independence of 1975, the Soviet Union's role in Third World politics increased dramatically. Some of the regions were important for national security, while other regions were important to the expansion of Soviet socialism to other countries. According to an anonymous Soviet writer, the national liberation struggle was the cornerstone of Soviet ideology, and therefore became a cornerstone for Soviet diplomatic activity in the Third World.[264]

Soviet influence in Latin America increased after Cuba became a communist state in 1961. The Cuban revolution was welcomed by Moscow since for once, they could point to a communist government established by indigenous forces instead of the Red Army. Cuba also became the Soviet Union's "front man" for promoting socialism in the Third World as the Havana regime was seen as more marketable and charismatic. By the late 1970s, Soviet influence in Latin America had reached crisis proportions according to several United States Congressmen.[265] Diplomatic and economic ties were established with several countries during the 1970s, and one of them, Peru bought external

Figure 67: *Iranian Emperor Mohammad Reza Pahlavi and Empress Farah Pahlavi meeting with Brezhnev in Moscow, 1970.*

goods from the Soviet Union. Mexico, and several countries in the Caribbean, forged increasingly strong ties with Comecon, an Eastern Bloc trading organisation established in 1949. The Soviet Union also strengthened its ties with the communist parties of Latin America.[266] Soviet ideologists saw the increasing Soviet presence as a part of the "mounting anti-imperialist struggle for democracy and social justice".[267]

The Soviet Union also played a key role in the secessionist struggle against the Portuguese Empire and the struggle for black majority rule in Southern Africa.[268] Control of Somalia was of great interest to both the Soviet Union and the United States, due to the country's strategic location at the mouth of the Red Sea. After the Soviets broke foreign relations with Siad Barre's regime in Somalia, the Soviets turned to the Derg Government in Ethiopia and supported them in their war against Somalia. Because the Soviets changed their allegiance, Barre expelled all Soviet advisers, tore up his friendship treaty with the Soviet Union, and switched allegiance to the West. The United States took the Soviet Union's place in the 1980s in the aftermath of Somalia's loss in the Ogaden War.

In Southeast Asia, Nikita Khrushchev had initially supported North Vietnam out of "fraternal solidarity", but as the war escalated he urged the North Viet-

namese leadership to give up the quest of liberating South Vietnam. He continued to reject offers to assist the North Vietnamese government, and instead told
them to enter negotiations in the United Nations Security Council.[269] Brezhnev, after taking power, started once again to aid the communist resistance in
Vietnam. In February 1965, Kosygin traveled to Hanoi with dozens of Soviet
air force generals and economic experts. During the Soviet visit, President
Lyndon B. Johnson had allowed US bombing raids on North Vietnamese soil
in retaliation of the recent Pleiku airbase attack by the Viet Cong.[270] In postwar Vietnam, Soviet aid became the cornerstone of socio-economic activity.
For example, in the early 1980s, 20–30% of the rice eaten by the Vietnamese
people was supplied by the Soviet Union. Since Vietnam never developed an
arms industry during the Cold War, it was the Soviet Union who assisted them
with weapons and materiel during the Sino-Vietnamese War.[271]

The Soviet Union supported the Vietnamese in their 1978 invasion of Cambodia, an invasion considered by the First World, most notably the United States,
and the People's Republic of China to be under the direct command of the Soviet Union. The USSR also became the largest backer of the new puppet state
in Cambodia, the People's Republic of Kampuchea (PRK). In a 1979 summit Jimmy Carter complained to Brezhnev about the presence of Vietnamese
troops in Cambodia, to which Brezhnev replied that the citizens of the PRK
were delighted about the overthrow of the Khmer Rouge-led government; in
this, as historian Archie Brown notes, he was right.[272]

Afghanistan

"   **"**
"We should tell Taraki and Amin to change their tactics. They still continue to
execute those people who disagree with them. They are killing nearly all of the
Parcham leaders, not only the highest rank, but of the middle rank, too."

— Alexei Kosygin, Chairman of the Council of Ministers.

Although the government of Democratic Republic of Afghanistan, formed in
the aftermath of the Saur Revolution of 1978, pursued several socialist policies, the country was "never considered socialist by the Soviet Union", according to historian Archie Brown.[273] Indeed, since the USSR had backed the previous regime under Mohammed Daoud Khan, the revolution, which had sur-
prised the Soviet leadership, created many difficulties for the Soviet Union.[273]
The People's Democratic Party of Afghanistan, the Afghan communist party,
consisted of two opposing factions, the khalqs and the parchams; the Soviet
leadership supported the latter, which had also join Moscow in backing the previous Daoud regime.[274] After engineering the coup, however it was the Khalq
faction that took over the reins of power. Nur Muhammad Taraki became

both President and Prime Minister of Afghanistan, while Hafizullah Amin became the Deputy Prime Minister of Afghanistan, and, from May 1979, Prime Minister. The new Khalq government ordered the execution of several high-standing and low-standing members of the Parcham faction. To make matters even worse, Taraki's and Hafizullah's relationship with each other soon turned sour as opposition against their government increased.[275] On 20 March 1979 Taraki travelled to the Soviet Union and met with Premier Kosygin, Dmitriy Ustinov (Defence Minister), Andrei Gromyko (Foreign Minister) and Boris Ponomarev (head of the International Department of the Central Committee), to discuss the possibilities of a Soviet intervention in Afghanistan. Kosygin opposed the idea, believing that the Afghan leadership had to prove it had the support of the people by combating opposition on its own, though he did agree to increase material aid to Afghanistan. When Taraki asked Kosygin about the possibilities of a military intervention led by the Eastern Bloc Kosygin rebuked him once more, again telling him that the Afghan leadership had to survive on its own.[276] However, in a closed meeting without Kosygin, the Politburo unanimously supported a Soviet intervention.[277]

In late 1979 Taraki failed to assassinate Amin, who, in a revenge attack, successfully engineering Taraki's own assassination on 9 October. Later, in December, the Soviet Union invaded Afghanistan at the behest of Khan. On 27 December a KGB unit killed Amin. Babrak Karmal, the leader of the Parcham faction, was chosen by the Soviet leadership as Amin's successor in the aftermath of the Soviet intervention.[278] Unfortunately for the Soviet leadership Karmal did not turn out to be the leader they expected, and he, just as his predecessors had arrested and killed several Parcham-members, arrested and killed several high-standing and low-standing Khalq members simply because they supported the wrong faction. With Soviet troops still in the country, however, he was forced to bow to Soviet pressure, and released all Khalq prisoners. To make matters even worse for Karmal several of the previously arrested Khalq-members were forced to join the new government.[278] At the time of Brezhnev's death, the Soviet Union was still bogged down in Afghanistan.[279]

Dissident movement

Soviet dissidents and human rights groups were routinely repressed by the KGB.[187] Overall, political repression tightened during the Brezhnev era and Stalin experienced a partial rehabilitation.[280] The two leading figures in the Soviet dissident movement during the Brezhnev Era were Aleksandr Solzhenitsyn and Andrei Sakharov. Despite their individual fame and widespread sympathy in the West, they attracted little support from the mass of the population. Sakharov was forced into internal exile in 1979, and Solzhenitsyn was forced out of the country in 1974.[281]

As a result, many dissidents became members of the Communist Party instead of protesting actively against the Soviet system throughout the 1970s and 1980s. These dissidents were defined by Archie Brown as "gradualists" who wanted to change the way the system worked in a slow manner.[282] The International Department of the Central Committee and the Socialist Countries Department of the Central Committee – departments considered by the First World media to be filled with conservative communists – were in fact the departments where Mikhail Gorbachev, as Soviet leader, would draw most of his "new thinkers" from. These officials had been influenced by Western culture and ideals by their travelling and reading.[283] Reformers were also in much greater numbers in the country's research institutes.[284]

The Brezhnev-era Soviet regime became notorious for using psychiatry as a means of silencing dissent. Many intellectuals, religious figures, and sometimes commoners protesting their low standard of living were ruled to be clinically insane and confined to mental hospitals.

Dissident success was mixed. Jews wanting to emigrate from the Soviet Union in the 1970s formed the most successful, and most organised, dissident movement. Their success can be attributed to the movement's support abroad, most notably from the Jewish community in the United States. In addition, as a group they were not advocating a transformation of Soviet society; the Jewish dissident movement was simply interested in leaving the Soviet Union for Israel. The Soviet Government subsequently sought to improve diplomatic ties with the First World by allowing the Jews to emigrate. The emigration flow was reduced dramatically as Soviet–American tension increased in the later half of the 1970s, though it was revived somewhat in 1979, peaking at 50,000. In the early 1980s, however, the Soviet leadership decided to block emigration completely.[285] Despite official claims that anti-Semitism was a bourgeois ideology incompatible with socialism, the truth was that Jews who openly practiced their religion or identified as Jewish from a cultural standpoint faced widespread discrimination from the Soviet system.

In 1978, a dissident movement of a different kind emerged when a group of unemployed miners led by Vladimir Klebanov attempted to form a labor union and demand collective bargaining. The main groups of Soviet dissidents, consisting mostly of intellectuals, remained aloof, and Klebanov was soon confined to a mental institution. Another attempt a month later to form a union of white collar professionals was also quickly broken up by authorities and its founder Vladimir Svirsky arrested.

"   **"**

"Every time when we speak about Solzhenitsyn as the enemy of the Soviet regime,
this just happens to coincide with some important [international] events and we
postpone the decision."

— Andrei Kirilenko, a Politburo member.

In general, the dissident movement had spurts of activity, including during
the Warsaw Pact invasion of Czechoslovakia, when several people demonstrated at Red Square in Moscow. With safety in numbers, dissidents who
were interested in democratic reform were able to show themselves, though
the demonstration, and the short-lived organised dissident group, were eventually repressed by the Soviet Government. The movement was then renewed
once again with the Soviet signing of the Helsinki Accords. Several Helsinki
Watch Groups were established across the country, all of which were routinely
repressed, and many closed down.[285] Due to the strong position of the Soviet
Government, many dissidents had problems reaching a "wide audience",[286]
and by the early 1980s, the Soviet dissident movement was in disarray: the
country's most notable dissidents had been exiled, either internally or exter-
nally, sent to prison or deported to the Gulags.[286]

The anti-religious course pursued by Khrushchev was toned down by the
Brezhnev/Kosygin leadership, with most Orthodox churches being staffed by
docile clergy often tied to the KGB. State propaganda tended to focus more
on promoting "scientific atheism" rather than active persecution of believers.
Nonetheless, minority faiths continued to be harassed relentlessly by the authorities, and particularly troubling to them was the continued resilience of
Islam in the Central Asian republics. This was worsened by their geographical
proximity to Iran, which fell under control of a fanatical Islamic government
in 1979 that professed hostility to both the United States and the Soviet Union.
While official figures put the number of believers at 9–10% of the population,
authorities were nonetheless baffled at the continued widespread presence of
religious belief in society, especially since by the start of the 1980s, the vast
majority of Soviet citizens alive had no memory of tsarist times.

Soviet society

Ideology and beliefs

Soviet society is generally regarded as having reached maturity under Brezhnev's rule. As noted by Edwin Bacon and Mark Sandle in their book *Brezhnev Reconsidered*, "a social revolution" was taking place in the Soviet Union
during his 18-year-long reign.[287] The increasingly modernized Soviet society was becoming more urban, and people became better educated and more

Figure 68: *Dancing during a break between sessions of
the 19th Komsomol Congress (photo taken in May 1982)*

professionalized. In contrast to previous periods dominated by "terrors, cat-
aclysms and conflicts", the Brezhnev Era constituted a period of continuous
development without interruption.[287] There was a fourfold growth in higher
education between the 1950s and 1980s; this development was referred to as
the "scientific-technological revolution".[287] In addition, women came to make
up half of the country's educated specialists.[287]

Following Khrushchev's controversial claim that (pure) communism could be
reached "within 20 years", the new Soviet leadership responded by fostering
the concept of developed socialism.[288] Brezhnev declared the onset of the era
developed socialism in 1971 at the 24th Congress of the Communist Party
of the Soviet Union. Developed socialism was described as socialism "at-
taining developed conditions", the result of "perfecting" the socialist society
which had been created. In short, it would be just another stage in the development of communism. Developed socialism evolved into the Brezhnev
regime's ideological cornerstone, and helped it to explain the situation of the
Soviet Union.[289] However, the theory of developed socialism theory also held
that the Soviet Union had reached a state in development where it was crisis-
free, and this proved to be incorrect. As a result, Yuri Andropov, Brezhnev's
successor, initiated the de-Brezhnevisation of the Soviet Union during his short
time in office, and introduced more realistic ideological theses. He did retain
developed socialism as a part of the state ideology, however.[290]

Culture

During the Brezhnev Era, pressure from below forced the Soviet leadership to alter some cultural policies, though the fundamental characteristics of the Communist system remained the same. Rock music and jeans, which had been criticized as hallmarks of Western culture, were legalized. The Soviet Union even started to manufacture its own jeans in the 1970s. As time progressed, however, the youth were more eager to buy Western products. The Soviet black market flourished during the Brezhnev Era, and "fake Western jeans" became very popular according to Archie Brown. Western rock groups such as The Beatles remained very popular throughout the Soviet Union and the Eastern Bloc, even if Soviet official policy remained wary of it.[291] Soviet rock music evolved, and became a form of dissidence against the Soviet system. Vladimir Vysotsky, Alexander Galich and Bulat Okudzhava were the most renowned rock musicians, and their lyrics, and music in general, were critical of the country's Stalinist past, as well as its undemocratic system.[292] In a 1981 editorial published in *Pravda*, Viktor Chebrikov, a deputy KGB head, commented on the apathy of Soviet youth towards the system and accused the West of using concepts such as consumerism, religion, and nationalism to encourage "pessimism, nihilism, and the pervasive view that life is better in the West." He also argued that foreign groups of Estonians, Latvians, and other ethnicities had a considerable influence on Soviet society.

Standard of living

From 1964 to 1973, the GDP per head in US dollars increased. Over the eighteen years Brezhnev ruled the Soviet Union, average income per head increased by half in equivalent US dollars.[294] In the first half of the Brezhnev period, income per head increased by 3.5 percent per annum, though this represented slightly less growth than in the last years of Khrushchev. This can be explained by the reversion of most of Khrushchev's policies when Brezhnev came to power.[295] Over time, however, citizens did find themselves better off than under Khrushchev. Consumption per head rose by an estimated 70% under Brezhnev, though three-quarters of this growth happened before 1973 and only one-quarter in the second half of his time in office.[296] Most of the increase in consumer production in the early Brezhnev era can be attributed to the Kosygin reform, according to an analysis on the performance of the reform carried out by the Moscow State University.

When the USSR's economic growth stalled in the 1970s, government focus shifted onto improving the standard of living and housing quality. The standard of living in Russia had fallen behind that of Georgia and Estonia under Brezhnev; this led many Russians to believe that the policies of the Soviet

Figure 69: *The official explanation for the ousting of Nikolai Podgorny, the head of state from 1965 to 1977, was his stance against détente and increasing the supply of consumer goods.*[293]

Government were hurting the Russian population.[297] To regain support, instead of paying more attention to the stagnant economy, the Soviet leadership under Brezhnev extended social benefits to boost the standard of living. This did indeed lead to an increase, albeit a minor one, in public support for the regime.[298]

In terms of advanced technology, the Soviet Union was far behind the United States, Western Europe, and Japan. Vacuum tube electronics remained in use long after they became obsolete elsewhere, and many factories in the 80s still used 1930s-vintage machine tools. General Nikolai Ogarkov in an unusually candid interview with an American journalist in 1982 admitted that "In America, even small children play with computers. We do not even have them in all the offices of the Defense Ministry. And for reasons you well know, we cannot make computers widely available in our society." Soviet manufacturing was not only primitive by Western standards, but extremely inefficient, often requiring 2–3 times the labor force of a mill or factory in the US.

During the Brezhnev era, there were material improvements for the Soviet citizen, but the Politburo was given no credit for this; the material improvements in the 1970s, i.e. the cheap provision of consumer goods, food, shelter, clothing, sanitation, health care and transport, were taken for granted by the common Soviet citizen. The common citizen associated Brezhnev's rule more with its limitation than its actual progress: as a result, Brezhnev earned neither affection nor respect. Most Soviet citizens had no power to change the existing system, so most of them tried to make the best of a bad situation. Rates of alcoholism, mental illness, divorce and suicide rose inexorably during the Brezhnev era.[229] Among ethnic Russians, the divorce rate by the late 70s was alarmingly high and 1 in 4 adults lived alone. Women lived particularly difficult lives as they performed most shopping, which could be an arduous task waiting in line for hours. Birthrates by 1982 were nearly flatline, with Muslims in the Central Asian republics being the only group in the nation with above-replacement fertility.

While investments in consumer goods were below projections, the expansion in output increased the Soviet people's standard of living. Refrigerators, owned by only 32 percent of the population in the early 1970s, had reached 86% of households by the late 1980s, and the ownership of color televisions increased from 51% in the early 1970s to 74% in the 1980s.[299] On the other hand, though some areas improved during the Brezhnev era, the majority of civilian services deteriorated, with the physical environment for the common Soviet citizen falling apart rapidly. Diseases were on the rise[229] because of the decaying health care system, and living space remained rather small by First World standards, with the common Soviet person living in 13.4 square metres. At the same time thousands of Moscow inhabitants were homeless, most of them living in shacks, doorways and parked trams. Authorities often conducted sweeps of movie theaters, restaurants, and saunas to locate people slacking off from work, particularly during major events like the 1980 Summer Olympics that attracted large numbers of foreign visitors. Nutrition ceased to improve in the late 1970s, with rationing of staple food products returning to locales such as Sverdlovsk. Environmental damage and pollution became a growing problem due to the Soviet government's policy of development at all costs, and some parts of the country such as the Kazakh SSR suffered particularly badly due to being used as a testing ground for nuclear weapons. While Soviet citizens in 1962 had enjoyed higher average life expectancy than the United States, by 1982 it had fallen by nearly five years.[300]

These effects were not felt uniformly, however. For example, by the end of the Brezhnev era, blue-collar workers had higher wages than professional workers in the Soviet Union. For example, the wage of a secondary school teacher in the Soviet Union was only 150 rubles while a bus driver's wage was 230.[299] As a whole, real wages increased from 96.5 rubles a month in 1965 to 190.1 rubles a month in 1985. A small minority benefited even more substantially. The state provided daily recreation and annual holidays for hard-working citizens.

Figure 70: *Private Nikolai Zaitsev being unanimously inducted into the Komsomol during a border guards' military drill in the Soviet Far East (photo taken in 1969).*

Soviet trade unions rewarded hard-working members and their families with beach vacations in Crimea and Georgia. Workers who fulfilled the monthly production quota set by the Soviet government were honored by placing their respective names on the factory's Roll of Honor. The state awarded badges for all manner of public services, and war veterans were allowed to go to the head of the shop queues. All members of the USSR Academy of Sciences were given a special badge and their own chauffeur-driven car. These awards, perks and privileges made it easier for some to find decent job placements, though they did not prevent the degeneration of Soviet society. Urbanization had led to unemployment in the Soviet agricultural sector, with most of the able workforce leaving villages for the local towns.[301]

Overall, it could be said that women had made marked social progress since the Bolshevik Revolution and by the Brezhnev era, comprised a considerable number of sole breadwinners in the country. Some professions such as the medical field had a considerable female workforce, although most of the best jobs (including academics, the state bureaucracy, and the military) remained almost exclusively the domain of men.

The agricultural sector continued to perform poorly and by Brezhnev's final year, food shortages were reaching disturbing levels of frequency. Particularly embarrassing to the regime was the fact that even bread had become rationed, one commodity that they always prided themselves on being available. One reason for this was excessive consumer demand as food prices remained artificially low while incomes had trebled over the last 20 years. Despite the miserable failure of collective farming, the Soviet government remained committed to reducing imports of foodstuffs from the West even though they cost less than domestic production, not only for reasons of national pride, but out of fear of becoming dependent on capitalist countries for basic necessities.

Social "rigidification" became a common feature in Soviet society. During the Stalin era in the 1930s and 1940s, a common laborer could expect promotion to a white-collar job if they studied and obeyed Soviet authorities. In Brezhnev's Soviet Union this was not the case. Holders of attractive offices clung to them as long as possible; mere incompetence was not seen as a good reason to dismiss anyone.[302] In this way, in addition to the others previously mentioned, the Soviet society Brezhnev passed on to his successors had become "static".[303]

Historical assessments

Despite Brezhnev's failures in domestic reforms, his foreign affairs and defense policies turned the Soviet Union into a superpower.[226] His popularity among citizens lessened during his last years, and support for the ideals of communism and Marxism-Leninism waned, even if the majority of Soviet citizens remained wary of liberal democracy and multi-party systems in general.[304]

The political corruption which had grown considerably during Brezhnev's tenure had become a major problem to the Soviet Union's economic development by the 1980s. In response, Andropov initiated a nationwide anti-corruption campaign. Andropov believed that the Soviet economy could possibly recover if the government were able to increase social discipline amongst workers.[305] Brezhnev was seen as very vain and self-obsessed,[305] but was praised for leading the Soviet Union into an unprecedented age of stability and domestic calm.[303]

Following Andropov's death, political wrangling led to harsh criticism of Brezhnev and his family. Mikhail Gorbachev, the last Soviet leader, drew support from hard-line communists and the Soviet population by criticizing Brezhnev's rule, and referred to his rule as the "Era of Stagnation".[306] Despite these attacks, in a poll taken in 2006, 61 percent of the people responded that they viewed the Brezhnev era as good for Russia.

Bibliography

- Baylis, Thomas A. (1989). *Governing by Committee: Collegial Leadership in Advanced Societies*. State University of New York Press. ISBN 978-0-88706-944-4.
- Brown, Archie (2009). *The Rise & Fall of Communism*. Bodley Head. ISBN 978-0-224-07879-5.
- Cocks, Paul; Daniels, Robert Vincent; Whittier Heer, Nancy (1976). *The Dynamics of Soviet Politics*. Harvard University Press. ISBN 0-674-21881-7.
- Daniels, Robert Vincent (1998). *Russia's Transformation: Snapshots of a Crumbling System*. Rowman & Littlefield. ISBN 0-8476-8709-0.
- Dellenbrant, Jan Åke (1986). *The Soviet Regional Dilemma: Planning, People, and Natural Resources*. M. E. Sharpe. ISBN 0-87332-384-X.
- Donaldson, Robert (2002). *The Soviet Union in the Third World: Successes and Failures*. Taylor & Francis. ISBN 0-89158-974-0.
- Evangelista, Matthew (2002). *Unarmed Forces: The Transnational Movement to End the Cold War*. Cornell University Press. ISBN 0-8014-8784-6.
- Frank, Willard (1992). *Soviet Military Doctrine from Lenin to Gorbachev, 1915–1991*. Greenwood Publishing Group. ISBN 0-313-27713-3.
- Kort, Michael (2010). *The Soviet Colossus: History and Aftermath*. M.E. Sharpe. ISBN 978-0-7656-2387-4.
- Kotz, David Michael; Weir, Fred (2007). *Russia's Path from Gorbachev to Putin: The Demise of the Soviet System and the New Russia*[307]. Taylor & Francis. ISBN 978-0-415-70146-4.
- Loth, Wilfried (2002). *Overcoming the Cold War: A History of Détente, 1950–1991*. Palgrave Macmillan. ISBN 978-0-333-97111-6.
- Low, Alfred D. (1976). *The Sino-Soviet Dispute: An Analysis of the Polemics*. Fairleigh Dickinson Univ Press. ISBN 0-8386-1479-5.
- McDowell, Bart; Conger, Dean (1977). *Journey Across Russia: The Soviet Union Today*. National Geographic Society. ISBN 0870442198.
- Sandle, Mark (1999). *A Short History of Soviet Socialism*. Routledge. ISBN 1-85728-355-4.
- Sandle, Mark; Bacon, Edwin (2002). *Brezhnev Reconsidered*. Palgrave Macmillan. ISBN 0-333-79463-X.
- Service, Robert (2003). *History of Modern Russia: From Tsarism to the Twenty-first Century*. Penguin Books Ltd. ISBN 0-14-103797-0.
- Sharlet, Robert S. (1992). *Soviet Constitutional Crisis: From De-Stalinization to Disintegration*. M. E. Sharpe. ISBN 978-1-56324-064-5.

- Sutela, Pekka (1991). *Economic Thought and Economic Reform in the Soviet Union*. Cambridge University Press. ISBN 0-521-38902-X.
- Wesson, Robert G. (1978). *Lenin's Legacy: The Story of the CPSU*. Hoover Press. ISBN 0-8179-6922-5.
- Zemtsov, Ilya (1989). *Chernenko: The Last Bolshevik: the Soviet Union on the eve of Perestroika*. Transaction Publishers. ISBN 0-88738-260-6.

1982–1991

History of the Soviet Union (1982–91)

Part of a series on the
History of the **Union of Soviet Socialist Republics** (Soviet Union)
1917–1927 **Revolutionary Beginnings**
• Revolution • Civil War • New Economic Policy • 1922 Treaty • National delimitation
1927–1953 **Stalinist rule**

- Socialism in One Country
- Great Purge

Soviet famine of 1932–33

- (Holodomor
- Kazakhstan famine of 1932-1933)

World War II

- (Molotov–Ribbentrop Pact
- Great Patriotic War
- Operation Barbarossa
- Occupation of the Baltic states
- Soviet occupation of Bessarabia and Northern Bukovina
- Battle of Berlin
- Soviet invasion of Manchuria)
- Soviet deportations
- Soviet famine of 1946–47
- Cold War
- Korean War

1953–1964
Post-Stalin era

- Berlin blockade
- 1954 transfer of Crimea
- Khrushchev Thaw
- On the Cult of Personality and Its Consequences
- We will bury you
- 9 March riots
- Wage reforms
- Cuban Revolution
- Sino-Soviet split
- Space program
- Cuban Missile Crisis

1964–1982
Brezhnev era

- Brezhnev Doctrine
- Era of Stagnation
- 50th anniversary of the Armenian Genocide protests
- Prague Spring

Vietnam War

- (Laotian Civil War
- Operation Menu
- Cambodian Civil War
- Fall of Saigon)
- Six-Day War
- Détente
- Yom Kippur War
- Dirty War

Wars in Africa

- (Angolan War of Independence
- Angolan Civil War
- Mozambican War of Independence
- Mozambican Civil War
- South African Border War
- Rhodesian Bush War)
- Cambodian-Vietnamese War
- Soviet–Afghan War
- 1980 Summer Olympics

Olympic boycotts

- (1980 Olympic boycott
- 1984 Olympic boycott)
- Polish strike
- Death and funeral of Brezhnev

1982–1991
Leadership changes and collapse

- Invasion of Grenada
- Glasnost
- Perestroika
- Soviet withdrawal from Afghanistan

Singing Revolution

- (Estonian Sovereignty Declaration
- Baltic Way
- Act of the Re-Establishment of the State of Lithuania
- On the Restoration of Independence of the Republic of Latvia)

Revolutions of 1989

- (Pan-European picnic
- Die Wende
- Peaceful Revolution
- Fall of the Berlin Wall
- Velvet Revolution
- End of communist rule in Hungary
- Romanian Revolution
- German reunification)

Dissolution

- (Jeltoqsan
- Nagorno-Karabakh War
- 9 April tragedy
- Black January
- Osh riots
- War of Laws
- Dushanbe riots
- January Events
- The Barricades
- Referendum
- Union of Sovereign States
- August Coup
- Ukrainian independence (referendum)
- Belavezha Accords
- Alma-Ata Protocol)

History of

- Russia
- Moscow
- Kiev
- Minsk
- Former Soviet Republics

Soviet leadership

- 1. Lenin
- 2. Stalin
- 3. Malenkov
- 4. Khrushchev
- 5. Brezhnev
- 6. Andropov
- 7. Chernenko
- 8. Gorbachev

- **Culture**
- **Economy**
- **Education**
- **Geography**
- **Politics**

▄▄ Soviet Union portal

- v
- t
- e[308]

The **history of the Soviet Union from 1982 through 1991** spans the period from Leonid Brezhnev's death and funeral until the dissolution of the Soviet Union. Due to the years of Soviet military buildup at the expense of domestic development, economic growth stagnated. Failed attempts at reform, a standstill economy, and the success of the United States against the Soviet Union's forces in the war in Afghanistan led to a general feeling of discontent, especially in the Baltic republics and Eastern Europe.[309]

Greater political and social freedoms, instituted by the last Soviet leader, Mikhail Gorbachev, created an atmosphere of open criticism of the communist regime. The dramatic drop of the price of oil in 1985 and 1986 profoundly influenced actions of the Soviet leadership.[310]

Nikolai Tikhonov, the Chairman of the Council of Ministers, was succeeded by Nikolai Ryzhkov, and Vasili Kuznetsov, the acting Chairman of the Presidium of the Supreme Soviet, was succeeded by Andrei Gromyko, the former Minister of Foreign Affairs.

Several republics began resisting central control, and increasing democratization led to a weakening of the central government. The Soviet Union finally collapsed in 1991 when Boris Yeltsin seized power in the aftermath of a failed coup that had attempted to topple reform-minded Gorbachev.

Leadership transition

By 1982, the stagnation of the Soviet economy was obvious, as evidenced by the fact that the Soviet Union had been importing grain from the U.S. throughout the 1970s, but the system was so firmly entrenched that any real change seemed impossible. A huge rate of defense spending consumed large parts of the economy. The transition period that separated the Brezhnev and Gorbachev eras resembled the former much more than the latter, although hints of reform emerged as early as 1983.

Andropov interregnum

Brezhnev died on 10 November 1982. Two days passed between his death and the announcement of the election of Yuri Andropov as the new General Secretary, suggesting to many outsiders that a power struggle had occurred in the Kremlin. Andropov maneuvered his way into power both through his KGB connections and by gaining the support of the military by promising not to cut defense spending. For comparison, some of his rivals such as Konstantin Chernenko were skeptical of a continued high military budget. Aged 69, he was the oldest person ever appointed as General Secretary and 11 years older than Brezhnev when he acquired that post. In June 1983, he assumed the post of chairman of the Presidium of the Supreme Soviet, thus becoming the ceremonial head of state. It had taken Brezhnev 13 years to acquire this post. Andropov began a thorough house-cleaning throughout the party and state bureaucracy, a decision made easy by the fact that the Central Committee had an average age of 69. He replaced more than one-fifth of the Soviet ministers and regional party first secretaries and more than one-third of the department heads within the Central Committee apparatus. As a result, he replaced the aging leadership with younger, more vigorous administrators. But Andropov's ability to reshape the top leadership was constrained by his own age and poor health and the influence of his rival (and longtime ally of Leonid Brezhnev) Konstantin Chernenko, who had previously supervised personnel matters in the Central Committee.

The transition of power from Brezhnev to Andropov was notably the first one in Soviet history to occur completely peacefully with no one being imprisoned, killed, or forced from office.

Andropov's domestic policy leaned heavily towards restoring discipline and order to Soviet society. He eschewed radical political and economic reforms, promoting instead a small degree of candor in politics and mild economic experiments similar to those that had been associated with the late Premier Alexei Kosygin's initiatives in the mid-1960s. In tandem with such economic experiments, Andropov launched an anti-corruption drive that reached high into the government and party ranks. Unlike Brezhnev, who possessed several mansions and a fleet of luxury cars, he lived quite simply. While visiting Budapest in early 1983, he expressed interest in Hungary's Goulash Communism and that the sheer size of the Soviet economy made strict top-down planning impractical. Changes were needed in a hurry for 1982 had witnessed the country's worst economic performance since World War II, with real GDP growth at almost zero percent.

In foreign affairs, Andropov continued Brezhnev's policies. US–Soviet relations deteriorated rapidly beginning in March 1983, when US President Ronald Reagan dubbed the Soviet Union an "evil empire". The official press agency TASS accused Reagan of "thinking only in terms of confrontation and bellicose, lunatic anti-communism". Further deterioration occurred as a result of the 1 Sep 1983 Soviet shootdown of Korean Air Lines Flight 007 near Moneron Island carrying 269 people including a sitting US congressman, Larry McDonald, and over Reagan's stationing of intermediate-range nuclear missiles in Western Europe. In Afghanistan, Angola, Nicaragua and elsewhere, under the Reagan Doctrine, the US began undermining Soviet-supported governments by supplying arms to anti-communist resistance movements in these countries.

President Reagan's decision to deploy medium-range Pershing II missiles in Western Europe met with mass protests in countries such as France and West Germany, sometimes numbering 1 million people at a time. Many Europeans became convinced that the US and not the Soviet Union was the more aggressive country, and there was fear over the prospect of a war, especially since there was a widespread conviction in Europe that the US, being separated from the Red Army by two oceans as opposed to a short land border, was insensitive to the people of Germany and other countries. Moreover, the memory of World War II was still strong and many Germans could not forget the destruction and mass rapes committed by Soviet troops in the closing days of that conflict. This attitude was helped along by the Reagan Administration's comments that a war between NATO and the Warsaw Pact would not necessarily result in the use of nuclear weapons.

Andropov's health declined rapidly during the tense summer and fall of 1983, and he became the first Soviet leader to miss the anniversary celebrations of the 1917 revolution that November.Wikipedia:Citation needed He died in February 1984 of kidney failure after disappearing from public view for several months. His most significant legacy to the Soviet Union was his discovery and promotion of Mikhail Gorbachev. Beginning in 1978, Gorbachev advanced in two years through the Kremlin hierarchy to full membership in the Politburo. His responsibilities for the appointment of personnel allowed him to make the contacts and distribute the favors necessary for a future bid to become general secretary. At this point, Western experts believed that Andropov was grooming Gorbachev as his successor. However, although Gorbachev acted as a deputy to the general secretary throughout Andropov's illness, Gorbachev's time had not yet arrived when his patron died early in 1984.

Chernenko interregnum

At 71, Konstantin Chernenko was in poor health, suffering from emphysema, and unable to play an active role in policy making when he was chosen, after lengthy discussion, to succeed Andropov. But Chernenko's short time in office did bring some significant policy changes. The personnel changes and investigations into corruption undertaken under Andropov's tutelage came to an end. Chernenko advocated more investment in consumer goods and services and in agriculture. He also called for a reduction in the CPSU's micromanagement of the economy and greater attention to public opinion. However, KGB repression of Soviet dissidents also increased. In February 1983, Soviet representatives withdrew from the World Psychiatric Organization in protest of that group's continued complaints about the use of psychiatry to suppress dissent. This policy was underlined in June when Vladimir Danchev, a broadcaster for Radio Moscow, referred to the Soviet troops in Afghanistan as "invaders" while conducting English-language broadcasts. After refusing to retract this statement, he was sent to a mental institution for several months. Valery Senderov, a leader of an unofficial union of professional workers, was sentenced to seven years in a labor camp early in the year for speaking out on discrimination practiced against Jews in education and the professions.

Although Chernenko had called for renewed *détente* with the West, little progress was made towards closing the rift in East–West relations during his rule. The Soviet Union boycotted the 1984 Summer Olympics in Los Angeles, retaliating for the United States-led boycott of the 1980 Summer Olympics in Moscow. In September 1984,[311] the Soviet Union also prevented a visit to West Germany by East German leader Erich Honecker. Fighting in Afghanistan also intensified, but in the late autumn of 1984 the United States and the Soviet Union did agree to resume arms control talks in early 1985.

Rise of Gorbachev

The war in Afghanistan, often referred to as the Soviet Union's "Vietnam War", led to increased public dissatisfaction with the Communist regime.Wikipedia:Citation needed Also, the Chernobyl disaster in 1986 added motive force to Gorbachev's glasnost and perestroika reforms, which eventually spiraled out of control and caused the Soviet system to collapse.

Changing of the guard

After years of stagnation, the "new thinking" (Anatoli Cherniaev, 2008: 131) of younger Communist apparatchik began to emerge. Following the death of terminally ill Konstantin Chernenko, the Politburo elected Mikhail Gorbachev to the position of General Secretary of the Communist Party of the Soviet Union (CPSU) in March 1985. At 54, Gorbachev was the youngest person since Joseph Stalin to become General Secretary and the country's first head of state born a Soviet citizen instead of a subject of the tsar. During his official confirmation on March 11, Foreign Minister Andrei Gromyko spoke of how the new Soviet leader had filled in for Chernenko as CC Secretariat, and praised his intelligence and flexible, pragmatic ideas instead of rigid adherence to party ideology. Gorbachev was aided by a lack of serious competition in the Politburo. He immediately began appointing younger men of his generation to important party posts, including Nikolai Ryzhkov, Secretary of Economics, Viktor Cherbrikov, KGB Chief, Foreign Minister Eduard Shevardnadze (replacing the 75-year-old Gromyko), Secretary of Defense Industries

Lev Zaikov, and Secretary of Construction Boris Yeltsin. Removed from the Politburo and Secretariat was Grigory Romanov, who had been Gorbachev's most significant rival for the position of General Secretary. Gromyko's removal as Foreign Minister was the most unexpected change given his decades of unflinching, faithful service compared to the unknown, inexperienced Shevardnadze.

More predictably, the 80-year-old Nikolai Tikhonov, the Chairman of the Council of Ministers, was succeeded by Nikolai Ryzhkov, and Vasili Kuznetsov, the acting Chairman of the Presidium of the Supreme Soviet, was succeeded by Andrei Gromyko, the former Minister of Foreign Affairs.

Further down the chain, up to 40% of the first secretaries of the *oblasts* (provinces) were replaced with younger, better educated, and more competent men. The defense establishment was also given a thorough shakeup with the commanders of all 16 military districts replaced along with all theaters of military operation, as well as the three Soviet fleets. Not since World War II had the Soviet military had such a rapid turnover of officers. Sixty-eight-year-old Marshal Nikolai Ogarkov was fully rehabilitated after having fallen from favor in 1983–84 due to his handling of the KAL 007 shootdown and his ideas about improving Soviet strategic and tactical doctrines were made into an official part of defense policy, although some of his other ambitions such as developing the military into a smaller, tighter force based on advanced technology were not considered feasible for the time being. Many, but not all, of the younger army officers appointed during 1985 were proteges of Ogarkov.

Gorbachev got off to an excellent start during his first months in power. He projected an aura of youth and dynamism compared to his aged predecessors and made frequent walks in the streets of the major cities answering questions from ordinary citizens. He became the first leader that spoke with the Soviet people in person. When he made public speeches, he made clear that he was interested in constructive exchanges of ideas instead of merely reciting lengthy platitudes about the excellence of the Soviet system. He also spoke candidly about the slackness and run-down condition of Soviet society in recent years, blaming alcohol abuse, poor workplace discipline, and other factors for these situations. Alcohol was a particular nag of Gorbachev's, especially as he himself did not drink, and he made one of his major policy aims curbing the consumption of it.

In terms of foreign policy, the most important one, relations with the United States, remained twitchy through 1985. In October, Gorbachev made his first visit to a non-communist country when he traveled to France and was warmly received. The fashion-conscious French were also captivated by his wife Raisa and political pundits widely believed that the comparatively young

Soviet leader would have a PR advantage over President Reagan, who was 20 years his senior.

Reagan and Gorbachev met for the first time in Geneva in November. The three weeks preceding the summit meeting were marked by an unprecedented Soviet media campaign against the Strategic Defense Initiative (SDI), taking advantage of opposition at home in the US to the program. When it finally took place, the two superpower leaders established a solid rapport that boded well for the future despite Reagan's refusal to compromise on abandonment of SDI. A joint communique by both parties stated that they were in agreement that nuclear war could not be won by either side and must never be allowed to happen. It was also agreed that Reagan and Gorbachev would carry out two more summit meetings in 1986–87.

Jimmy Carter had officially ended the policy of détente, by financially aiding the Mujahideen movement in neighboring Afghanistan, which served as a pretext for the Soviet intervention in Afghanistan six months later, with the aims of supporting the Afghan government, controlled by the People's Democratic Party of Afghanistan. Tensions between the superpowers increased during this time, when Carter placed trade embargoes on the Soviet Union and stated that the Soviet invasion of Afghanistan was "the most serious threat to the peace since the Second World War."

East-West tensions increased during the first term of U.S. President Ronald Reagan (1981–85), reaching levels not seen since the Cuban Missile Crisis as Reagan increased US military spending to 7% of the GDP.Wikipedia:Citation needed To match the USA's military buildup, the Soviet Union increased its own military spending to 27% of its GDP and froze production of civilian goods at 1980 levels, causing a sharp economic decline in the already failing Soviet economy. However, it is not clear where the number 27% of the GDP-Wikipedia:Citation needed came from. This thesis is not confirmed by the extensive study on the causes of the dissolution of the Soviet Union by two prominent economists from the World Bank—William Easterly and Stanley Fischer from the Massachusetts Institute of Technology. "... the study concludes that the increased Soviet defense spending provoked by Mr. Reagan's policies was not the straw that broke the back of the Empire. The Afghan war and the Soviet response to Mr. Reagan's Star Wars program caused only a relatively small rise in defense costs. And the defense effort throughout the period from 1960 to 1987 contributed only marginally to economic decline."

Economically, the soviet leaders attempted to adopt the Chinese option—economic liberalization with preservation of political system instead of the Shock therapy (economics) that was going on in Latin America and Poland. However, Gorbachev reforms did not work because the Soviet Union economy was almost 80% state owned compared to the 20–30% in China. The gradual opening of markets was too slow and not deep enough to leave any significant economic reforms until it was too late to prevent the collapse of the USSR.

The US financed the training for the Mujahideen warlords such as Jalaluddin Haqqani, Gulbudin Hekmatyar and Burhanuddin Rabbani eventually culminated to the fall of the Soviet satellite the Democratic Republic of Afghanistan. While the CIA and MI6 and the People's Liberation Army of China financed the operation along with the Pakistan government against the Soviet Union,[312] eventually the Soviet Union began looking for a withdrawal route and in 1988 the Geneva Accords were signed between Communist-Afghanistan and the Islamic Republic of Pakistan; under the terms Soviet troops were to withdraw. Once the withdrawal was complete the Pakistan ISI continued to support the Mujahideen against the Communist Government and by 1992, the government collapsed. US President Reagan also actively hindered the Soviet Union's ability to sell natural gas to Europe whilst simultaneously actively working to keep gas prices low, which kept the price of Soviet oil low and further starved the Soviet Union of foreign capital. This "long-term strategic offensive," which "contrasts with the essentially reactive and defensive strategy of "containment", accelerated the fall of the Soviet Union by encouraging it to overextend its economic base. The proposition that special operations by the CIA in Saudi Arabia affected the prices of Soviet oil was refuted by Marshall Goldman—one of the leading experts on the economy of the Soviet Union—in his latest book. He pointed out that the Saudis decreased their production of oil in 1985 (it reached a 16-year low), whereas the peak of oil production was reached in 1980. They increased the production of oil in 1986, reduced it in 1987 with a subsequent increase in 1988, but not to the levels of 1980 when production reached its highest level. The real increase happened in 1990, by which time the Cold War was almost over. In his book he asked why, if Saudi Arabia had such an effect on Soviet oil prices, did prices not fall in 1980 when the production of oil by Saudi Arabia reached its highest level—three times as much oil as in the mid-eighties—and why did the Saudis wait till 1990 to increase their production, five years after the CIA's supposed intervention? Why didn't the Soviet Union collapse in 1980 then?

However, this theory ignores the fact that the Soviet Union had already suffered several important setbacks during "reactive and defensive strategy" of "containment". In 1972, Nixon normalized US relations with China, thus creating pressure on the Soviet Union. In 1979, Egyptian president Anwar Sadat severed military and economic relations with the USSR after signing the Camp David Accords (by that time the USSR provided a lot of assistance to Egypt and supported it in all its military operations against Israel).

By the time Gorbachev ushered in the process that would lead to the dismantling of the Soviet administrative planned economy through his programs of

Figure 71: *Soviet Union administrative divisions, 1989*

glasnost (political openness), *uskoreniye* (speed-up of economic development) and *perestroika* (political and economic restructuring) announced in 1986, the Soviet economy suffered from both hidden inflation and pervasive supply shortages aggravated by an increasingly open black market that undermined the official economy.Wikipedia:Citation needed Additionally, the costs of superpower status—the military, space program, subsidies to client states—were out of proportion to the Soviet economy. The new wave of industrialization based upon information technology had left the Soviet Union desperate for Western technology and credits in order to counter its increasing backwardness.Wikipedia:Citation needed

Reforms

The Law on Cooperatives enacted in May 1988 was perhaps the most radical of the economic reforms during the early part of the Gorbachev era. For the first time since Vladimir Lenin's New Economic Policy, the law permitted private ownership of businesses in the services, manufacturing, and foreign-trade sectors. Under this provision, cooperative restaurants, shops, and manufacturers became part of the Soviet scene.

Glasnost resulted in greater freedom of speech and the press becoming far less controlled. Thousands of political prisoners and many dissidents were also released.Wikipedia:Citation needed Soviet social science became free to explore and publish on many subjects that had previously been off limits, including conducting public opinion polls. The All–Union Center for Public Opinion Research (VCIOM)—the most prominent of several polling organizations that were started then— was opened. State archives became more accessible, and some social statistics that had been kept secret became open for research and publication on sensitive subjects such as income disparities, crime, suicide, abortion, and infant mortality. The first center for gender studies was opened within a newly formed Institute for the Socio–Economic Study of Human Population.

In January 1987, Gorbachev called for democratization: the infusion of democratic elements such as multi-candidate elections into the Soviet political process. A 1987 conference convened by Soviet economist and Gorbachev adviser Leonid Abalkin, concluded: "Deep transformations in the management of the economy cannot be realized without corresponding changes in the political system."[313]

In June 1988, at the CPSU's Nineteenth Party Conference,Wikipedia:Citation needed Gorbachev launched radical reforms meant to reduce party control of the government apparatus. On 1 December 1988, the Supreme Soviet amended the Soviet constitution to allow for the establishment of a Congress of People's Deputies as the Soviet Union's new supreme legislative body.Wikipedia:Citation needed

Elections to the new Congress of People's Deputies were held throughout the USSR in March and April 1989. Gorbachev, as General Secretary of the Communist Party, could be forced to resign at any moment if the communist elite became dissatisfied with him. To proceed with reforms opposed by the majority of the communist party, Gorbachev aimed to consolidate power in a new position, President of the Soviet Union, which was independent from the CPSU and the soviets (councils) and whose holder could be impeached only in case of direct violation of the law.[314] On 15 March 1990, Gorbachev was elected as the first executive president. At the same time, Article 6 of the constitution was changed to deprive the CPSU of a monopoly on political power.

Unintended consequences

Gorbachev's efforts to streamline the Communist system offered promise, but ultimately proved uncontrollable and resulted in a cascade of events that eventually concluded with the dissolution of the Soviet Union. Initially intended as tools to bolster the Soviet economy, the policies of *perestroika* and *glasnost* soon led to unintended consequences.

Relaxation under *glasnost* resulted in the Communist Party losing its absolute grip on the media. Before long, and much to the embarrassment of the authorities, the media began to expose severe social and economic problems the

Soviet government had long denied and actively concealed. Problems receiving increased attention included poor housing, alcoholism, drug abuse, pollution, outdated Stalin-era factories, and petty to large-scale corruption, all of which the official media had ignored. Media reports also exposed crimes committed by Joseph Stalin and the Soviet regime, such as the gulags, his treaty with Adolf Hitler, and the Great Purges, which had been ignored by the official media. Moreover, the ongoing war in Afghanistan, and the mishandling of the 1986 Chernobyl disaster, further damaged the credibility of the Soviet government at a time when dissatisfaction was increasing.

In all, the positive view of Soviet lifelong presented to the public by the official media was rapidly fading, and the negative aspects of life in the Soviet Union were brought into the spotlight.[315] This undermined the faith of the public in the Soviet system and eroded the Communist Party's social power base, threatening the identity and integrity of the Soviet Union itself.

Fraying amongst the members of the Warsaw Pact countries and instability of its western allies, first indicated by Lech Wałęsa's 1980 rise to leadership of the trade union Solidarity, accelerated, leaving the Soviet Union unable to depend upon its Eastern European satellite states for protection as a buffer zone. By 1989, following hid doctrine of "new political thinking", Gorbachev had repudiated the Brezhnev Doctrine in favor of non-intervention in the internal affairs of its Warsaw Pact allies ("Sinatra Doctrine"). Gradually, each of the Warsaw Pact countries saw their communist governments fall to popular elections and, in the case of Romania, a violent uprising. By 1990, the governments of Bulgaria, Czechoslovakia, East Germany, Hungary, Poland and Romania, all of which had been imposed after World War II, were brought down as revolutions swept Eastern Europe.

The Soviet Union also began experiencing upheaval as the political consequences of *glasnost* reverberated throughout the country. Despite efforts at containment, the upheaval in Eastern Europe inevitably spread to nationalities within the USSR. In elections to the regional assemblies of the Soviet Union's constituent republics, nationalists as well as radical reformers swept the board. As Gorbachev had weakened the system of internal political repression, the ability of the USSR's central Moscow government to impose its will on the USSR's constituent republics had been largely undermined. Massive peaceful protests in the Baltic republics such as the Baltic Way and the Singing Revolution drew international attention and bolstered independence movements in various other regions.

The rise of nationalism under *freedom of speech* soon re-awakened simmering ethnic tensions in various Soviet republics, further discrediting the ideal of a unified Soviet people. One instance occurred in February 1988, when the government in Nagorno-Karabakh, a predominantly ethnic Armenian region in the Azerbaijan SSR, passed a resolution calling for unification with the Armenian SSR. Violence against local Azerbaijanis was reported on Soviet television, provoking massacres of Armenians in the Azerbaijani city of Sumgait.

Emboldened by the liberalized atmosphere of *glasnost*, public dissatisfaction with economic conditions was much more overt than ever before in the Soviet period. Although *perestroika* was considered bold in the context of Soviet history, Gorbachev's attempts at economic reform were not radical enough to restart the country's chronically sluggish economy in the late 1980s. The reforms made some inroads in decentralization, but Gorbachev and his team left intact most of the fundamental elements of the Stalinist system, including price controls, inconvertibility of the ruble, exclusion of private property ownership, and the government monopoly over most means of production.

The value of all consumer goods manufactured in 1990 in retail prices was about 459 billion rubles ($2.1 trillion). Nevertheless, the Soviet government had lost control over economic conditions. Government spending increased sharply as an increasing number of unprofitable enterprises required state support and consumer price subsidies to continue. Tax revenues declined as republic and local governments withheld tax revenues from the central government under the growing spirit of regional autonomy. The anti–alcohol campaign reduced tax revenues as well, which in 1982 accounted for about 12% of all state revenue. The elimination of central control over production decisions, especially in the consumer goods sector, led to the breakdown in traditional supplier–producer relationships without contributing to the formation of new ones. Thus, instead of streamlining the system, Gorbachev's decentralization caused new production bottlenecks.

Dissolution of the USSR

The **dissolution of the Soviet Union** was a process of systematic disintegration, which occurred in the economy, social structure and political structure. It resulted in the abolition of the Soviet Federal Government ("the Union center") and independence of the USSR's republics on 25 December 1991. The process was caused by a weakening of the Soviet government, which led to disintegration and took place from about 19 January 1990 to 31 December 1991. The process was characterized by many of the republics of the Soviet Union declaring their independence and being recognized as sovereign nation-states.

Andrei Grachev, the Deputy Head of the Intelligence Department of the Central Committee, summed up the denouement of the downfall quite cogently:

"Gorbachev actually put the sort of final blow to the resistance of the Soviet Union by killing the fear of the people. It was still that this country was governed and kept together, as a structure, as a government structure, by the fear from Stalinist times."

Summary

The principal elements of the old Soviet political system were Communist Party dominance, the hierarchy of soviets, state socialism, and ethnic federalism. Gorbachev's programs of *perestroika* (restructuring) and *glasnost* (openness) produced radical unforeseen effects that brought that system down. As a means of reviving the Soviet state, Gorbachev repeatedly attempted to build a coalition of political leaders supportive of reform and created new arenas and bases of power. He implemented these measures because he wanted to resolve serious economic problems and political inertia that clearly threatened to put the Soviet Union into a state of long-term stagnation.

But by using structural reforms to widen opportunities for leaders and popular movements in the union republics to gain influence, Gorbachev also made it possible for nationalist, orthodox communist, and populist forces to oppose his attempts to liberalize and revitalize Soviet communism. Although some of the new movements aspired to replace the Soviet system altogether with a liberal democratic one, others demanded independence for the national republics. Still others insisted on the restoration of the old Soviet ways. Ultimately, Gorbachev could not forge a compromise among these forces and the consequence was the dissolution of the Soviet Union.

Post-Soviet restructuring

To restructure the Soviet administrative command system and implement a transition to a market economy, Yeltsin's shock program was employed within days of the dissolution of the Soviet Union. The subsidies to money-losing farms and industries were cut, price controls abolished, and the ruble moved towards convertibility. New opportunities for Yeltsin's circle and other entrepreneurs to seize former state property were created, thus restructuring the old state-owned economy within a few months.

After obtaining power, the vast majority of "idealistic" reformers gained huge possessions of state property using their positions in the government and became business oligarchs in a manner that appeared antithetical to an emerging democracy. Existing institutions were conspicuously abandoned prior to the establishment of new legal structures of the market economy such as those governing private property, overseeing financial markets, and enforcing taxation.

Market economists believed that the dismantling of the administrative command system in Russia would raise GDP and living standards by allocating resources more efficiently. They also thought the collapse would create new production possibilities by eliminating central planning, substituting a decentralized market system, eliminating huge macroeconomic and structural distortions through liberalization, and providing incentives through privatization.

Since the USSR's collapse, Russia faced many problems that free market proponents in 1992 did not expect. Among other things, 25% of the population lived below the poverty line, life expectancy had fallen, birthrates were low, and the GDP was halved. There was a sharp increase in economic inequality: between 1988/1989 and 1993/1995, the Gini ratio increased by an average of 9 points for all former socialist countries. These problems led to a series of crises in the 1990s, which nearly led to the election of Yeltsin's Communist challenger, Gennady Zyuganov, in the 1996 presidential election. In recent years, the economy of Russia has begun to improve greatly, due to major investments and business development and also due to high prices of natural resources.

Further reading

- Hélène Carrère d'Encausse, *The End of the Soviet Empire: The Triumph of the Nations*, Basic Books, 1992, ISBN 0-465-09818-5
- Gaidar, Yegor (19 April 2007). "The Soviet Collapse: Grain and Oil"[316]. *AEI Online*. Archived from the original[317] on 22 July 2009. Retrieved 9 July 2009.
- Gaidar, Yegor (2006). *Gibel' Imperii: Uroki dlya sovremennoi Rossii* [*The Collapse of an Empire: Lessons for Modern Russia*]. Gaidar, Yegor Gaidar (2007). *Collapse of an Empire: Lessons for Modern Russia*[318]. Antonina W. Bouis (trans.). Washington D.C.: Brookings Institution Press. ISBN 978-0-8157-3114-6.
- Jack F. Matlock, Jr., *Autopsy on an Empire: The American Ambassador's Account of the Collapse of the Soviet Union*, Random House, 1995, ISBN 0-679-41376-6
- David Remnick, *Lenin's Tomb: The Last Days of the Soviet Empire*, Vintage Books, 1994, ISBN 0-679-75125-4
- Ronald Grigor Suny, *The Revenge of the Past: Nationalism, Revolution, and the Collapse of the Soviet Union*, Stanford University Press, 1993, ISBN 0-8047-2247-1

- Anatoli Cherniaev, 'Gorbachev's Foreign Policy: The Concept' in Skinner, Kiron (ed.) Turning Points in Ending the Cold War[319], (Hoover Institution Press: 2008), pp. 111–140, p. 111; [online] [accessed 22–23 February 2012]. Also for 'new thinking' see Ibid., p. 131.

External links

- Reform, Coup and Collapse: The End of the Soviet State[320] by Professor Archie Brown
- Soviet Archives[321] collected by Vladimir Bukovsky
- End of the Soviet Union[322] from the Dean Peter Krogh Foreign Affairs Digital Archives[323]
- Candid photos of the Eastern Bloc[324] September–December 1991, in the last months of the USSR
- Kuliabin A. Semine S. Some of aspects of state national economy evolution in the system of the international economic order.- USSR ACADEMY OF SCIENCES FAR EAST DIVISION INSTITUTE FOR ECONOMIC & INTERNATIONAL OCEAN STUDIES Vladivostok, 1991[325]
- Making the History of 1989[326]

Appendix

References

[1] //en.wikipedia.org/wiki/Soviet_Union#endnote_1

[2] *De facto* before 1990

[3] //en.wikipedia.org/wiki/Soviet_Union#endnote_3

[4] Historical Dictionary of Socialism. James C. Docherty, Peter Lamb. Page 85. "The Soviet Union was a one-party Marxist-Leninist state".

[5] Ideology, Interests, and Identity http://csis.org/files/media/csis/pubs/ruseur_wp_010.pdf. Stephen H. Hanson. Page 14. "the USSR was officially a Marxist-Leninist state".

[6] The Fine Line between the Enforcement of Human Rights Agreements and the Violation of National Sovereignty: The Case of Soviet Dissidents http://digitalcommons.lmu.edu/cgi/viewcontent.cgi?article=1078&context=ilr. Jennifer Noe Pahre. p. 336. "[...] the Soviet Union, as a Marxist-Leninist state [...]". p. 348. "The Soviet Union is a Marxist–Leninist state".

[7] Leninist National Policy: Solution to the "National Question"? http://www.epa.hu/00000/00010/00020/pdf/HSR_1989_1-2_023-046.pdf. Walker Connor. Page 31. "[...] four Marxist-Leninist states (the Soviet Union, China, Czechoslovakia and Yugoslavia)[...]".

[8] //en.wikipedia.org/wiki/Soviet_Union#endnote_4

[9] Part III of the 1977 Soviet Constitution "THE NATIONAL-STATE STRUCTURE OF THE USSR"

[10] Davies & Wheatcroft 2004, pp. xiv https://books.google.com/books?id=4s1lCwAAQBAJ&pg=PR14#v=onepage&q&f=false, 401 https://books.google.com/books?id=4s1lCwAAQBAJ&lpg=PR14&pg=PA401#v=onepage&q&f=false 441 https://books.google.com/books?id=4s1lCwAAQBAJ&lpg=PR14&pg=PA441#v=onepage&q&f=false.

[11] The term "successor state of the Soviet Union" for the Russian Federation was laid down in paragraph 3 of article 1 and paragraph 7 of article 37 of the Federal law "On international treaties of the Russian Federation" of 15 July 1995 No. 101-FZ (adopted by the State Duma on 16 June 1995). — See Federal law of July 15, 1995 № 101-FZ On international treaties of the Russian Federation http://constitution.garant.ru/act/base/10103790/

[12] [The case of Mikhail Suprun: the story of political repression as an invasion of privacy http://echo.msk.ru/programs/kulshok/822592-echo/#element-text]

[13] On 13 January 1992 the Russian MFA dispatched to heads of diplomatic missions in Moscow a note in which it was stated that the Russian Federation continues to exercise rights and perform obligations under all agreements concluded by the Soviet Union. On the basis of the specified notes the international community implicitly recognized in the Russian Federation the status of a successor state of the Soviet Union. See International treaties in the legal system of the Russian Federation http://constitution.garant.ru/science-work/modern/3540062/

[14] //en.wikipedia.org/w/index.php?title=Template:History_of_Russia&action=edit

[15] (*rada*); ; ; ; ; ; ; ; ; ; ; ;

[16] Fischer 1964, p. 608; Lewin 1969, p. 50; Leggett 1981, p. 354; Volkogonov 1994, p. 421; Service 2000, p. 455; White 2001, p. 175.

[17] Russia – Encyclopædia Britannica http://www.britannica.com/EBchecked/topic/513251/Russia. Britannica.com (27 April 2010). Retrieved on 29 July 2013.

[18] //en.wikipedia.org/w/index.php?title=Template:History_of_the_Soviet_Union&action=edit

[19] Richard Sakwa *The Rise and Fall of the Soviet Union, 1917–1991: 1917–1991*. Routledge, 1999. pp. 140–143.

[20] Julian Towster. *Political Power in the U.S.S.R., 1917–1947: The Theory and Structure of Government in the Soviet State* Oxford Univ. Press, 1948. p. 106.

[21] Voted Unanimously for the Union. http://region.adm.nov.ru/pressa.nsf/0c7534916fcf6028c3256b3700243eac/4302e4941fb6a6bfc3256c99004faea5!OpenDocument

[22] Creation of the USSR http://www.hronos.km.ru/sobyt/cccp.html at Khronos.ru.

[23] On GOELRO Plan – at Kuzbassenergo. http://www.kuzbassenergo.ru/goelro/

[24]The consolidation into a one-party regime took place during the first three and a half years after the revolution, which included the period of War communism and an election in which multiple parties competed. See Leonard Schapiro, *The Origin of the Communist Autocracy: Political Opposition in the Soviet State, First Phase 1917–1922*. Cambridge, MA: Harvard University Press, 1955, 1966.

[25]Hitler vs. Stalin: Who Was Worse? http://www.nybooks.com/daily/2011/01/27/hitler-vs-stalin-who-was-worse/, *The New York Review of Books*, 27 January 2011

[26]Wheatcroft 1996, pp. 1334,1348.

[27]Religion and the State in Russia and China: Suppression, Survival, and Revival, by Christopher Marsh, page 47. Continuum International Publishing Group, 2011.

[28]Inside Central Asia: A Political and Cultural History, by Dilip Hiro. Penguin, 2009.

[29]USGOV1

[30]Geoffrey Blainey; A Short History of Christianity; Viking; 2011; p.494"

[31]Ukrainian 'Holodomor' (man-made famine) Facts and History http://www.holodomorct.org/history.html. Holodomorct.org (28 November 2006). Retrieved on 29 July 2013.

[32]J. Arch Getty, "State and Society Under Stalin: Constitutions and Elections in the 1930s," *Slavic Review* 50#1 (1991), pp. 18-35 online https://www.jstor.org/stable/2500596

[33]Mel'tiukhov, Mikhail. *Upushchennyi shans Stalina: Sovetskii Soiuz i bor'ba za Evropu 1939–1941*. Moscow: Veche, 2000.

[34]Denunciation of the neutrality pact http://avalon.law.yale.edu/wwii/s3.asp 5 April 1945. (Avalon Project at Yale University)

[35]Soviet Declaration of War on Japan http://avalon.law.yale.edu/wwii/s4.asp, 8 August 1945. (Avalon Project at Yale University)

[36]Daniel Goldhagen, *Hitler's Willing Executioners* (p. 290) — "2.8 million young, healthy Soviet POWs" killed by the Germans, "mainly by starvation ... in less than eight months" of 1941–42, before "the decimation of Soviet POWs ... was stopped" and the Germans "began to use them as laborers".

[37]Mark Kramer, "The Soviet Bloc and the Cold War in Europe," in

[38]Kenneth S. Deffeyes, Beyond Oil: The View from Hubbert's Peak.

[39]The red blues — Soviet politics https://web.archive.org/web/20050324050607/http://findarticles.com/p/articles/mi_m1282/is_n12_v42/ai_9119705 by Brian Crozier, *National Review*, 25 June 1990.

[40]Origins of Moral-Ethical Crisis and Ways to Overcome it http://www.rspp.su/sobor/conf_2006/istoki_duh_nrav_crisis.html by V.A.Drozhin Honoured Lawyer of Russia.

[41]Country Profile: Russia http://www.fco.gov.uk/servlet/Front?pagename=OpenMarket/Xcelerate/ShowPage&c=Page&cid=1007029394365&a=KCountryProfile&aid=1019744935436 Foreign & Commonwealth Office of the United Kingdom.

[42]"Child poverty soars in eastern Europe" http://news.bbc.co.uk/1/hi/business/966616.stm, BBC News, 11 October 2000

[43]Theodore P. Gerber & Michael Hout, "More Shock than Therapy: Market Transition, Employment, and Income in Russia, 1991–1995", AJS Volume 104 Number 1 (July 1998): 1–50.

[44]David Stuckler, Lawrence King, and Martin McKee. "Mass privatisation and the post-communist mortality crisis: a cross-national analysis." *The Lancet* 373.9661 (2009): 399–407.

[45]Privatisation 'raised death rate' http://news.bbc.co.uk/2/hi/health/7828901.stm. *BBC*, 15 January 2009. Retrieved 19 November 2014.

[46]Adam B. Ulam, *Expansion and coexistence: the history of Soviet foreign policy, 1917-73* (1974)

[47]Duncan Hallas, *The Comintern: The History of the Third International* (1985).

[48]"Germany (East)", Library of Congress Country Study, Appendix B: The Council for Mutual Economic Assistance http://memory.loc.gov/frd/cs/germany_east/gx_appnb.html

[49]Michael C. Kaser, *Comecon: Integration problems of the planned economies* (Oxford University Press, 1967).

[50]Laurien Crump, *The Warsaw Pact Reconsidered: International Relations in Eastern Europe, 1955-1969* (Routledge, 2015).

[51] Michał Jerzy Zacharias, "The Beginnings of the Cominform: The Policy of the Soviet Union towards European Communist Parties in Connection with the Political Initiatives of the United States of America in 1947." *Acta Poloniae Historica* 78 (1998): 161-200.

[52] Nikos Marantzidis, "The Greek Civil War (1944–1949) and the International Communist System." *Journal of Cold War Studies* 15.4 (2013): 25-54.

[53] Heinz Timmermann, "The cominform effects on Soviet foreign policy." *Studies in Comparative Communism* 18.1 (1985): 3-23.

[54] Ulam, *Expansion and Coexistence* (1974) pp 111-79.

[55] Gordon H. Mueller, "Rapallo Reexamined: a new look at Germany's secret military collaboration with Russia in 1922." *Military Affairs: The Journal of Military History* (1976): 109-117. online https://www.jstor.org/stable/1986524

[56] Christine A. White, *British and American Commercial Relations with Soviet Russia, 1918-1924* (UNC Press Books, 2017).

[57] Joan Hoff Wilson, "American Business and the Recognition of the Soviet Union." *Social Science Quarterly* (1971): 349-368. online https://www.jstor.org/stable/42860014

[58] Chris Ward, *Stalin's Russia* (2nd ed. 1999) pp 148-88.

[59] Barbara Jelavich, *St.Petersburg and Moscow: Czarist and Soviet Foreign Policy, 1814-1974* (1974) pp 342-46.

[60] //en.wikipedia.org/w/index.php?title=Template:Marxism%E2%80%93Leninism_sidebar&action=edit

[61] Sakwa, Richard. *Soviet Politics in Perspective.* 2nd ed. London – N.Y.: Routledge, 1998.

[62] The Occupation of Latvia http://www.am.gov.lv/en/latvia/history/occupation-aspects/ at Ministry of Foreign Affairs of the Republic of Latvia

[63] Estonia says Soviet occupation justifies it staying away from Moscow celebrations - Pravda.Ru http://newsfromrussia.com/cis/2005/05/03/59549.html

[64] Motion for a resolution on the Situation in Estonia http://www.europarl.europa.eu/sides/getDoc.do?pubRef=-//EP//NONSGML+MOTION+B6-2007-0215+0+DOC+PDF+V0//EN by the EU

[65] European Court of Human Rights cases on Occupation of Baltic States

[66] Hanson, Philip. *The Rise and Fall of the Soviet Economy: An Economic History of the USSR from 1945.* London: Longman, 2003.

[67] Rose Eveleth (12 December 2013). Soviet Russia Had a Better Record of Training Women in STEM Than America Does Today http://www.smithsonianmag.com/smart-news/soviet-russia-had-a-better-record-of-training-women-in-stem-than-america-does-today-180948141/?no-ist. *Smithsonian.com.* Retrieved 26 June 2014.

[68] Ambler, Shaw and Symons 1985, p. 166–67.

[69] Ambler, Shaw and Symons 1985, p. 168.

[70] Ambler, Shaw and Symons 1985, p. 165.

[71] Ambler, Shaw and Symons 1985, p. 167.

[72] Ambler, Shaw and Symons 1985, p. 169.

[73] International Monetary Fund and Organisation for Economic Co-operation and Development 1991, p. 56.

[74] Paper presented at the International Conference on Health, Morbidity and Mortality by Cause of Death in Europe.

[75] Sheila Fitzpatrick, *Education and Social Mobility in the Soviet Union 1921–1934* http://www.cambridge.org/us/academic/subjects/history/twentieth-century-european-history/education-and-social-mobility-soviet-union-19211934, Cambridge University Press (16 May 2002),

[76] Comrie 1981, p. 2.

[77] (pay-fee)

[78] 'On the other hand...' See the index of *Stalin and His Hangmen* by Donald Rayfield, 2004, Random House

[79] https://books.google.com/books?id=Rpg9AAAAIAAJ&dq

[80] https://books.google.com/books?id=QTU7AAAAIAAJ&dq

[81] http://www.palgrave.com/us/book/9780333311073

[82] https://books.google.com/books?id=EUVwrcnXwBsC

[83] https://books.google.com/books?id=rcXafOqyxgQC&dq

[84] https://books.google.com/books?id=sTLc8H3b4vUC

[85] https://books.google.com/books?id=1qgOAAAAQAAJ&dq

[86] https://books.google.com/books?id=fiDpE5M9jRAC&dq

[87] https://books.google.com/books?id=T-d_QgAACAAJ

[88] http://sovietinfo.tripod.com/WCR-German_Soviet.pdf

[89] //doi.org/10.1080/09668139608412415

[90] //www.jstor.org/stable/152781

[91] http://rs6.loc.gov/frd/cs/sutoc.html

[92] https://www.amazon.com/Routledge-Russian-History-Historical-Atlases/dp/0415394848/

[93] https://www.amazon.com/dp/0679745440

[94] https://www.amazon.com/dp/0521616530

[95] https://www.questia.com/PM.qst?a=o&d=109468478

[96] https://www.amazon.com/dp/0521565219

[97] https://www.questia.com/read/108215209?title=Stalin%20and%20the%20Soviet%20Union

[98] https://www.questia.com/PM.qst?a=o&d=103246514

[99] http://www.humanitiesebook.org/

[100] https://www.amazon.com/dp/0375724710/

[101] https://www.amazon.com/Motherland-Danger-Soviet-Propaganda-during/dp/0674049241/

[102] https://www.amazon.com/Little-Soldiers-Soviet-Children-1941-1945/dp/0199585555/

[103] https://www.amazon.com/gp/reader/0140271694/

[104] https://www.amazon.com/dp/0140271694/

[105] https://web.archive.org/web/20120525095312/http://www.questia.com/PM.qst?a=o&d=100872346

[106] https://www.jstor.org/stable/3092980

[107] https://www.amazon.com/dp/0804725217

[108] https://www.questia.com/read/105899376

[109] https://www.amazon.com/dp/0300066643

[110] https://www.amazon.com/dp/0195126599

[111] https://www.questia.com/read/98422373

[112] https://www.amazon.com/dp/0393324842

[113] http://search.live.com/results.aspx?q=&scope=books#q=zubok&filter=all&start=1

[114] https://www.amazon.com/dp/0745643450/

[115] https://www.amazon.com/dp/0195368630/

[116] http://lcweb2.loc.gov/frd/cs/

[117] http://ariwatch.com/VS/JD/ImpressionsOfSovietRussia.htm

[118] http://lcweb2.loc.gov/frd/cs/sutoc.html

[119] http://rt.com/news/ussr-collapse-mistake-poll-585/

[120] //en.wikipedia.org/w/index.php?title=Template:History_of_the_Soviet_Union&action=edit

[121] Voted Unanimously for the Union http://region.adm.nov.ru/pressa.nsf/0c7534916fcf6028c3256b3700243eac/4302e4941fb6a6bfc3256c99004faea5!OpenDocument

[122] Creation of the USSR http://www.hronos.km.ru/sobyt/cccp.html at Khronos.ru

[123] https://www.jstor.org/stable/10.1086/343412

[124] https://www.questia.com/PM.qst?a=o&d=103246514

[125] https://web.archive.org/web/20000707012840/http://www.historyebook.org/

[126] //en.wikipedia.org/w/index.php?title=Template:History_of_the_Soviet_Union&action=edit

[127] Martin Mccauley, *The Soviet Union 1917–1991* (Routledge, 2014). p. 81.

[128] Martin Mccauley, *Stalin and Stalinism* (3rd ed. 2013) p. 39.

[129] E. A. Rees, *Decision-making in the Stalinist Command Economy, 1932–37* (Palgrave Macmillan, 1997) 212–13.

[130] Andrew B. Somers, *History of Russia* (Monarch Press, 1965) p. 77.

[131] *Problems of Communism* (1989) – Volume 38 p. 137

[132] Mark Harrison and Robert W. Davies. "The Soviet military-economic effort during the second five-year plan (1933–1937)." *Europe-Asia Studies* 49.3 (1997): 369–406.

[133] Vadim Birstein *Smersh: Stalin's Secret Weapon* (Biteback Publishing, 2013) pp. 80–81.

[134] Robert Service, *Comrades! A History of World Communism* (2007) p 145

[135] R. W. Davies, Stephen G. Wheatcroft, *The Industrialisation of Soviet Russia Volume 5: The Years of Hunger: Soviet Agriculture 1931–1933* (2nd ed. 2010) p xiv online https://www.amazon.com/Industrialisation-Soviet-Russia-Agriculture-1931-1933/dp/0230238556/

[136] Tucker 1990, p. 96.

[137] Tucker 1990, p. 228.

[138] Davies (1986), p. 451.

[139] Polian (2004), p. 119.

[140] Hope (2005), p. 29.

[141] Malcher (1993), pp. 8–9.

[142] Piesakowski (1990), pp. 50–51.

[143] Mikolajczyk (1948).

[144] Piotrowski (2004).

[145] Gross (2002), p. xiv.

[146] Cienciala (2007), p. 139.

[147] Polian (2004), p. 118.

[148] L. E. Reshin, "Year of 1941", vol. 2, p. 152.

[149] Population transfer in the Soviet Union, Wikipedia.

[150] Although the 1946 drought was severe, government mismanagement of its grain reserves largely accounted for the population losses.<ref>.

[151] Russia and the USSR, 1855–1991: Autocracy and Dictatorship p.147

[152] https://www.amazon.com/dp/0521616530

[153] https://www.questia.com/PM.qst?a=o&d=109468478

[154] https://www.amazon.com/dp/0521565219

[155] https://www.questia.com/read/108215209?title=Stalin%20and%20the%20Soviet%20Union

[156] https://www.questia.com/PM.qst?a=o&d=103246514

[157] https://web.archive.org/web/20000707012840/http://www.historyebook.org/

[158] https://www.amazon.com/Moscow-Fourth-Rome-Stalinism-Cosmopolitanism/dp/0674057872/

[159] https://www.amazon.com/Stalins-Peasants-Resistance-Survival-Collectivization/dp/0195104595/

[160] https://www.amazon.com/dp/0375724710/

[161] https://www.amazon.com/Motherland-Danger-Soviet-Propaganda-during/dp/0674049241/

[162] https://www.amazon.com/dp/0140271694/

[163] https://www.questia.com/PM.qst?a=o&d=100872346

[164] https://www.amazon.com/dp/0804725217

[165] https://www.questia.com/read/105899376

[166] https://www.amazon.com/dp/0300066643

[167] https://www.questia.com/read/98422373

[168] https://www.amazon.com/dp/0393324842

[169] https://web.archive.org/web/20080121085401/http://deweytextsonline.area501.net/ImpressionsOfSovietRussia.htm

[170] http://deweytextsonline.area501.net/ImpressionsOfSovietRussia.htm

[171] http://www.globalpost.com/video/commerce/100722/stalin-russia-soviet-union

[172] http://library2.usask.ca/USSRConst/

[173] //en.wikipedia.org/w/index.php?title=Template:History_of_the_Soviet_Union&action=edit

[174] //en.wikipedia.org/w/index.php?title=Template:History_of_the_Soviet_Union&action=edit

[175] //en.wikipedia.org/w/index.php?title=Template:Leonid_Brezhnev_series&action=edit

[176] Baylis 1989, p. 97.

[177] Service 2009, p. 375.

[178] Cocks, Daniels & Heer 1997, pp. 56–57.

[179] Bacon & Sandle 2002, p. 54.

[180] Brown 2009, p. 403.

[181] Daniels 1998, p. 36.

[182] Brown 2009, p. 402.

[183] Zemtsov 1989, p. 119.

[184] Mitchell 1990, p. 72.

[185] Baylis 1989, p. 98.
[186] Evangelista 2002, p. 152.
[187] Bacon & Sandle 2002, p. 19.
[188] Frank 1992, p. 9.
[189] Evangelista 2002, p. 178.
[190] Evangelista 2002, pp. 178–179.
[191] Evangelista 2002, p. 179.
[192] Evangelista 2002, p. 181.
[193] Frank 1992, p. 182.
[194] Frank 1992, p. 46.
[195] Frank 1992, p. 240.
[196] Frank 1992, p. 200.
[197] Bacon & Sandle 2002, p. 11.
[198] Bacon & Sandle 2002, p. 12.
[199] Service 2009, p. 380.
[200] Service 2009, p. 392.
[201] Service 2009, pp. 380–381.
[202] Service 2009, pp. 404–405.
[203] Daniels 1998, pp. 52–53.
[204] Daniels 1998, p. 53.
[205] Wesson 1978, p. 252.
[206] Zemtsov 1989, pp. 97–98.
[207] Sharlet 1992, p. 18.
[208] Sharlet 1992, pp. 18–19.
[209] Sharlet 1992, p. 19.
[210] Sharlet 1992, p. 20.
[211] Sharlet 1992, p. 21.
[212] Service 2009, p. 403.
[213] Brown 2009, p. 404.
[214] Brown 2009, p. 405.
[215] Brown 2009, p. 398.
[216] Service 2009, p. 404.
[217] Service 2009, p. 426.
[218] Sutela 1991, pp. 70–71.
[219] Sutela 1991, p. 71.
[220] Sutela 1991, p. 72.
[221] Bacon & Sandle 2002, p. 40.
[222] Western specialists believe that the net material product (NMP; Soviet version of gross national product (GNP)) contained distortions and could not accurately determine a country's economic growth; according to some, it greatly exaggerated growth. Because of this, several specialists created GNP figures to estimate Soviet growth and to compare Soviet growth with the growth of capitalist countries.<ref name="FOOTNOTEKotz & Weir35">Kotz & Weir, p. 35.
[223] Kotz & Weir, p. 39.
[224] Kotz & Weir, p. 40.
[225] Manufactured goods sector was worth 118 billion rubles in 1972 https//books.google.com
[226] Bacon & Sandle 2002, pp. 1–2.
[227] Bacon & Sandle 2002, p. 45.
[228] Service 2009, p. 416.
[229] Service 2009, p. 417.
[230] Dellenbrant 1986, p. 75.
[231] Dellenbrant 1986, p. 112.
[232] Wesson 1978, p. 248.
[233] Brown 2009, p. 460.
[234] Brown 2009, p. 399.
[235] Brown 2009, pp. 460–461.
[236] Brown 2009, p. 461.

[237] Brown 2009, pp. 462–463.
[238] Brown 2009, pp. 464–465.
[239] Brown 2009, p. 465.
[240] Lüthi 2008, p. 288.
[241] Lüthi 2008, p. 290.
[242] Radchenko 2009, p. 131.
[243] Radchenko 2009, pp. 132 and 134.
[244] Radchenko 2009, p. 144.
[245] Lüthi 2008, p. 293.
[246] Lüthi 2008, p. 294.
[247] Radchenko 2009, p. 145.
[248] Radchenko 2009, p. 146.
[249] Low 1976, p. 320.
[250] Low 1976, p. 321.
[251] Low 1976, p. 322.
[252] Service 2009, pp. 385–386.
[253] Service 2009, p. 385.
[254] Service 2009, p. 386.
[255] Service 2009, p. 387.
[256] Service 2009, p. 388.
[257] Brown 2009, p. 430.
[258] Brown 2009, p. 431.
[259] Brown 2009, p. 432.
[260] Brown 2009, p. 433.
[261] Brown 2009, p. 435.
[262] Brown 2009, p. 364.
[263] Brown 2009, p. 365.
[264] Donaldson 1981, p. 5.
[265] Donaldson 1981, p. 1.
[266] Donaldson 1981, p. 2.
[267] Donaldson 1981, p. 3.
[268] Donaldson 1981, p. 69.
[269] Loth 2002, pp. 85–86.
[270] Loth 2002, p. 86.
[271] Donaldson 1981, p. 255.
[272] Brown 2009, p. 349.
[273] Brown 2009, p. 351.
[274] Brown 2009, pp. 350–351.
[275] Brown 2009, p. 352.
[276] Brown 2009, pp. 352–353.
[277] Brown 2009, p. 354.
[278] Brown 2009, p. 355.
[279] Brown 2009, pp. 355–356.
[280] Kort 2010, p. 325.
[281] Kort 2010, pp. 325–326.
[282] Brown 2009, p. 412.
[283] Brown 2009, pp. 413–414.
[284] Brown 2009, p. 414.
[285] Kort 2010, p. 328.
[286] Kort 2010, p. 329.
[287] Bacon & Sandle 2002, p. 17.
[288] Sandle 1999, p. 337.
[289] Sandle 1999, p. 338.
[290] Sandle 1999, pp. 360–361.
[291] Brown 2009, p. 410.
[292] Brown 2009, p. 411.

293 Daniels 1998, p. 38.
294 Bacon & Sandle 2002, pp. 45–46.
295 Bacon & Sandle 2002, p. 47.
296 Bacon & Sandle 2002, p. 48.
297 Service 2009, p. 423.
298 Bacon & Sandle 2002, p. 28.
299 Service 2009, p. 409.
300 Service 2009, p. 418.
301 Service 2009, p. 421.
302 Service 2009, p. 422.
303 Service 2009, p. 427.
304 Kort 2010, p. 357.
305 Service 2009, p. 429.
306 Bacon & Sandle 2002, p. 1.
307 https://books.google.com/books?id=-KG1ALgx8rUC
308 //en.wikipedia.org/w/index.php?title=Template:History_of_the_Soviet_Union&action=edit
309 WorldBook online
310 (Edited version of a speech given November **, **** at the American Enterprise Institute.)
311 Honecker's West German Visit: Divided Meaning https://www.nytimes.com/1987/09/07/world/
honecker-s-west-german-visit-divided-meaning.html?pagewanted=all, *The New York Times*,
7 September 1987
312 S. Frederick Starriditor=S. Frederick Starr (2004).
[/books?id=GXj4a3gss8wC&pg=PA158#v=onepage&q&f=false Xinjiang: China's
Muslim Borderland] (illustrated ed.). M.E. Sharpe. p. 158.
313 *Voprosy Ekonomiki* (Moscow), no. 2 (1988), p. 79.
314 Российская история I Персонажи I Горбачев Михаил Сергеевич http://www.sgu.ru/rus_
hist/people/?pid=226
315 Acton, Edward,, (1995) *Russia, The Tsarist and Soviet Legacy*, Longmann Group Ltd (1995)
316 https://web.archive.org/web/20090722091512/http://www.aei.org/issue/25991
317 http://www.aei.org/issue/25991
318 http://www.brookings.edu/press/Books/2007/collapseofanempire.aspx
319 https://www.hoover.org/research/turning-points-ending-cold-war
320 http://www.bbc.co.uk/history/worldwars/coldwar/soviet_end_01.shtml
321 http://psi.ece.jhu.edu/~kaplan/IRUSS/BUK/GBARC/buk.html
322 http://repository.library.georgetown.edu/handle/10822/552542
323 https://www.library.georgetown.edu/digitalgeorgetown/krogh
324 http://www.4020.net/eastbloc/
325 http://simon31.narod.ru/syndromeofsocialism.htm
326 http://chnm.gmu.edu/1989/

Article Sources and Contributors

The sources listed for each article provide more detailed licensing information including the copyright status, the copyright owner, and the license conditions.

Soviet Union *Source:* https://en.wikipedia.org/w/index.php?oldid=854006634 *License:* Creative Commons Attribution-Share Alike 3.0 *Contributors:* 0211 SKDGAKUCHO, A.h. king, AMLNet49, Absolutelypuremilk, AdaCiccone, Aleksandr Grigoryev, AmazingJus, AmericanAir88, Anonymous427, ArticCynda, Asd1233456, BelAirWhale, Bmarotta8, Boeing720, Bokmanrocks01, Boop 1025, Brandmeister, Brianvan, Buhniania, C.J. Griffin, CASSIOPEIA, CapLiber, ClueBot NG, CommonsDelinker, Coolguy22468, Crawiki, Cskamoscow100, Davemck, DavidLynchFan19, Davide King, Dawnseeker2000, Derek R Bullamore, Diannaa, Dimadick, Dr.K., Eggishorn, ElpJo84, Erkinalp9035, Ernio48, EvilxFish, Finnusertop, Flix11, Fruitloop11, FuzhouneseMinpride, Galobtter, Goldsztajn, Gravuritas, Guy Macon, Hairygrim, HangingCurve, HeathIsling, HiLo48, Hoof Hearted, Hopquabian, Illegitimate Barrister, ImperatorPublius, JD Bigs, JDuggan101, JackofOz, Jacob Middleton, Jandalhandler, Jarble, Jax 0677, Jdaloner, Jeromi Mikhael, Jurassicjae, Ka24872482Akeakamai, Kaihsu, Kaiserkarl13, Karmanatory, Ke an, Khajidha, Kind Tennis Fan, Kurzon, Laszlo Panaflex, Laytar1, Leftwinguy92, Lopifalko, Lord Gorbachev, MB298, MadMax3249, Mandruss, Markg729, Matt Fitzpatrick, Max Arosev, Max.Moore, Mboyd71, Mega Fixer Lee, MereTechnicality, MouseCatDog, Moxy, Mr KEBAB, Mswarner2016, Mundopopular, My very best wishes, Neko-chan, NightShadow23, Oiygg, Omnipaedista, Onel5969, Openlydialectic, Oranjelo100, Otterstone, Paine Ellsworth, Paul2520, Perunslava, Pgan002, Piperh, Plumber, Polmande, Popcornduff, Power~enwiki, Ppdbt2001, Pwnerast, Redalert2fan, RhinoMind, Ricbep, Rjensen, Robert Brockway, Russian Ukraine, Ryan1783, SUM1, Sammartinlai, Sammimack, Schwede66, Shadowzpaev, ShakespeareFan00, Sjö, Sortsdam, SpanishSnake, Ssbbplayer, St.nerol, Starwarsalp, Stephen Hui, Strikerman, Suhd, Sunshineisles2, Supreme Dragon, Tónis, TU-nor, Takayazhe, The Professor (Time Lord), TheCrazyWhovian, TheFreeWorld, TheGeneralUser, Timmyshin, Tobby72, TompaDompa, Torchiest, Tyvic, Uglemat, Uhj122, Ulscfd, Ukrainetz1, Vanamonde93, Vanjagenije, Vitopavlovivit, Vmavanti, Wakari07, Wrestlingring, XanaduZepp2112, Xenophrenic, Xindeho, Xx236, Yekshemesh, Yggdrasilsroot, Уⲥⲩⲗⲁⲛⲓⲁ, 九議千九公主 1

History of Soviet Russia and the Soviet Union (1917–27) *Source:* https://en.wikipedia.org/w/index.php?oldid=854093129 *License:* Creative Commons Attribution-Share Alike 3.0 *Contributors:* 2D, AbigailAbernathy, AdaCiccone, Aivazovsky, Aktron, Aleksandr Grigoryev, Alexf, Altenmann, Avicennasis, Baddady12, Battlemonk, Bazonka, BigrTex, Billinghurst, Biruitorul, Bluemoose, Bobet, Brad E. Williams, Brutannica, CLCStudent, Carrite, Caseyrd1, Cattus, Chris the speller, ChristianCommunist, ClueBot NG, Cmapm, ComradeRyan, Cxdh, DDima, DHN, DHN-bot~enwiki, DVdm, Dave Dial, Dewritech, DI2000, DonnieSwanson, Dr zEllow, Dthomsen8, Duja, Dzied Bulbash, Edward, Eopsid, Epozokatrib, Everyking, Finnusertop, HaeB, HalfShadow, Hayfordoleary, Hedviberit, Hmains, Hydrogen Iodide, Imagine Wizard, Iridescent, Iritakamas, J.delanoy, J36miles, JHunter1, Jane McCann, Jaro.p~enwiki, Jim1138, John Maynard Friedman, John of Reading, JorisvS, Juliancolton, Just a guy from the KP, Kahkonen, Khazar2, Kingfish, Koko-Phantom, Kwertii, LWG, Larry Mafi, Ledmonkey, LilHelpa, Logical2u, Loginnigol, Lycurgus, MTSbot~enwiki, MacGyverMagic, Magna khan, Magog the Ogre, Mark Schierbecker, Materialscientist, Mr legumoto, Muhends, Mzajac, Notwist, ONEder Boy, Ohconfucius, Optichan, Pat Payne, Pharmakon, Phl3djo, Polly Tunnel, RandomCritic, Rebrane, RexNL, Rhinestone K, Rich Farmbrough, Rjensen, Rjwilmsi, Robotman1974, Ron2, Schgooda, Schumin-Web, Seryo93, Seth Whales, SilverStar, SnoozeKing, Spyder53Part, Steven Crossin, Sundostund, Tawkerbot2, Tehvata~enwiki, Templarion, Tgrain, The Illusive Man, The smart one27, TheFreeWorld, The Vault, Themightyquill, Tladendo, Trezil, Tulandro, Tutmosis, Valip, Vary, VolatileChemical, Wiki alf, Wrestlingring, Wywin, Yopie, YoursT, Zachlipton, Zzauzz, PKII, 225 anonymous edits 71

History of the Soviet Union (1927–1953) *Source:* https://en.wikipedia.org/w/index.php?oldid=852721839 *License:* Creative Commons Attribution-Share Alike 3.0 *Contributors:* 0x5849857, 1990'sguy, AbidinCan, AdaCiccone, Alansohn, Allens, Altenmann, Ariya Shajii, Armenius vambery, Arthur Rubin, Belchman, Bender235, Beta7, Bobanni, Caula, Chase me ladies, I'm the Cavalry, ChezwickKolfanz, Chris the speller, Citation bot 1, ClueBot NG, Colonies Chris, CommonsDelinker, DDima, Davenoon, David Schaich, Dawnseeker2000, Dewritech, Dig under deep, Doh5678, Duomer60, Drewmutt, Ducknish, DuncanHill, Edward321, Epicgenius, Eumolpo, Everyking, Flyte35, Golodg, Good Olfactory, Ground Zero, Gujuguy, Gulumeemee, Hamish59, Hmains, Hmainsbot1, InedibleHulk, Iritakamas, Italia2006, J Milburn, JIK1975, JWNoctis, Jamesmcmahon0, Jkeaton, Jncraton, Jniech, Jonesey95, Just Chilling, KConWiki, Kevlar67, Khazar2, King Vic 2, Koavf, KorinoChikara, Kubasrock, LokiiT, Mack2, Mash99, Materialscientist, Miacek, Michaelwuzthere, Mild Bill Hiccup, Mosedschurte, Mycos, NawlinWiki, Neznakom, Nightenbelle, Nug, Onel5969, Orphan Wiki, OwenBlacker, Paul Siebert, PhnomPencil, Piotrus, Polly Tunnel, QwertyxP2000, R'n'B, Radhaknkr, Rcsprinter123, Redthoreau, Rhinestone K, Rjensen, Rjwilmsi, RoboticLasers, Rocketrod1960, Ronhjones, Sadads, Sakura Cartelet, Sbabones, Sean Heron, Senjuto, Seth Whales, Shellwood, Skamecrazy123, Sole Soul, Sundostund, Super48paul, Surv1v411st, Thismightbezach, Timmyshin, Tladendo, Toccata quarta, Toobner2001, Topbanana, Trappist the monk, Trust Is All You Need, Tulandro, Tungsten, Uglemat, VVPushkin, Vagr7, Vecrumba, VeryCrocker, Victor falk, Vlad fedorov, Volunteer Marek, Wavelength, Whiteroll, Widefox, Woohhoo, Wrestlingring, Xx236, Yourmom69696, Yvwv, Тиверополник, 158 anonymous edits 89

History of the Soviet Union (1953–64) *Source:* https://en.wikipedia.org/w/index.php?oldid=853465911 *License:* Creative Commons Attribution-Share Alike 3.0 *Contributors:* 172, Aaaaaaannddjdjewnw, Abdulrahimb, Abune, AdaCiccone, Aetil, Afrique, Aivazovsky, Aksi great, Ale700, Alexander Dubois, Altenmann, Andrevan, Andris, Asharidu, AvicAWB, Bahamat, Bert Schlossberg, Bob the Wikipedian, BotMultichill, Brockert, C:d, CJK, Chris the speller, Citanuleht, ClueBot NG, ComradeWiki, CredoFromStart, Csamuel, Curpsbot-unicodify, Czalex, DARTH SIDIOUS 2, DJ Sturm, DabMachine, Damiens.rf, DarkLink, DarkThought, Davenoon, Deb, Deor, Digwuren, Dlyons493, DocWatson42, EdmundT, Elsmlie, EncephalonSeven, Everyking, Formeruser-81, Fvw, G-Man, Gianttrombone, Good Olfactory, Goudzovski, Ground Zero, Halgin, HarryHenryGebel, Hayfordoleary, Hmains, Humus sapiens, Iridescent, Iritakamas, Irpen, Jeepday, JiMidnite, Jkelly, Jn52lee, Joseph Solis in Australia, Joy, Jprg1966, Jsan, Jtmichcock, KapilTagore, Kingfish, Kjetil r, Knowledgebycoop, Konstable, Krenair, LOL, Leandrod, Leeswoo00, LeoO3, LilHelpa, Little Mountain 5, Lovok Sovok, MDfoo, MaGioZal, Maphisto86, Marcocapelle, Marknew, MaxBech1975, Maxaf, Maxim, Medhat moussa, Mhazard9, Mike2000~enwiki, Mister X, Modster, Mzajac, Narky Blert, Nikai, Nikodemos, Nishkid64, Onopearls, PeR, Pearle, Pegship, Pennst110, Peripitus, Peyre, Piotrus, Postdlf, PottersWood, Producercunningham, Pt314156, Quadruplum, RFBailey, Radhaknkr, RadioKirk, Randy Kryn, Rbonvall, RedWolf, Rjwilmsi, Robth, Romanm, Rufferto, Sam Korn, SchuminWeb, Severo, Signinman, Signinmans, Silver hr, Silverback, Slashme, Slyguy, Snowdog, Steveshelokhonov, Stinkehund, Sundostund, Superzohar, TAnthony, TDC, Tda 666, Template namespace initialisation script, Terbayang, Themightyquill, Torn, Tommy2010, Toobner2001, Trust Is All You Need, Tulandro, Valip, VeryVerily, Warsmith, Waxwing slain, Wordisample, Wrestlingring, Xezbeth, Тиверополник, בורד"אלק, 173 anonymous edits 121

History of the Soviet Union (1964–82) *Source:* https://en.wikipedia.org/w/index.php?oldid=849711284 *License:* Creative Commons Attribution-Share Alike 3.0 *Contributors:* AdaCiccone, AjaxSmack, Altenmann, BethNaught, Bjf, Bte99, ChezwickKolfanz, Cinnamullma, CommonsDelinker, Comrade Wiki, ComradeWiki, Cplakidas, Dcirovic, Dthomsen8, Firefly4342, Frietjes, Gaius Cornelius, Gob Lofa, GoingBatty, Good Olfactory, Ground Zero, Hedwig in Washington, Ianblair23, Incnis Mrsi, Jarry1250, John of Reading, Kbolino, Khazar2, Kwamikagami, LittleJsayH, Marcocapelle, Materialscientist, Miacek, Mikeblas, Mogism, Moorlock, Nightflyer, Nyttend, Pax85, Polly Tunnel, Rjwilmsi, Runner1928, ShelfSkewed, Sundostund, Superzohar, Suryawarman1950, TheFreeWorld, Three-quarter-ten, Trust Is All You Need, Wavelength, Whiteroll, Woohookitty, Wrestlingring, Алексей Галушкин, Тиверополник, 26 anonymous edits 139

History of the Soviet Union (1982–91) *Source:* https://en.wikipedia.org/w/index.php?oldid=849712020 *License:* Creative Commons Attribution-Share Alike 3.0 *Contributors:* 1990'sguy, Ad2626, 7Sidz, A little insignificant, Abdulrahimb, Ace of Raves, AdaCiccone, Afrique, AjaxSmack, Al83tito, Alaney2k, Altenmann, Amorymeltzer, Balph Eubank, Basawala, Bender235, Bert Schlossberg, BrianDohm2, C.J. Griffin, CarlGGHamilton, Calemur, Citation bot 1, ClueBot NG, Comrade Wiki, ComradeWiki, Cory11m, Courcelles, Cybercobra, DARTH SIDIOUS 2, DDima, Deerfield66, Darkwind, Dawnseeker2000, Denisarona, Dewritech, Drbrezmjev, Dsp13, Dthomsen8, Dzlinker, Edward, Ejensyd, Epbr123, Eskandarany, Excirial, Faizan, Favonian, FlieGerFaUstMe262, Flyte35, Gary, Ginsuloft, Gire 3pich2005, Good Olfactory, Ground Zero, Hmains, Illegitimate Barrister, InverseHypercube, Iritakamas, Ja 62, Jc86035, Jean.l.spear, Jim1138, Jodon1971, Jogundas Armaitis, Jpwhitney, Jschnur, KConWiki, Kintetsubuffalo, Klu, Kmw2700, Kris159, Kuralyov, Kuru, LOL, Leutha, Lovok Sovok, Lugia2453, MAXXX-309, Macogle, Magnazeh, Marcocapelle, Materialscientist, Matěj Grabovský, Mboverload, Morning277, Mursel, Mythbusterlover, NewHikaru07, Newone, NicatronTg, Niceguyedc, Noblerinthemind, Noyster, Ocaasi, Ohconfucius, Orenburg1, Oxana879, Penguinfilter, Peyre, Ptbotgourou, Quark1005, RA0808, Rhatsa26X, Rich Farmbrough, Rjensen, Russavia, Sader, Seaphoto, Sha-H-Ire, Skizzik, Slon02, Smalljim, Sundostund, TAnthony, Tassedethe, Tide rolls, Tommy2010, Trappist the monk, Triggerhippie4, Trust Is All You Need, Tulandro, Tuscumbia, Unedel, Usb10, Valenciano, Wavelength, Wiki id2, Wolfkeeper, Wrestlingring, ҮHYH, Σ, Тиверополник, דוד ש, 246 anonymous edits 181

Image Sources, Licenses and Contributors

The sources listed for each image provide more detailed licensing information including the copyright status, the copyright owner, and the license conditions.

Image *Source:* https://en.wikipedia.org/w/index.php?title=File:Padlock-silver.svg *Contributors:* AzaToth, BotMultichill, BotMultichillT, Gurch, Jarekt, Kallerna, Multichill, Perhelion, Rd232, Riana, Sarang, Siebrand, Steinsplitter, 4 anonymous edits ... 1

Image *Source:* https://en.wikipedia.org/w/index.php?title=File:Flag_of_the_Soviet_Union.svg *License:* Public Domain *Contributors:* A1, Ahmadi∼commonswiki, Akihiro Nagai 2, Alex Smotrov, Alvis Jean, Art-top, BagnoHax, Beetsyres34, Benzoyl, Brandmeister∼commonswiki, Cathy Richards, Counny, Cycn, Daphne Lantier, Denniss, Dynamicwork, ELeschev, Endless-tripper, Ericmetro, EugeneZelenko, F l a n k e r, FDRMRZUSA, Fred J, FreshCorp619, Fry1989, G.dallorto, Garynysmon∼commonswiki, Herbythyme, Homo lupus, Illegitimate Barrister, Jake Wartenberg, Li-sung, Loic26, MaggotMaster, Michaelversatile, MrAustin390, Ms2ger, Nightstallion, Palosirkka, Patrickpedia, PeaceKeeper97, Pianist, R-41∼commonswiki, RainbowSilver2ndBackup, Rainforest tropicana, S.A. Julio (old), Sammimack, Sangjinhwa, Sarang, Sebyugez, Skeezix1000, Solbris, Storkk, Str4nd, Tabasco∼commonswiki, ThomasPusch, Tiven2240, Toben, Twilight Chill, User000name, Xgeorg, Zscout370, Илья Драконов, Полиционер, Ранко Николић, Серп, Тоны4, ,ייהל'ז'ושמר 65 anonymous edits ... 1

Image *Source:* https://en.wikipedia.org/w/index.php?title=File:State_Emblem_of_the_Soviet_Union.svg *License:* Public Domain *Contributors:* User:C records ... 1

Image *Source:* https://en.wikipedia.org/w/index.php?title=File:Gimn_Sovetskogo_Soyuza_(1944_Stalinist_lyrics).oga *License:* Public Domain *Contributors:* Red Army choirs ... 2

Image *Source:* https://en.wikipedia.org/w/index.php?title=File:Gimn_Sovetskogo_Soyuza_(1977_Vocal).oga *License:* Public Domain *Contributors:* Alex Bakharev, Georg I.Andreev, Illegitimate Barrister, Jusjih, Marcus Cyron, Pedro8790, Siebrand, Xiengyod∼commonswiki, Zscout370, 3 anonymous edits ... 2

Image *Source:* https://en.wikipedia.org/w/index.php?title=File:Union_of_Soviet_Socialist_Republics_(orthographic_projection).svg *License:* GNU Free Documentation License *Contributors:* Ssolbergj ... 2

Image *Source:* https://en.wikipedia.org/w/index.php?title=File:Flag_RSFSR_1918.svg *Contributors:* - ... 3

Image *Source:* https://en.wikipedia.org/w/index.php?title=File:Flag_of_Transcaucasian_SFSR.svg *License:* Public Domain *Contributors:* Aivazovsky ... 3

Image *Source:* https://en.wikipedia.org/w/index.php?title=File:Flag_of_the_Ukrainian_SSR_(1919-1929).svg *Contributors:* - ... 3

Image *Source:* https://en.wikipedia.org/w/index.php?title=File:Flag_of_the_Byelorussian_SSR_(1919).svg *Contributors:* - ... 3

Image *Source:* https://en.wikipedia.org/w/index.php?title=File:Flag_of_the_Bukharan_People's_Soviet_Republic.svg *License:* Public Domain *Contributors:* Mysid ... 3

Image *Source:* https://en.wikipedia.org/w/index.php?title=File:Flag_of_Khiva_1920-1923.svg *License:* Public Domain *Contributors:* Aivazovsky∼commonswiki, Benzoyl, Cycn, Foroa, Homo lupus, NuclearVacuum, Primus1x, Sergey Rufanov, TRAJAN 117, Torsch, 2 anonymous edits 3

Image *Source:* https://en.wikipedia.org/w/index.php?title=File:Flag_of_Estonia.svg *License:* Public Domain *Contributors:* Originally drawn by User:SKopp. Blue colour changed by User:PeepP to match the image at 3

Image *Source:* https://en.wikipedia.org/w/index.php?title=File:Flag_of_Latvia.svg *License:* Public Domain *Contributors:* Anime Addict AA, Cathy Richards, Ciervo258, Common Good, Cycn, Dark Eagle, David1010, Edgars2007, Editor at Large, Fred J, Fry1989, Homo lupus, IvanOS, Kalnroze, Klemen Kocjancic, Ludger1961, MAXXX-309, Mattes, Ninane, OAlexander∼commonswiki, RainbowSilver2ndBackup, Renessaince, Ricordisamoa, Rocket000, SKopp, Sarang, TFerenczy, V. Turchaninov, Wester, Zscout370, 12 anonymous edits ... 3

Image *Source:* https://en.wikipedia.org/w/index.php?title=File:Flag_of_Lithuania_(1918-1940).svg *License:* Public Domain *Contributors:* Altales Teriadem, Andreyyshore, Anime Addict AA, Conti, Erlenmeyer, GiW, Marcus Cyron, Sangjinhwa, Ранко Николић, 1 anonymous edits ... 3

Image *Source:* https://en.wikipedia.org/w/index.php?title=File:Flag_of_Romania.svg *Contributors:* AdiJapan ... 3

Image *Source:* https://en.wikipedia.org/w/index.php?title=File:Flag_of_the_Tuvan_People's_Republic_(1943-1944).svg *License:* Public Domain *Contributors:* , vectorization by Orange Tuesday ... 3

Image *Source:* https://en.wikipedia.org/w/index.php?title=File:Flag_of_Russia_(1991-1993).svg *Contributors:* - ... 3

Image *Source:* https://en.wikipedia.org/w/index.php?title=File:Flag_of_Ukraine.svg *License:* Public Domain *Contributors:* Ahonc, Akhristov, Albedo-ukr, Andrew J.Kurbiko, Antonanton∼commonswiki, Chase I, Cycn, Denelson83, Diánmondin, Dzordzm, Fred J, GoldenRainbow, Homo lupus, Ilyaroz, IvanOS, Jdx, Jon Harald Søby, Justass, Klemen Kocjancic, Kwasura, LIsnykMaria, Mattes, Maximaximax, Mormegil, Neq00, Odder, PsichoPuzo, Sangjinhwa, Sarang, SeNeKa∼commonswiki, Serhio∼commonswiki, SiBr4, Steinsplitter, TFerenczy, Tat1642, User000name, Yann, Zcout1993, ZooFari, Zscout370, Живот Олегович, МЕИ, Ранко Николић, علی المزارقه, 夢蝶葬花 , 15 anonymous edits ... 3

Image *Source:* https://en.wikipedia.org/w/index.php?title=File:Flag_of_Belarus_(1991-1995).svg *Contributors:* - ... 3

Image *Source:* https://en.wikipedia.org/w/index.php?title=File:Flag_of_Armenia.svg *License:* Public Domain *Contributors:* Alex Great, Cathy Richards, ChongDae, Cycn, Céréales Killer, Denelson83, Enbéká, Fail Khasay, Fry1989, Gikü, Golden Bosnian Lily, GoldenRainbow, Hayk, Hedwig in Washington, Homo lupus, Hosmich, Ilfga, Klemen Kocjancic, Mattes, Mikewazhere, Mikrobølgeovn, Mogelzahn, Neq00, O (bot), Prev, SKopp, Sarang, SiBr4, Sir Iain, Smaug the Golden, TFCforever, TFerenczy, Takahara Osaka, ThomasPusch, TigerTjäder, UberHalogen, Valentinian, Vzb83∼commonswiki, Zscout370, 10 anonymous edits ... 3

Image *Source:* https://en.wikipedia.org/w/index.php?title=File:Flag_of_Azerbaijan.svg *License:* Public Domain *Contributors:* SKopp and others 3

Image *Source:* https://en.wikipedia.org/w/index.php?title=File:Flag_of_Georgia_(1990-2004).svg *Contributors:* - ... 3

Image *Source:* https://en.wikipedia.org/w/index.php?title=File:Flag_of_the_Kazakh_SSR_(reverse).svg *License:* Public Domain *Contributors:* User:Volks Das Auto ... 3

Image *Source:* https://en.wikipedia.org/w/index.php?title=File:Flag_of_Kyrgyzstan_(1991-1992).svg *License:* Public Domain *Contributors:* User:Urmas ... 3

Image *Source:* https://en.wikipedia.org/w/index.php?title=File:Flag_of_Lithuania_1989-2004.svg *Contributors:* - ... 3

Image *Source:* https://en.wikipedia.org/w/index.php?title=File:Flag_of_Moldova.svg *License:* Public Domain *Contributors:* User:Nameneko ... 3

Image *Source:* https://en.wikipedia.org/w/index.php?title=File:Flag_of_Tajikistan_1991-1992.svg *License:* Public Domain *Contributors:* Alkari, Cathy Richards, Erlenmeyer, Fry1989, Homo lupus, Man77, Sangjinhwa, StalwartUK, Tcfc2349, Urmas ... 3

Image *Source:* https://en.wikipedia.org/w/index.php?title=File:Flag_of_the_Turkmen_SSR_(reverse).svg *License:* Public Domain *Contributors:* Amit6 ... 3

Image *Source:* https://en.wikipedia.org/w/index.php?title=File:Flag_of_Uzbekistan.svg *License:* Public Domain *Contributors:* User:Zscout370 . 3

Image *Source:* https://en.wikipedia.org/w/index.php?title=File:Loudspeaker.svg *License:* Public Domain *Contributors:* User:Dbenbenn, User:Optimager, User:Tsca, User:Dbenbenn, User:Optimager, User:Tsca, User:Dbenbenn, User:Optimager, User:Tsca ... 4

Image *Source:* https://en.wikipedia.org/w/index.php?title=File:Coat_of_Arms_of_the_Russian_Federation.svg *License:* Creative Commons Attribution-Sharealike 2.0 *Contributors:* Е. Ухналёв // Федеральный конституционный закон от 25.12.2000 г. № 2-ФКЗ «О Государственном гербе Российской Федерации» ... 6

Image *Source:* https://en.wikipedia.org/w/index.php?title=File:Flag_of_Russia.svg *License:* Public Domain *Contributors:* Anomie, Jo-Jo Eumerus, Zscout370 ... 7

Figure 1 *Source:* https://en.wikipedia.org/w/index.php?title=File:19191107-lenin_second_anniversary_october_revolution_moscow.jpg *License:* Public Domain *Contributors:* L.Y. Leonidov ... 14

Figure 2 *Source:* https://en.wikipedia.org/w/index.php?title=File:Soviet_Union_-_Russian_SFSR_(1922).svg *License:* Creative Commons Attribution-Sharealike 3.0 *Contributors:* Soviet_Union_-_Transcaucasia.svg: Shadowxfox derivative work: TarzanASG ... 15

Figure 3 *Source:* https://en.wikipedia.org/w/index.php?title=File:Soviet_Union_-_Russian_SFSR_(1936).svg *Contributors:* User:Shadowxfox 16

Image *Source:* https://en.wikipedia.org/w/index.php?title=File:Voroshilov,_Molotov,_Stalin,_with_Nikolai_Yezhov.jpg *License:* Public Domain *Contributors:* Ajfweb, Alonso de Mendoza, Butko, DIREKTOR, Dencey, Eusebius, Gkml, Ingolfson, Jdx, Jonkerz, Josve05a, Kl833x9∼commonswiki, Lklundin, Mtsmallwood, Mutter Erde, Rowanwindwhistler, Starscream, Stolbovsky, Svajcr, WhisperToMe, Wieralee, Yann, Zielniok, 2 anonymous edits 17

Image *Source:* https://en.wikipedia.org/w/index.php?title=File:The_Commissar_Vanishes_2.jpg *License:* Public Domain *Contributors:* 17

Figure 4 *Source:* https://en.wikipedia.org/w/index.php?title=File:"Strengthen_working_discipline_in_collective_farms"_–_Uzbek,_Tashkent,_1933_(Mardjani).jpg *License:* Public Domain *Contributors:* Butko, Cekli829, Watchduck ... 19

Figure 5 *Source:* https://en.wikipedia.org/w/index.php?title=File:Korolev_posle_aresta_1938.jpg *License:* Public Domain *Contributors:* Diezeitung, Ivtorov, J824h, SpaceRu ... 20

Figure 6 *Source:* https://en.wikipedia.org/w/index.php?title=File:RIAN_archive_44732_Soviet_soldiers_attack_house.jpg *Contributors:* Zelma / Георгий Зельма ... 21

Image *Source:* https://en.wikipedia.org/w/index.php?title=File:PD-icon.svg *License:* Public Domain *Contributors:* Alex.muller, Anomie, Anonymous Dissident, CBM, Jo-Jo Eumerus, MBisanz, PBS, Quadell, Rocket000, Strangerer, Timotheus Canens, 1 anonymous edits 68

Image *Source:* https://en.wikipedia.org/w/index.php?title=File:Gnome-globe.svg *Contributors:* Abu badali~commonswiki, Adambro, Cathy Richards, Lijealso, Odder, Perhelion, Reseletti, Seahen, Steinsplitter, Thibaut120094, Thomas Linard, Tkgd2007, Tulsi Bhagat, 4 anonymous edits ... 69

Figure 43 *Source:* https://en.wikipedia.org/w/index.php?title=File:Lenin_and_stalin.jpg *Contributors:* Alex Bakharev, Aschroet, Augiasstallputzer~commonswiki, Before My Ken, Bestalex, Beyond My Ken, Csman, Diwas, Docu, Dzięcioł 3, Edward, File Upload Bot (Magnus Manske), Infrogmation, Jonkerz, KOKUYO, Kl833x9~commonswiki, Materialscientist, PanchoS, Shakko, Waldemar~commonswiki, 6 anonymous edits 72

Figure 44 *Source:* https://en.wikipedia.org/w/index.php?title=File:Russian_Revolutionary_Poster,_Red_Cavalry.jpg *License:* Public Domain *Contributors:* According to contemporary art expert Dmitry Gorbachov, this poster belongs to a series created in Kiev in 1920 by Boris 79

Figure 45 *Source:* https://en.wikipedia.org/w/index.php?title=File:Rubel_1924.png *License:* Public Domain *Contributors:* User:Jaro.p~commonswiki 81

Figure 46 *Source:* https://en.wikipedia.org/w/index.php?title=File:Tscherwonetz.jpg *License:* Public Domain *Contributors:* Cirt, Gumruch, Jaro.p~commonswiki, Kaganer, Karl432, MGA73bot2, Russian Rocky, Vaga-am, Winterheart, Викимонетчик, 2 anonymous edits 82

Figure 47 *Source:* https://en.wikipedia.org/w/index.php?title=File:McCormick-Deering_15-30_The_First_Tractor_Propaganda_Shot.jpg *Contributors:* Armenius vambery 96

Figure 48 *Source:* https://en.wikipedia.org/w/index.php?title=File:Smoke_of_chimneys_is_the_breath_of_Soviet_Russia.jpg *License:* Public Domain *Contributors:* Alan Liefting, Alex Bakharev, Butko, Edward, FrancisTyers~commonswiki, Humus sapiens~commonswiki, Morgan Riley, Odder, Russavia, Shakko, SunOfErat, Trilliumz 97

Figure 49 *Source:* https://en.wikipedia.org/w/index.php?title=File:State_Emblem_of_the_Soviet_Union.svg *License:* Public Domain *Contributors:* User:C records 98

Figure 50 *Source:* https://en.wikipedia.org/w/index.php?title=File:Armia_Czerwona,_Wehrmacht_22.09.1939_wspólna_parada.jpg *License:* Creative Commons Attribution-Sharealike 3.0 Germany *Contributors:* A1, Andros64, BD2412, Bundesarchiv-B6, Colchicum~commonswiki, Coldplay Expert, Cucumber, Drdoht, Duch, EWriter, Gkml, Gorgo, Helgi-S, Jarekt, Jianhui67, JotaCartas, Kameraad Pjotr, Kl833x9~commonswiki, Kozolup, Lycaon, Matiia, Mike.lifeguard, Mogelzahn, Nemo5576, Nxx~commonswiki, Piotrus, Randbewohner, Sergkarman, Tryphon, Väsk, Wolfmann, 9 anonymous edits 103

Figure 51 *Source:* https://en.wikipedia.org/w/index.php?title=File:On_the_eve.jpg *License:* Public Domain *Contributors:* Author unknown. . 105

Figure 52 *Source:* https://en.wikipedia.org/w/index.php?title=File:EasternBloc_BorderChange38-48.svg *License:* GNU Free Documentation License *Contributors:* Mosedschurte 109

Figure 53 *Source:* https://en.wikipedia.org/w/index.php?title=File:Soviet_empire_1960.png *License:* GNU Free Documentation License *Contributors:* User:MaGioZal 126

Image *Source:* https://en.wikipedia.org/w/index.php?title=File:Symbol_support_vote.svg *License:* Public Domain *Contributors:* Anomie, Fastily, Jo-Jo Eumerus 139

Image *Source:* https://en.wikipedia.org/w/index.php?title=File:1977_CPA_4774(Cutted).jpg *License:* Public Domain *Contributors:* Post of the Soviet Union, designer Ye. Aniskin; scanned and processed by Andrei Sdobnikov, cropped by DanielTM 143

Figure 54 *Source:* https://en.wikipedia.org/w/index.php?title=File:Glassboro-meeting1967.jpg *License:* Public Domain *Contributors:* Bossanoven, Clusternote, Governor Jerchel, Jatkins, Leppus, Maks Stirlitz, Trust Is All You Need 144

Figure 55 *Source:* https://en.wikipedia.org/w/index.php?title=File:1988_CPA_6001.jpg *License:* Public Domain *Contributors:* Scanned and processed by Mariluna 147

Figure 56 *Source:* https://en.wikipedia.org/w/index.php?title=File:Mikhail_Gorbachev_1985_Geneva_Summit.jpg *License:* Public Domain *Contributors:* White House Photo Office 149

Figure 57 *Source:* https://en.wikipedia.org/w/index.php?title=File:1977_CPA_4774.jpg *License:* Public Domain *Contributors:* Post of the Soviet Union, designer Ye. Aniskin 151

Figure 58 *Source:* https://en.wikipedia.org/w/index.php?title=File:1981_CPA_5216.jpg *License:* Public Domain *Contributors:* Scanned and processed by A. Sdobnikov 152

Figure 59 *Source:* https://en.wikipedia.org/w/index.php?title=File:Kosygin_at_the_Glassboro_Summit.jpg *License:* Public Domain *Contributors:* Apollo1758, Bossanoven, Clusternote, Docu, Governor Jerchel, Trust Is All You Need 156

Figure 60 *Source:* https://en.wikipedia.org/w/index.php?title=File:Andrej_Gromyko_1978.jpg *License:* Public Domain *Contributors:* White House Staff Photographer 157

Figure 61 *Source:* https://en.wikipedia.org/w/index.php?title=File:Carter_Brezhnev_sign_SALT_II.jpg *License:* Public Domain *Contributors:* Photo Credit: Bill Fitz-Patrick 158

Figure 62 *Source:* https://en.wikipedia.org/w/index.php?title=File:Kossygin_Glassboro.jpg *License:* Public Domain *Contributors:* Apollo1758, Bossanoven, Colchicum~commonswiki, POY~commonswiki, Trust Is All You Need 160

Figure 63 *Source:* https://en.wikipedia.org/w/index.php?title=File:Bundesarchiv_Bild_183-F0417-0001-011,_Berlin,_VII._SED-Parteitag,_Eröffnung.jpg *License:* Creative Commons Attribution-Sharealike 3.0 Germany *Contributors:* Boston9, BotMultichill, Fredy.00, Gumruch, Janbies, Ludmila Pilecka, Martin H., Materialscientist, Mbdortmund, Trust Is All You Need, Yzarg, Барвенковский 162

Figure 64 *Source:* https://en.wikipedia.org/w/index.php?title=File:Kosygin_and_Ceausescu.jpg *Contributors:* not credited 163

Figure 65 *Source:* https://en.wikipedia.org/w/index.php?title=File:Stamps_of_Germany_(DDR)_1972,_MiNr_1760.jpg *License:* Public Domain *Contributors:* Hochgeladen und Bearbeitet von ~Nightflyer (talk) 09:54, 20 February 2011 (UTC) 164

Figure 66 *Source:* https://en.wikipedia.org/w/index.php?title=File:Freundschaftsvertrag_Kossygin_al-Bakr_1972.jpg *License:* Public Domain *Contributors:* Roxanna, Trust Is All You Need 166

Figure 67 *Source:* https://en.wikipedia.org/w/index.php?title=File:Pahlavi_meets_Brezhnev_in_1970.jpg *License:* Public Domain *Contributors:* Americophile, BotAdventures, Brejnev, Butko, Chyah, Ervaude, Foroa, Idranstel, Infrogmation, Klemen Kocjancic, Materialscientist, Rrohdin, Wvk, Yzarg, 2 anonymous edits 167

Figure 68 *Source:* https://en.wikipedia.org/w/index.php?title=File:RIAN_archive_535377_Dancing_during_break_between_sessions_of_19th_Komsomol_congress.jpg *Contributors:* Boris Kaufman / Борис Кауфман 172

Figure 69 *Source:* https://en.wikipedia.org/w/index.php?title=File:Nicolai_Podgorny.jpg *License:* Creative Commons Attribution-Sharealike 3.0 Germany *Contributors:* Bundesarchiv_Bild_183-B0114-0010-038, Berlin, VI._SED-Parteitag,_Ulbricht,_Chruschtschow.jpg: Junge, Peter Heinz derivat 174

Figure 70 *Source:* https://en.wikipedia.org/w/index.php?title=File:RIAN_archive_696233_Border_guard_Nikolai_Zaitsev_is_inducted_into_Komsomol.jpg *Contributors:* Lev Oustinov / Лев Устинов 176

Figure 71 *Source:* https://en.wikipedia.org/w/index.php?title=File:Soviet_Union_Administrative_Divisions_1989.jpg *License:* Public Domain *Contributors:* Alexius08, Boivie, Electionworld, Illegitimate Barrister, Russian Rocky, Shadowxfox 192

License

Index

Expatriate, 95

Fairleigh Dickinson Univ Press, 178
Fall of Saigon, 11, 73, 91, 123, 141, 183
Fall of the Wall, 12, 74, 92, 124, 142, 184
Farah Pahlavi, 167
Fascism, 36, 102
Fatty liver disease, 113
February Revolution, 13, 14, 76
Federal government of the United States, 157
Federalism, 2
Federal republic, 2
Federation, 4
Fidel Castro, 33, 156
Financial crisis, 154
Finland, 8, 20
Finnish Declaration of Independence, 15
First All-Union Census of the Soviet Union, 54
First Deputy Premier of the Soviet Union, 145, 155
First five-year plan, 17, 49
First World, 46–48, 156, 158, 160, 162, 168, 170, 175
Five-year plans for the national economy of the Soviet Union, 4, 16, 39, 45
Flag of Russia, 29
Flag of Soviet Union, 1
Forced labor in the Soviet Union, 4
Foreign trade of the Soviet Union, 45
Formosa Strait, 131
Four Policemen, 21
France, 77
Francoist Spain, 19
Franklin D. Roosevelt, 22
Freedom of expression, 61
Free market, 197
Free trade, 44
Free World, 116
French Indochina, 116
French Third Republic, 102
Friedrich Engels, 76
Fyodor Kulakov, 150
Fyodorov Eye Microsurgery Complex, 57

General line of the party, 85
General of the army (USSR), 105
General Secretary, 164
General Secretary of the Communist Party of the Soviet Union, 2, 17, 37, 84, 125, 143, 145, 156, 165, 185
Geneva, 102, 190
Geneva Accords (1988), 191
Gennady Voronov, 148
Gennady Zyuganov, 197
Genrikh Yagoda, 101
Geoffrey Hosking, 18

Geography of the Soviet Union, 13, 76, 93, 124, 142, 184
George F. Kennan, 115
George H. W. Bush, 34
Georgia (country), 3
Georgian Affair, 7
Georgian language, 8
Georgians, 54
Georgian Soviet Socialist Republic, 29, 41, 42, 54, 173, 176
Georgi Malenkov, 125
Georgy Arbatov, 147
Georgy Chicherin, 32
Georgy Lvov, 77
Georgy Malenkov, 13, 23, 39, 75, 93, 112, 124, 133, 142, 184
Georgy Zhukov, 105, 106, 133
Gerald Ford, 33, 157
German–Soviet Axis talks, 20
German–Soviet Commercial Agreement (1940), 20, 104
German mistreatment of Soviet prisoners of war, 21
German reunification, 12, 74, 92, 124, 142, 184
Gerontocracy, 144, 149
Gini ratio, 31, 197
Glasnost, 5, 11, 26, 61, 74, 91, 124, 142, 184, 192, 196
Glassboro Summit Conference, 144, 156
Global Post, 119
GOELRO plan, 16
Golden Horde, 6
Gosplan, 45, 154
Goulash Communism, 186
Government budget, 39, 50
Government of China, 161
Government of the Soviet Union, 4, 51, 170, 174, 195
Gradualism, 170
Grand Duchy of Moscow, 6
Grand Kremlin Palace, 38
Great Depression, 111
Great Leap Forward, 135
Great Purge, 4, 9, 18, 20, 39, 72, 90, 93, 100, 122, 140, 150, 182
Great Purges, 194
Great Russia, 7
Great Society, 137
Greenwood Publishing Group, 178
Grigorii Khanin, 154
Grigory Petrovsky, 16, 81
Grigory Romanov, 149, 150, 189
Grigory Zinoviev, 17, 100, 130
Gross domestic product, 111, 186
Gross national income, 154

www.ingramcontent.com/pod-product-compliance
Lightning Source LLC
Chambersburg PA
CBHW021503090426
42739CB00007B/444